JOHN MILTON'S

SAMSON AGONISTES

JOHN MILTON'S SAMSON AGONISTES

The Poem and Materials for Analysis

SELECTED AND EDITED BY
RALPH E. HONE
UNIVERSITY OF REDLANDS

CHANDLER PUBLISHING COMPANY
124 Spear Street
San Francisco, California 94105

COVER ILLUSTRATION: *Woodcut by Hans Burgkmair, courtesy of the Achenbach Foundation for Graphic Arts.*

Library of Congress Catalog Card No. 66-11621
Printed in the United States of America

CONTENTS

APPENDIX

PREFACE

It is ironic that the poetry of Milton, who is considered by most students of English literature to be second only to Shakespeare in greatness, should be so slightly read by undergraduates in America. Anthologies tend to represent Milton by his lyrics (the sonnets or *Lycidas* chiefly) or by selected portions only of *Paradise Lost.* All too often, also, the present generation's illiteracy of the Bible and classical mythology stymies any depth acquaintance by undergraduates with Milton's major epic. Twentieth-century criticism, moreover, has so frequently challenged Milton's position (not without able replies from stalwart champions) that he has occasionally been ignored or, what is worse, patronized. Literature thus suffers in the house of its friends.

With the conviction that an *entire* work of greater length than the lyric poems, or of greater continuity than selections from *Paradise Lost,* will be a fairer way than the usual of presenting Milton to undergraduates, I have brought together this edition of *Samson Agonistes,* Milton's majestic drama, and selected related studies as a contribution to the Materials for Analysis texts for college students. The college English teacher has here a volume which is literature-centered, making available a number of study and writing assignments on the analysis of theme and structure, the texture of imagery, the development of characterization, the use of sources, the date of composition, the perspectives of criticism, the identity of tone or spirit, and the basis for comparative-literature study. A list of suggested topics for student work is to be found in the Appendix, as well as a bibliography for further reading.

Acknowledgment of copyright permissions will be found on the copyright page of this volume. I have been delighted by the kindness of fellow scholars and their publishers. To my secretary, Mrs. Magdalene Hester, I must express resounding gratitude for her patient helpfulness. Members of the staffs of the University of Redlands Library and the Huntington Library have been consistently gracious in their assistance. It is my hope that every reader "with new acquist / Of true experience from this great event" may discover a measure of "What the unsearchable dispose / Of Highest Wisdom brings about."

The picture used on the cover is from the collection of the Achenbach Foundation for Graphic Arts at the California Palace of the Legion of Honor in San Francisco, and was obtained with the kind cooperation of E. Gunter Troche, Director of the Foundation.

JOHN MILTON'S

SAMSON AGONISTES

PART I

THE TEXT OF *SAMSON AGONISTES*

JOHN MILTON

SAMSON AGONISTES: A DRAMATIC POEM

David Masson (1822-1907), whose edition of Milton's drama Samson Agonistes *is printed in this volume, was the most voluminous writer on the poet in the nineteenth century. He compiled* The Life of John Milton, Narrated in Connexion with the Political, Ecclesiastical, and Literary History of His Time *(London and New York, 1871-1894), in seven volumes. The Text of* Samson Agonistes *appears in* The Poetical Works of John Milton, Edited with Introduction, Notes, and an Essay on Milton's English *(3 vols., London, 1874), II, 97-153.*

Of that Sort of Dramatic Poem Called Tragedy

Tragedy, as it was anciently composed, hath been ever held the gravest, moralest, and most profitable of all other poems; therefore said by Aristotle to be of power, by raising pity and fear, or terror, to purge the mind of those and such-like passions—that is, to temper and reduce them to just measure with a kind of delight, stirred up by reading or seeing those passions well imitated. Nor is Nature wanting in her own effects to make good his assertion; for so, in physic, things of melancholic hue and quality are used against melancholy, sour against sour, salt to remove salt humours. Hence philosophers and other gravest writers, as Cicero, Plutarch, and others, frequently cite out of tragic poets, both to adorn and illustrate their discourse. The Apostle Paul himself thought it not unworthy to insert a verse of Euripides into the text of Holy Scripture, I Cor. xv. 33; and Paræus, commenting on the *Revelation,* divides the whole book, as a tragedy, into acts, distinguished each by a Chorus of heavenly harpings and song between. Heretofore men in highest dignity have laboured not a little to be thought able to compose a tragedy. Of that honour Dionysius the elder was no less ambitious than before of his attaining to the tyranny. Augustus Cæsar also had begun his *Ajax,* but, unable to please his own judgment with what he had begun, left it unfinished. Seneca, the philosopher, is by some thought the author of those tragedies (at least the best of them) that go under that name. Gregory Nazianzen, a Father of the Church, thought it not unbeseeming the sanctity of his person to write a tragedy, which he entitled *Christ Suffering.* This is mentioned to vindicate Tragedy from the small esteem, or rather infamy, which in the account of many it undergoes at this day, with other common interludes; happening through the poet's error of intermixing comic stuff with tragic sadness and gravity, or introducing trivial and vulgar persons: which by all judicious hath been counted absurd, and brought in without discretion, corruptly to gratify the people. And, though ancient Tragedy use no Prologue, yet using sometimes, in case of self-defence or explanation, that which Martial calls an Epistle, in behalf of this tragedy, coming forth after the ancient manner, much different from what among us passes for best, thus much beforehand may be *epistled*—that Chorus is here introduced after the Greek manner, not ancient only, but modern, and still in use among the Italians. In the modelling therefore of this poem, with good reason, the Ancients and Italians are rather followed, as of much more authority and fame. The measure of verse used in the Chorus is of all sorts, called by the Greeks *Monostrophic,* or rather *Apolelymenon,* without regard had to Strophe, Antistrophe, or Epode—which were a kind of stanzas framed only for the music, then used with the Chorus that sung; not essential to the poem, and therefore not material; or, being divided into stanzas or pauses, they may be called *Allæostropha.*

Division into act and scene, referring chiefly to the stage (to which this work never was intended), is here omitted.

It suffices if the whole drama be found not produced beyond the fifth act. Of the style and uniformity, and that commonly called the plot, whether intricate or explicit—which is nothing indeed but such economy, or disposition of the fable, as may stand best with verisimilitude and decorum—they only will best judge who are not unacquainted with Æschylus, Sophocles, and Euripides, the three tragic poets unequalled yet by any, and the best rule to all who endeavour to write Tragedy. The circumscription of time, wherein the whole drama begins and ends, is, according to ancient rule and best example, within the space of twenty-four hours.

The Argument

Samson, made captive, blind, and now in the prison at Gaza, there to labour as in a common workhouse, on a festival day, in the general cessation from labour, comes forth into the open air, to a place nigh, somewhat retired, there to sit a while and bemoan his condition. When he happens at length to be visited by certain friends and equals of his tribe, which make the Chorus, who seek to comfort him what they can; then by his old father, Manoa, who endeavours the like, and withal tells him his purpose to procure his liberty by ransom; lastly, that this feast was proclaimed by the Philistines as a day of thanksgiving for their deliverance from the hands of Samson—which yet more troubles him. Manoa then departs to prosecute his endeavour with the Philistian lords for Samson's redemption: who, in the meanwhile, is visited by other persons, and, lastly, by a public officer to require his coming to the feast before the lords and people, to play or show his strength in their presence. He at first refuses, dismissing the public officer with absolute denial to come; at length, persuaded inwardly that this was from God, he yields to go along with him, who came now the second time with great threatenings to fetch him. The Chorus yet remaining on the place, Manoa returns full of joyful hope to procure ere long his son's deliverance; in the midst of which discourse an Ebrew comes in haste, confusedly at first, and afterwards more distinctly, relating the catastrophe—what Samson had done to the Philistines, and by accident to himself; wherewith the Tragedy ends.

THE PERSONS

SAMSON

MANOA, *the father of* SAMSON

DALILA, *his wife*

HARAPHA *of Gath*

PUBLIC OFFICER

MESSENGER

CHORUS *of Danites*

[The Scene, before the Prison in Gaza.]

SAMPSON AGONISTES

SAMSON A little onward lend thy guiding hand
To these dark steps, a little further on;
For yonder bank hath choice of sun or shade.
There I am wont to sit, when any chance
Relieves me from my task of servile toil,
Daily in the common prison else enjoined me,
Where I, a prisoner chained, scarce freely draw
The air, imprisoned also, close and damp,
Unwholesome draught. But here I feel amends—
The breath of heaven fresh blowing, pure and sweet,
With day-spring born; here leave me to respire.
This day a solemn feast the people hold
To Dagon, their sea-idol, and forbid
Laborious works. Unwillingly this rest
Their superstition yields me; hence, with leave
Retiring from the popular noise, I seek
This unfrequented place to find some ease—
Ease to the body some, none to the mind
From restless thoughts, that, like a deadly swarm
Of hornets armed, no sooner found alone
But rush upon me thronging, and present
Times past, what once I was, and what am now.
Oh, wherefore was my birth from Heaven foretold
Twice by an angel, who at last, in sight
Of both my parents, all in flames ascended
From off the altar where an offering burned,
As in a fiery column charioting
His godlike presence, and from some great act
Or benefit revealed to Abraham's race?
Why was my breeding ordered and prescribed
As of a person separate to God,
Designed for great exploits, if I must die

Betrayed, captived, and both my eyes put out,
Made of my enemies the scorn and gaze,
To grind in brazen fetters under task
With this heaven-gifted strength? O glorious strength,
Put to the labour of a beast, debased
Lower than bond-slave! Promise was that I
Should Israel from Philistian yoke deliver!
Ask for this great deliverer now, and find him
Eyeless in Gaza, at the mill with slaves,
Himself in bonds under Philistian yoke.
Yet stay; let me not rashly call in doubt
Divine prediction. What if all foretold
Had been fulfilled but through mine own default?
Whom have I to complain of but myself,
Who this high gift of strength committed to me,
In what part lodged, how easily bereft me,
Under the seal of silence could not keep,
But weakly to a woman must reveal it,
O'ercome with importunity and tears?
O impotence of mind in body strong!
But what is strength without a double share
Of wisdom? Vast, unwieldy, burdensome,
Proudly secure, yet liable to fall
By weakest subtleties; not made to rule,
But to subserve where wisdom bears command.
God, when he gave me strength, to show withal
How slight the gift was, hung it in my hair.
But peace! I must not quarrel with the will
Of highest dispensation, which herein
Haply had ends above my reach to know.
Suffices that to me strength is my bane,
And proves the source of all my miseries—
So many, and so huge, that each apart
Would ask a life to wail. But, chief of all,
O loss of sight, of thee I most complain!
Blind among enemies! O worse than chains,
Dungeon, or beggary, or decrepit age!

Light, the prime work of God, to me is extinct,
And all her various objects of delight
Annulled, which might in part my grief have eased.
Inferior to the vilest now become
Of man or worm, the vilest here excel me:
They creep, yet see; I, dark in light, exposed
To daily fraud, contempt, abuse, and wrong,
Within doors, or without, still as a fool,
In power of others, never in my own—
Scarce half I seem to live, dead more than half.
O dark, dark, dark, amid the blaze of noon,
Irrecoverably dark, total eclipse
Without all hope of day!
O first-created beam, and thou great Word,
"Let there be light, and light was over all,"
Why am I thus bereaved thy prime decree?
The Sun to me is dark
And silent as the Moon,
When she deserts the night,
Hid in her vacant interlunar cave.
Since light so necessary is to life,
And almost life itself, if it be true
That light is in the soul,
She all in every part, why was the sight
To such a tender ball as the eye confined,
So obvious and so easy to be quenched,
And not, as feeling, through all parts diffused,
That she might look at will through every pore?
Then had I not been thus exiled from light,
As in the land of darkness, yet in light,
To live a life half dead, a living death,
And buried; but, O yet more miserable!
Myself my sepulchre, a moving grave;
Buried, yet not exempt,
By privilege of death and burial,
From worst of other evils, pains, and wrongs;
But made hereby obnoxious more

To all the miseries of life,
Life in captivity
Among inhuman foes.
But who are these? for with joint pace I hear
The tread of many feet steering this way;
Perhaps my enemies, who come to stare
At my affliction, and perhaps to insult—
Their daily practice to afflict me more.

CHORUS This, this is he; softly a while;
Let us not break in upon him.
O change beyond report, thought, or belief!
See how he lies at random, carelessly diffused,
With languished head unpropt,
As one past hope abandoned,
And by himself given over,
In slavish habit, ill-fitted weeds
O'er-worn and soiled.
Or do my eyes misrepresent? Can this be he,
That heroic, that renowned,
Irresistible Samson? whom, unarmed,
No strength of man, or fiercest wild beast, could withstand;
Who tore the lion as the lion tears the kid;
Ran on embattled armies clad in iron,
And, weaponless himself,
Made arms ridiculous, useless the forgery
Of brazen shield and spear, the hammered cuirass,
Chalybean-tempered steel, and frock of mail
Adamantean proof:
But safest he who stood aloof,
When insupportably his foot advanced,
In scorn of their proud arms and warlike tools,
Spurned them to death by troops. The bold Ascalonite
Fled from his lion ramp; old warriors turned
Their plated backs under his heel,
Or grovelling soiled their crested helmets in the dust.
Then with what trivial weapon came to hand,

The jaw of a dead ass, his sword of bone,
A thousand foreskins fell, the flower of Palestine,
In Ramath-lechi, famous to this day:
Then by main force pulled up, and on his shoulders bore,
The gates of Azza, post and massy bar,
Up to the hill by Hebron, seat of giants old—
No journey of a sabbath-day, and loaded so—
Like whom the Gentiles feign to bear up Heaven.
Which shall I first bewail—
Thy bondage or lost sight,
Prison within prison
Inseparably dark?
Thou art become (O worst imprisonment!)
The dungeon of thyself; thy soul
(Which men enjoying sight oft without cause complain)
Imprisoned now indeed,
In real darkness of the body dwells,
Shut up from outward light
To incorporate with gloomy night;
For inward light, alas!
Puts forth no visual beam.
O mirror of our fickle state,
Since man on earth, unparalleled,
The rarer thy example stands,
By how much from the top of wondrous glory,
Strongest of mortal men,
To lowest pitch of abject fortune thou art fallen.
For him I reckon not in high estate
Whom long descent of birth,
Or the sphere of fortune, raises;
But thee, whose strength, while virtue was her mate,
Might have subdued the Earth,
Universally crowned with highest praises.

SAMSON I hear the sound of words; their sense the air
Dissolves unjointed ere it reach my ear.

CHORUS He speaks: let us draw nigh. Matchless in might,

The glory late of Israel, now the grief!
We come, thy friends and neighbors not unknown,
From Eshtaol and Zora's fruitful vale,
To visit or bewail thee; or, if better,
Counsel or consolation we may bring,
Salve to thy sores; apt words have power to swage
The tumours of a troubled mind,
And are as balm to festered wounds.

SAMSON Your coming, friends, revives me; for I learn
Now of my own experience, not by talk,
How counterfeit a coin they are who 'friends'
Bear in their superscription (of the most
I would be understood). In prosperous days
They swarm, but in adverse withdraw their head,
Not to be found, though sought. Ye see, O friends,
How many evils have enclosed me round;
Yet that which was the worst now least afflicts me,
Blindness; for, had I sight, confused with shame,
How could I once look up, or heave the head,
Who, like a foolish pilot, have shipwracked
My vessel trusted to me from above,
Gloriously rigged, and for a word, a tear,
Fool! have divulged the secret gift of God
To a deceitful woman? Tell me, friends,
Am I not sung and proverbed for a fool
In every street? Do they not say, 'How well
Are come upon him his deserts'? Yet why?
Immeasurable strength they might behold
In me; of wisdom nothing more than mean.
This with the other should at least have paired;
These two, proportioned ill, drove me transverse.

CHORUS Tax not divine disposal. Wisest men
Have erred, and by bad women been deceived;
And shall again, pretend they ne'er so wise.
Deject not, then, so overmuch thyself,
Who hast of sorrow thy full load besides.

Yet, truth to say, I oft have heard men wonder
Why thou should'st wed Philistian women rather
Than of thine own tribe fairer, or as fair,
At least of thy own nation, and as noble.

SAMSON The first I saw at Timna, and she pleased
Me, not my parents, that I sought to wed
The daughter of an infidel. They knew not
That what I motioned was of God; I knew
From intimate impulse, and therefore urged
The marriage on, that, by occasion hence,
I might begin Israel's deliverance—
The work to which I was divinely called.
She proving false, the next I took to wife
(O that I never had! fond wish too late!)
Was in the vale of Sorec, Dalila,
That specious monster, my accomplished snare.
I thought it lawful from my former act,
And the same end, still watching to oppress
Israel's oppressors. Of what now I suffer
She was not the prime cause, but I myself,
Who, vanquished with a peal of words (O weakness!),
Gave up my fort of silence to a woman.

CHORUS In seeking just occasion to provoke
The Philistine, thy country's enemy,
Thou never wast remiss, I bear thee witness;
Yet Israel still serves with all his sons.

SAMSON That fault I take not on me, but transfer
On Israel's governors and heads of tribes,
Who, seeing those great acts which God had done
Singly by me against their conquerors,
Acknowledged not, or not at all considered,
Deliverance offered. I, on the other side,
Used no ambition to commend my deeds;
The deeds themselves, though mute, spoke loud the doer.
But they persisted deaf, and would not seem
To count them things worth notice, till at length

Their lords, the Philistines, with gathered powers,
Entered Judea, seeking me, who then
Safe to the rock of Etham was retired—
Not flying, but forecasting in what place
To set upon them, what advantaged best.
Meanwhile the men of Judah, to prevent
The harass of their land, beset me round;
I willingly on some conditions came
Into their hands, and they as gladly yield me
To the Uncircumcised a welcome prey,
Bound with two cords. But cords to me were threads
Touched with the flame: on their whole host I flew
Unarmed, and with a trivial weapon felled
Their choicest youth; they only lived who fled.
Had Judah that day joined, or one whole tribe,
They had by this possessed the towers of Gath,
And lorded over them whom now they serve.
But what more oft, in nations grown corrupt,
And by their vices brought to servitude,
Than to love bondage more than liberty—
Bondage with ease than strenuous liberty—
And to despise, or envy, or suspect,
Whom God hath of his special favour raised
As their deliverer? If he aught begin,
How frequent to desert him, and at last
To heap ingratitude on worthiest deeds!

CHORUS Thy words to my remembrance bring
How Succoth and the fort of Penuel
Their great deliverer contemned,
The matchless Gideon, in pursuit
Of Madian, and her vanquished kings;
And how ingrateful Ephraim
Had dealt with Jephtha, who by argument,
Not worse than by his shield and spear,
Defended Israel from the Ammonite,
Had not his prowess quelled their pride

In that sore battle when so many died
Without reprieve, adjudged to death
For want of well pronouncing *Shibboleth*.
SAMSON Of such examples add me to the roll.
Me easily indeed mine may neglect,
But God's proposed deliverance not so.
CHORUS Just are the ways of God,
And justifiable to men,
Unless there be who think not God at all.
If any be, they walk obscure;
For of such doctrine never was there school,
But the heart of the fool,
And no man therein doctor but himself.
Yet more there be who doubt his ways not just,
As to his own edicts found contradicting;
Then give the reins to wandering thought,
Regardless of his glory's diminution,
Till, by their own perplexities involved,
They ravel more, still less resolved,
But never find self-satisfying solution.
As if they would confine the Interminable,
And tie him to his own prescript,
Who made our laws to bind us, not himself,
And hath full right to exempt
Whomso it pleases him by choice
From national obstriction, without taint
Of sin, or legal debt;
For with his own laws he can best dispense.
He would not else, who never wanted means,
Nor in respect of the enemy just cause,
To set his people free,
Have prompted this heroic Nazarite,
Against his vow of strictest purity,
To seek in marriage that fallacious bride,
Unclean, unchaste.
Down, Reason, then; at least, vain reasonings down;

Though Reason here aver
That moral verdit quits her of unclean:
Unchaste was subsequent; her stain, not his.
  But see! here comes thy reverend sire,
With careful step, locks white as down,
Old Manoa: advise
Forthwith how thou ought'st to receive him.
SAMSON Ay me! another inward grief, awaked
With mention of that name, renews the assault.
MANOA Brethren and men of Dan (for such ye seem,
Though in this uncouth place), if old respect,
As I suppose, towards your once gloried friend,
My son, now captive, hither hath informed
Your younger feet, while mine, cast back with age,
Came lagging after, say if he be here.
CHORUS As signal now in low dejected state
As erst in highest, behold him where he lies.
MANOA O miserable change! Is this the man,
That invincible Samson, far renowned,
The dread of Israel's foes, who with a strength
Equivalent to Angels' walked their streets,
None offering fight; who, single combatant,
Duelled their armies ranked in proud array,
Himself an army—now unequal match
To save himself against a coward armed
At one spear's length? O ever-failing trust
In mortal strength! and, oh, what not in man
Deceivable and vain? Nay, what thing good
Prayed for, but often proves our woe, our bane?
I prayed for children, and thought barrenness
In wedlock a reproach; I gained a son,
And such a son as all men hailed me happy:
Who would be now a father in my stead?
Oh, wherefore did God grant me my request,
And as a blessing with such pomp adorned?
Why are his gifts desirable, to tempt

Our earnest prayers, then, given with solemn hand
As graces, draw a scorpion's tail behind?
For this did the Angel twice descend? for this
Ordained thy nurture holy, as of a plant
Select and sacred? glorious for a while,
The miracle of men; then in an hour
Ensnared, assaulted, overcome, led bound,
Thy foes' derision, captive, poor and blind,
Into a dungeon thrust, to work with slaves!
Alas! methinks whom God hath chosen once
To worthiest deeds, if he through frailty err,
He should not so o'erwhelm, and as a thrall
Subject him to so foul indignities,
Be it but for honour's sake of former deeds.

SAMSON Appoint not heavenly disposition, father.
Nothing of all these evils hath befallen me
But justly; I myself have brought them on;
Sole author I, sole cause. If aught seem vile,
As vile hath been my folly, who have profaned
The mystery of God, given me under pledge
Of vow, and have betrayed it to a woman,
A Canaanite, my faithless enemy.
This well I knew, nor was at all surprised,
But warned by oft experience. Did not she
Of Timna first betray me, and reveal
The secret wrested from me in her highth
Of nuptial love professed, carrying it straight
To them who had corrupted her, my spies
And rivals? In this other was there found
More faith, who, also in her prime of love,
Spousal embraces, vitiated with gold,
Though offered only, by the scent conceived,
Her spurious first-born, Treason against me?
Thrice she assayed, with flattering prayers and sighs,
And amorous reproaches, to win from me
My capital secret, in what part my strength

Lay stored, in what part summed, that she might know;
Thrice I deluded her, and turned to sport
Her importunity, each time perceiving
How openly and with what impudence
She purposed to betray me, and (which was worse
Than undissembled hate) with what contempt
She sought to make me traitor to myself.
Yet, the fourth time, when, mustering all her wiles,
With blandished parleys, feminine assaults,
Tongue-batteries, she surceased not day nor night
To storm me, over-watched and wearied out,
At times when men seek most repose and rest,
I yielded, and unlocked her all my heart,
Who, with a grain of manhood well resolved,
Might easily have shook off all her snares;
But foul effeminacy held me yoked
Her bond-slave. O indignity, O blot
To honour and religion! servile mind
Rewarded well with servile punishment!
The base degree to which I now am fallen,
These rags, this grinding, is not yet so base
As was my former servitude, ignoble,
Unmanly, ignominious, infamous,
True slavery; and that blindness worse than this,
That saw not how degenerately I served.
MANOA I cannot praise thy marriage-choices, son—
Rather approved them not; but thou didst plead
Divine impulsion prompting how thou might'st
Find some occasion to infest our foes.
I state not that; this I am sure—our foes
Found soon occasion thereby to make thee
Their captive, and their triumph; thou the sooner
Temptation found'st, or over-potent charms,
To violate the sacred trust of silence
Deposited within thee—which to have kept
Tacit was in thy power. True; and thou bear'st

Enough, and more, the burden of that fault;
Bitterly hast thou paid, and still art paying,
That rigid score. A worse thing yet remains:—
This day the Philistines a popular feast
Here celebrate in Gaza, and proclaim
Great pomp, and sacrifice, and praises loud,
To Dagon, as their god who hath delivered
Thee, Samson, bound and blind, into their hands—
Them out of thine, who slew'st them many a slain.
So Dagon shall be magnified, and God,
Besides whom is no god, compared with idols,
Disglorified, blasphemed, and had in scorn
By the idolatrous rout amidst their wine;
Which to have come to pass by means of thee,
Samson, of all thy sufferings think the heaviest,
Of all reproach the most with shame that ever
Could have befallen thee and thy father's house.

SAMSON Father, I do acknowledge and confess
That I this honour, I this pomp, have brought
To Dagon, and advanced his praises high
Among the Heathen round—to God have brought
Dishonour, obloquy, and oped the mouths
Of idolists and atheists; have brought scandal
To Israel, diffidence of God, and doubt
In feeble hearts, propense enough before
To waver, or fall off and join with idols:
Which is my chief affliction, shame and sorrow,
The anguish of my soul, that suffers not
Mine eye to harbour sleep, or thoughts to rest.
This only hope relieves me, that the strife
With me hath end. All the contest is now
'Twixt God and Dagon. Dagon hath presumed,
Me overthrown, to enter lists with God,
His deity comparing and preferring
Before the God of Abraham. He, be sure,
Will not connive, or linger, thus provoked,

But will arise, and his great name assert.
Dagon must stoop, and shall ere long receive
Such a discomfit as shall quite despoil him
Of all these boasted trophies won on me,
And with confusion blank his worshipers.

MANOA With cause this hope relieves thee; and these words
I as a prophecy receive; for God
(Nothing more certain) will not long defer
To vindicate the glory of his name
Against all competition, nor will long
Endure it doubtful whether God be Lord
Or Dagon. But for thee what shall be done?
Thou must not in the meanwhile, here forgot,
Lie in this miserable loathsome plight
Neglected. I already have made way
To some Philistian lords, with whom to treat
About thy ransom. Well they may by this
Have satisfied their utmost of revenge,
By pains and slaveries, worse than death, inflicted
On thee, who now no more canst do them harm.

SAMSON Spare that proposal, father; spare the trouble
Of that solicitation. Let me here,
As I deserve, pay on my punishment,
And expiate, if possible, my crime,
Shameful garrulity. To have revealed
Secrets of *men*, the secrets of a friend,
How heinous had the fact been, how deserving
Contempt and scorn of all—to be excluded
All friendship, and avoided as a blab,
The mark of fool set on his front! But I
God's counsel have not kept, his holy secret
Presumptuously have published, impiously,
Weakly at least and shamefully—a sin
That Gentiles in their parables condemn
To their Abyss and horrid pains confined.

MANOA Be penitent, and for thy fault contrite;

But act not in thy own affliction, son.
Repent the sin; but, if the punishment
Thou canst avoid, self-preservation bids;
Or the execution leave to high disposal,
And let another hand, not thine, exact
Thy penal forfeit from thyself. Perhaps
God will relent, and quit thee all his debt;
Who ever more approves and more accepts
(Best pleased with humble and filial submission)
Him who, imploring mercy, sues for life,
Than who, self-rigorous, chooses death as due;
Which argues over-just, and self-displeased
For self-offence more than for God offended.
Reject not, then, what offered means who knows
But God hath set before us to return thee
Home to thy country and his sacred house,
Where thou may'st bring thy offerings, to avert
His further ire, with prayers and vows renewed.

SAMSON His pardon I implore; but, as for life,
To what end should I seek it? When in strength
All mortals I excelled, and great in hopes,
With youthful courage, and magnanimous thoughts
Of birth from Heaven foretold and high exploits,
Full of divine instinct, after some proof
Of acts indeed heroic, far beyond
The sons of Anak, famous now and blazed,
Fearless of danger, like a petty god
I walked about, admired of all, and dreaded
On hostile ground, none daring my affront–
Then, swollen with pride, into the snare I fell
Of fair fallacious looks, venereal trains,
Softened with pleasure and voluptuous life,
At length to lay my head and hallowed pledge
Of all my strength in the lascivious lap
Of a deceitful concubine, who shore me,
Like a tame wether, all my precious fleece,

Then turned me out ridiculous, despoiled,
Shaven, and disarmed among my enemies.
CHORUS Desire of wine and all delicious drinks,
Which many a famous warrior overturns,
Thou could'st repress; nor did the dancing ruby,
Sparkling out-poured, the flavour or the smell,
Or taste, that cheers the heart of gods and men,
Allure thee from the cool crystalline stream.
SAMSON Wherever fountain or fresh current flowed
Against the eastern ray, translucent, pure
With touch ethereal of Heaven's fiery rod,
I drank, from the clear milky juice allaying
Thirst, and refreshed; nor envied them the grape
Whose heads that turbulent liquor fills with fumes.
CHORUS O madness! to think use of strongest wines
And strongest drinks our chief support of health,
When God with these forbidden made choice to rear
His mighty champion, strong above compare,
Whose drink was only from the liquid brook!
SAMSON But what availed this temperance, not complete
Against another object more enticing?
What boots it at one gate to make defence,
And at another to let in the foe,
Effeminately vanquished? by which means,
Now blind, disheartened, shamed, dishonoured, quelled,
To what can I be useful? wherein serve
My nation, and the work from Heaven imposed?
But to sit idle on the household hearth,
A burdenous drone; to visitants a gaze,
Or pitied object; these redundant locks,
Robustious to no purpose, clustering down,
Vain monument of strength; till length of years
And sedentary numbness craze my limbs
To a contemptible old age obscure.
Here rather let me drudge, and earn my bread,
Till vermin, or the draff of servile food,

Consume me, and oft-invocated death
Hasten the welcome end of all my pains.

MANOA Wilt thou then serve the Philistines with that gift
Which was expressly given thee to annoy them?
Better at home lie bed-rid, not only idle,
Inglorious, unemployed, with age outworn.
But God, who caused a fountain at thy prayer
From the dry ground to spring, thy thirst to allay
After the brunt of battle, can as easy
Cause light again within thy eyes to spring,
Wherewith to serve him better than thou hast.
And I persuade me so. Why else this strength
Miraculous yet remaining in those locks?
His might continues in thee not for naught,
Nor shall his wondrous gifts be frustrate thus.

SAMSON All otherwise to me my thoughts portend—
That these dark orbs no more shall treat with light,
Nor the other light of life continue long,
But yield to double darkness nigh at hand;
So much I feel my genial spirits droop,
My hopes all flat: Nature within me seems
In all her functions weary of herself;
My race of glory run, and race of shame,
And I shall shortly be with them that rest.

MANOA Believe not these suggestions, which proceed
From anguish of the mind, and humours black
That mingle with thy fancy. I, however,
Must not omit a father's timely care
To prosecute the means of thy deliverance
By ransom or how else: meanwhile be calm,
And healing words from these thy friends admit.

SAMSON Oh, that torment should not be confined
To the body's wounds and sores,
With maladies innumerable
In heart, head, breast, and reins,
But must secret passage find

To the inmost mind,
There exercise all his fierce accidents,
And on her purest spirits prey,
As on entrails, joints, and limbs,
With answerable pains, but more intense,
Though void of corporal sense!
My griefs not only pain me
As a lingering disease,
But, finding no redress, ferment and rage;
Nor less than wounds immedicable
Rankle, and fester, and gangrene,
To black mortification.
Thoughts, my tormentors, armed with deadly stings,
Mangle my apprehensive tenderest parts,
Exasperate, exulcerate, and raise
Dire inflammation, which no cooling herb
Or medicinal liquor can assuage,
Nor breath of vernal air from snowy Alp.
Sleep hath forsook and given me o'er
To death's benumbing opium as my only cure;
Thence faintings, swoonings of despair,
And sense of Heaven's desertion.
I was his nursling once and choice delight,
His destined from the womb,
Promised by heavenly message twice descending.
Under his special eye
Abstemious I grew up and thrived amain;
He led me on to mightiest deeds,
Above the nerve of mortal arm,
Against the Uncircumcised, our enemies:
But now hath cast me off as never known,
And to those cruel enemies,
Whom I by his appointment had provoked,
Left me all helpless, with the irreparable loss
Of sight, reserved alive to be repeated
The subject of their cruelty or scorn.

Nor am I in the list of them that hope;
Hopeless are all my evils, all remediless.
This one prayer yet remains, might I be heard,
No long petition—speedy death,
The close of all my miseries and the balm.

CHORUS Many are the sayings of the wise,
In ancient and in modern books enrolled,
Extolling patience as the truest fortitude,
And to the bearing well of all calamities,
All chances incident to man's frail life,
Consolatories writ
With studied argument, and much persuasion sought,
Lenient of grief and anxious thought.
But with the afflicted in his pangs their sound
Little prevails, or rather seems a tune
Harsh, and of dissonant mood from his complaint,
Unless he feel within
Some source of consolation from above,
Secret refreshings that repair his strength
And fainting spirits uphold.
God of our fathers! what is Man,
That thou towards him with hand so various—
Or might I say contrarious?—
Temper'st thy providence through his short course:
Not evenly, as thou rul'st
The angelic orders, and inferior creatures mute,
Irrational and brute?
Nor do I name of men the common rout,
That, wandering loose about,
Grow up and perish as the summer fly,
Heads without name, no more remembered;
But such as thou hast solemnly elected,
With gifts and graces eminently adorned,
To some great work, thy glory,
And people's safety, which in part they effect.
Yet toward these, thus dignified, thou oft,

Amidst their highth of noon,
Changest thy countenance and thy hand, with no regard
Of highest favours past
From thee on them, or them to thee of service.
  Nor only dost degrade them, or remit
To life obscured, which were a fair dismission,
But throw'st them lower than thou didst exalt them high—
Unseemly falls in human eye,
Too grievous for the trespass or omission;
Oft leav'st them to the hostile sword
Of heathen and profane, their carcasses
To dogs and fowls a prey, or else captived,
Or to the unjust tribunals, under change of times,
And condemnation of the ungrateful multitude.
If these they scape, perhaps in poverty
With sickness and disease thou bow'st them down,
Painful diseases and deformed,
In crude old age;
Though not disordinate, yet causeless suffering
The punishment of dissolute days. In fine,
Just or unjust alike seem miserable,
For oft alike both come to evil end.
  So deal not with this once thy glorious champion,
The image of thy strength, and mighty minister.
What do I beg? how hast thou dealt already!
Behold him in this state calamitous, and turn
His labours, for thou canst, to peaceful end.
  But who is this? what thing of sea or land—
Female of sex it seems—
That, so bedecked, ornate, and gay,
Comes this way sailing,
Like a stately ship
Of Tarsus, bound for the isles
Of Javan or Gadier,
With all her bravery on, and tackle trim,
Sails filled, and streamers waving,

Courted by all the winds that hold them play;
An amber scent of odorous perfume
Her harbinger, a damsel train behind?
Some rich Philistian matron she may seem;
And now, at nearer view, no other certain
Than Dalila thy wife.

SAMSON My wife! my traitress! let her not come near me.

CHORUS Yet on she moves; now stands and eyes thee fixed,
About to have spoke; but now, with head declined,
Like a fair flower surcharged with dew, she weeps,
And words addressed seem into tears dissolved,
Wetting the borders of her silken veil.
But now again she makes address to speak.

DALILA With doubtful feet and wavering resolution
I came, still dreading thy displeasure, Samson;
Which to have merited, without excuse,
I cannot but acknowledge. Yet, if tears
May expiate (though the fact more evil drew
In the perverse event than I foresaw),
My penance hath not slackened, though my pardon
No way assured. But conjugal affection,
Prevailing over fear and timorous doubt,
Hath led me on, desirous to behold
Once more thy face, and know of thy estate,
If aught in my ability may serve
To lighten what thou suffer'st, and appease
Thy mind with what amends is in my power—
Though late, yet in some part to recompense
My rash but more unfortunate misdeed.

SAMSON Out, out hyæna! These are thy wonted arts,
And arts of every woman false like thee—
To break all faith, all vows, deceive, betray;
Then, as repentant, to submit, beseech,
And reconcilement move with feigned remorse,
Confess, and promise wonders in her change—
Not truly penitent, but chief to try

Her husband, how far urged his patience bears,
His virtue or weakness which way to assail:
Then, with more cautious and instructed skill,
Again transgresses, and again submits;
That wisest and best men, full oft beguiled,
With goodness principled not to reject
The penitent, but ever to forgive,
Are drawn to wear out miserable days,
Entangled with a poisonous bosom-snake,
If not by quick destruction soon cut off,
As I by thee, to ages an example.

DALILA Yet hear me, Samson; not that I endeavour
To lessen or extenuate my offence,
But that, on the other side, if it be weighed
By itself, with aggravations not surcharged,
Or else with just allowance counterpoised,
I may, if possible, thy pardon find
The easier towards me, or thy hatred less.
First granting, as I do, it was a weakness
In me, but incident to all our sex,
Curiosity, inquisitive, importune
Of secrets, then with like infirmity
To publish them—both common female faults—
Was it not weakness also to make known
For importunity, that is for naught,
Wherein consisted all thy strength and safety?
To what I did thou show'dst me first the way.
But I to enemies revealed, and should not!
Nor should'st thou have trusted that to woman's frailty:
Ere I to thee, thou to thyself wast cruel.
Let weakness, then, with weakness come to parle,
So near related, or the same of kind;
Thine forgive mine, that men may censure thine
The gentler, if severely thou exact not
More strength from me than in thyself was found.
And what if love, which thou interpret'st hate,

The jealousy of love, powerful of sway
In human hearts, nor less in mine towards thee,
Caused what I did? I saw thee mutable
Of fancy; feared lest one day thou would'st leave me
As her at Timna; sought by all means, therefore,
How to endear, and hold thee to me firmest:
No better way I saw than by importuning
To learn thy secrets, get into my power
Thy key of strength and safety. Thou wilt say,
'Why, then, revealed?' I was assured by those
Who tempted me that nothing was designed
Against thee but safe custody and hold.
That made for me; I knew that liberty
Would draw thee forth to perilous enterprises,
While I at home sat full of cares and fears,
Wailing thy absence in my widowed bed;
Here I should still enjoy thee, day and night,
Mine and love's prisoner, not the Philistines',
Whole to myself, unhazarded abroad,
Fearless at home of partners in my love.
These reasons in Love's law have passed for good,
Though fond and reasonless to some perhaps;
And love hath oft, well meaning, wrought much woe,
Yet always pity or pardon hath obtained.
Be not unlike all others, not austere
As thou art strong, inflexible as steel.
If thou in strength all mortals dost exceed,
In uncompassionate anger do not so.

SAMSON How cunningly the sorceress displays
Her own transgressions, to upbraid me mine!
That malice, not repentance, brought thee hither,
By this appears. I gave, thou say'st, the example,
I led the way—bitter reproach, but true;
I to myself was false ere thou to me.
Such pardon, therefore, as I give my folly
Take to thy wicked deed; which when thou seest

Impartial, self-severe, inexorable,
Thou wilt renounce thy seeking, and much rather
Confess it feigned. Weakness is thy excuse,
And I believe it—weakness to resist
Philistian gold. If weakness may excuse,
What murtherer, what traitor, parricide,
Incestuous, sacrilegious, but may plead it?
All wickedness is weakness; that plea, therefore,
With God or man will gain thee no remission.
But love constrained thee! Call it furious rage
To satisfy thy lust. Love seeks to have love;
My love how could'st thou hope, who took'st the way
To raise in me inexpiable hate,
Knowing, as needs I must, by thee betrayed?
In vain thou striv'st to cover shame with shame,
Or by evasions thy crime uncover'st more.

DALILA Since thou determin'st weakness for no plea
In man or woman, though to thy own condemning,
Hear what assaults I had, what snares besides,
What sieges girt me round, ere I consented;
Which might have awed the best-resolved of men,
The constantest, to have yielded without blame.
It was not gold, as to my charge thou lay'st,
That wrought with me. Thou know'st the magistrates
And princes of my country came in person,
Solicited, commanded, threatened, urged,
Adjured by all the bonds of civil duty
And of religion—pressed how just it was,
How honourable, how glorious, to entrap
A common enemy, who had destroyed
Such numbers of our nation: and the priest
Was not behind, but ever at my ear,
Preaching how meritorious with the gods
It would be to ensnare an irreligious
Dishonourer of Dagon. What had I
To oppose against such powerful arguments?

typically Samson

Paper idea - weakness - as viewed by Samson, Dilila, Milton, God, Manoa

Only my love of thee held long debate,
And combated in silence all these reasons
With hard contest. At length, that grounded maxim,
So rife and celebrated in the mouths
Of wisest men, that to the public good
Private respects must yield, with grave authority
Took full possession of me, and prevailed;
Virtue, as I thought, truth, duty, so enjoining.

SAMSON I thought where all thy circling wiles would end—
In feigned religion, smooth hypocrisy!
But, had thy love, still odiously pretended,
Been, as it ought, sincere, it would have taught thee
Far other reasonings, brought forth other deeds.
I, before all the daughters of my tribe
And of my nation, chose thee from among
My enemies, loved thee, as too well thou knew'st;
Too well; unbosomed all my secrets to thee,
Not out of levity, but overpowered
By thy request, who could deny thee nothing;
Yet now am judged an enemy. Why, then,
Didst thou at first receive me for thy husband—
Then, as since then, thy country's foe professed?
Being once a wife, for me thou wast to leave
Parents and country; nor was I their subject,
Nor under their protection, but my own;
Thou mine, not theirs. If aught against my life
Thy country sought of thee, it sought unjustly,
Against the law of nature, law of nations;
No more thy country, but an impious crew
Of men conspiring to uphold their state
By worse than hostile deeds, violating the ends
For which our country is a name so dear;
Not therefore to be obeyed. But zeal moved thee;
To please thy gods thou didst it! Gods unable
To acquit themselves and prosecute their foes
But by ungodly deeds, the contradiction

Of their own deity, Gods cannot be—
Less therefore to be pleased, obeyed, or feared.
These false pretexts and varnished colours failing,
Bare in thy guilt, how foul must thou appear!

DALILA In argument with men a woman ever
Goes by the worse, whatever be her cause.

SAMSON For want of words, no doubt, or lack of breath!
Witness when I was worried with thy peals.

DALILA I was a fool, too rash, and quite mistaken
In what I thought would have succeeded best.
Let me obtain forgiveness of thee, Samson;
Afford me place to show what recompense
Towards thee I intend for what I have misdone,
Misguided. Only what remains past cure
Bear not too sensibly, nor still insist
To afflict thyself in vain. Though sight be lost,
Life yet hath many solaces, enjoyed
Where other senses want not their delights—
At home, in leisure and domestic ease,
Exempt from many a care and chance to which
Eyesight exposes, daily, men abroad.
I to the lords will intercede, not doubting
Their favourable ear, that I may fetch thee
From forth this loathsome prison-house, to abide
With me, where my redoubled love and care,
With nursing diligence, to me glad office,
May ever tend about thee to old age,
With all things grateful cheered, and so supplied
That what by me thou hast lost thou least shalt miss.

SAMSON No, no; of my condition take no care;
It fits not; thou and I long since are twain;
Nor think me so unwary or accursed
To bring my feet again into the snare
Where once I have been caught. I know thy trains,
Though dearly to my cost, thy gins, and toils.
Thy fair enchanted cup, and warbling charms,

No more on me have power; their force is nulled;
So much of adder's wisdom I have learned,
To fence my ear against thy sorceries.
If in my flower of youth and strength, when all men
Loved, honoured, feared me, thou alone could hate me,
Thy husband, slight me, sell me, and forgo me,
How would'st thou use me now, blind and thereby
Deceivable, in most things as a child
Helpless, thence easily contemned and scorned,
And last neglected! How would'st thou insult,
When I must live uxorious to thy will
In perfect thraldom! how again betray me,
Bearing my words and doings to the lords
To gloss upon, and, censuring, frown or smile!
This jail I count the house of liberty
To thine, whose doors my feet shall never enter.

DALILA Let me approach at least, and touch thy hand.

SAMSON Not for thy life, lest fierce remembrance wake
My sudden rage to tear thee joint by joint.
At distance I forgive thee; go with that;
Bewail thy falsehood, and the pious works
It hath brought forth to make thee memorable
Among illustrious women, faithful wives;
Cherish thy hastened widowhood with the gold
Of matrimonial treason: so farewell.

DALILA I see thou art implacable, more deaf
To prayers than winds and seas. Yet winds to seas
Are reconciled at length, and sea to shore:
Thy anger, unappeasable, still rages,
Eternal tempest never to be calmed.
Why do I humble thus myself, and suing
For peace, reap nothing but repulse and hate,
Bid go with evil omen, and the brand
Of infamy upon my name denounced?
To mix with thy concernments I desist
Henceforth, nor too much disapprove my own.

Fame, if not double-faced, is double-mouthed,
And with contrary blast proclaims most deeds;
On both his wings, one black, the other white,
Bears greatest names in his wild aery flight.
My name, perhaps, among the Circumcised
In Dan, in Judah, and the bordering tribes,
To all posterity may stand defamed,
With malediction mentioned, and the blot
Of falsehood most unconjugal traduced.
But in my country, where I most desire,
In Ecron, Gaza, Asdod, and in Gath,
I shall be named among the famousest
Of women, sung at solemn festivals,
Living and dead recorded, who, to save
Her country from a fierce destroyer, chose
Above the faith of wedlock bands; my tomb
With odours visited and annual flowers;
Not less renowned than in Mount Ephraim
Jael, who, with inhospitable guile,
Smote Sisera sleeping, through the temples nailed.
Nor shall I count it heinous to enjoy
The public marks of honour and reward
Conferred upon me for the piety
Which to my country I was judged to have shown.
At this whoever envies or repines,
I leave him to his lot, and like my own.

CHORUS She's gone—a manifest serpent by her sting
Discovered in the end, till now concealed.

SAMSON So let her go. God sent her to debase me,
And aggravate my folly, who committed
To such a viper his most sacred trust
Of secrecy, my safety, and my life.

CHORUS Yet beauty, though injurious, hath strange power,
After offence returning, to regain
Love once possessed, nor can be easily
Repulsed, without much inward passion felt,

And secret sting of amorous remorse.
SAMSON Love-quarrels oft in pleasing concord end;
Not wedlock-treachery endangering life.
CHORUS It is not virtue, wisdom, valour, wit,
Strength, comeliness of shape, or amplest merit,
That woman's love can win, or long inherit;
But what it is, hard is to say,
Harder to hit,
Which way soever men refer it,
(Much like thy riddle, Samson) in one day
Or seven though one should musing sit.
If any of these, or all, the Timnian bride
Had not so soon preferred
Thy paranymph, worthless to thee compared,
Successor in thy bed,
Nor both so loosely disallied
Their nuptials, nor this last so treacherously
Had shorn the fatal harvest of thy head.
Is it for that such outward ornament
Was lavished on their sex, that inward gifts
Were left for haste unfinished, judgment scant,
Capacity not raised to apprehend
Or value what is best
In choice, but oftest to affect the wrong?
Or was too much of self-love mixed,
Of constancy no root infixed,
That either they love nothing, or not long?
Whate'er it be, to wisest men and best
Seeming at first all heavenly under virgin veil,
Soft, modest, meek, demure,
Once joined, the contrary she proves—a thorn
Intestine, far within defensive arms
A cleaving mischief, in his way to virtue
Adverse and turbulent; or by her charms
Draws him awry, enslaved
With dotage, and his sense depraved

To folly and shameful deeds, which ruin ends.
What pilot so expert but needs must wreck,
Embarked with such a steers-mate at the helm?
  Favoured of Heaven who finds
One virtuous, rarely found,
That in domestic good combines!
Happy that house! his way to peace is smooth:
But virtue which breaks through all opposition,
And all temptation can remove,
Most shines and most is acceptable above.
  Therefore God's universal law
Gave to the man despotic power
Over his female in due awe,
Nor from that right to part an hour,
Smile she or lour:
So shall he least confusion draw
On his whole life, not swayed
By female usurpation, nor dismayed.
  But had we best retire? I see a storm.

SAMSON Fair days have oft contracted wind and rain.
CHORUS But this another kind of tempest brings.
SAMSON Be less abstruse; my riddling days are past.
CHORUS Look now for no enchanting voice, nor fear
The bait of honeyed words; a rougher tongue
Draws hitherward; I know him by his stride,
The giant Harapha of Gath, his look
Haughty, as in his pile high-built and proud.
Comes he in peace? What wind hath blown him hither
I less conjecture than when first I saw
The sumptuous Dalila floating this way:
His habit carries peace, his brow defiance.
SAMSON Or peace or not, alike to me he comes.
CHORUS His fraught we soon shall know: he now arrives.
HARAPHA I come not, Samson, to condole thy chance,
As these perhaps, yet wish it had not been,
Though for no friendly intent. I am of Gath;

Men call me Harapha, of stock renowned
As Og, or Anak, and the Emims old
That Kiriathaim held. Thou know'st me now,
If thou at all art known. Much I have heard
Of thy prodigious might and feats performed,
Incredible to me, in this displeased,
That I was never present on the place
Of those encounters, where we might have tried
Each other's force in camp or listed field;
And now am come to see of whom such noise
Hath walked about, and each limb to survey,
If thy appearance answer loud report.
SAMSON The way to know were not to see, but taste.
HARAPHA Dost thou already single me? I thought
Gyves and the mill had tamed thee. O that fortune
Had brought me to the field where thou art famed
To have wrought such wonders with an ass's jaw!
I should have forced thee soon with other arms,
Or left thy carcass where the ass lay thrown;
So had the glory of prowess been recovered
To Palestine, won by a Philistine
From the unforeskinned race, of whom thou bear'st
The highest name for valiant acts. That honour,
Certain to have won by mortal duel from thee,
I lose, prevented by thy eyes put out.
SAMSON Boast not of what thou would'st have done, but do
What then thou would'st; thou seest it in thy hand.
HARAPHA To combat with a blind man I disdain,
And thou hast need much washing to be touched.
SAMSON Such usage as your honourable lords
Afford me, assassinated and betrayed;
Who durst not with their whole united powers
In fight withstand me single and unarmed,
Nor in the house with chamber-ambushes
Close-banded durst attack me, no, not sleeping,
Till they had hired a woman with their gold,

Breaking her marriage-faith, to circumvent me.
Therefore, without feign'd shifts, let be assigned
Some narrow place enclosed, where sight may give thee,
Or rather flight, no great advantage on me;
Then put on all thy gorgeous arms, thy helmet
And brigandine of brass, thy broad habergeon,
Vant-brace and greaves and gauntlet; add thy spear,
A weaver's beam, and seven-times-folded shield:
I only with an oaken staff will meet thee,
And raise such outcries on thy clattered iron,
Which long shall not withhold me from thy head,
That in a little time, while breath remains thee,
Thou oft shalt wish thyself at Gath, to boast
Again in safety what thou would'st have done
To Samson, but shalt never see Gath more.

HARAPHA Thou durst not thus disparage glorious arms
Which greatest heroes have in battle worn,
Their ornament and safety, had not spells
And black enchantments, some magician's art,
Armed thee or charmed thee strong, which thou from Heaven
Feign'dst at thy birth was given thee in thy hair,
Where strength can least abide, though all thy hairs
Were bristles ranged like those that ridge the back
Of chafed wild boars or ruffled porcupines.

SAMSON I know no spells, use no forbidden arts;
My trust is in the Living God, who gave me,
At my nativity, this strength, diffused
No less through all my sinews, joints, and bones,
Than thine, while I preserved these locks unshorn,
The pledge of my unviolated vow.
For proof hereof, if Dagon be thy god,
Go to his temple, invocate his aid
With solemnest devotion, spread before him
How highly it concerns his glory now
To frustrate and dissolve these magic spells,
Which I to be the power of Israel's God

Avow, and challenge Dagon to the test,
Offering to combat thee, his champion bold,
With the utmost of his godhead seconded:
Then thou shalt see, or rather to thy sorrow
Soon feel, whose God is strongest, thine or mine.

HARAPHA Presume not on thy God. Whate'er he be,
Thee he regards not, owns not, hath cut off
Quite from his people, and delivered up
Into thy enemies' hand; permitted them
To put out both thine eyes, and fettered send thee
Into the common prison, there to grind
Among the slaves and asses, thy comrades,
As good for nothing else, no better service
With those thy boisterous locks; no worthy match
For valour to assail, nor by the sword
Of noble warrior, so to stain his honour,
But by the barber's razor best subdued.

SAMSON All these indignities, for such they are
From thine, these evils I deserve and more,
Acknowledge them from God inflicted on me
Justly, yet despair not of his final pardon,
Whose ear is ever open, and his eye
Gracious to re-admit the suppliant;
In confidence whereof I once again
Defy thee to the trial of mortal fight,
By combat to decide whose god is God,
Thine, or whom I with Israel's sons adore.

HARAPHA Fair honour that thou dost thy God, in trusting
He will accept thee to defend his cause,
A murtherer, a revolter, and a robber!

SAMSON Tongue-doughty giant, how dost thou prove me these?

HARAPHA Is not thy nation subject to our lords?
Their magistrates confessed it when they took thee
As a league-breaker, and delivered bound
Into our hands; for hadst thou not committed
Notorious murder on those thirty men

At Ascalon, who never did thee harm,
Then, like a robber, stripp'dst them of their robes?
The Philistines, when thou hadst broke the league,
Went up with armed powers thee only seeking,
To others did no violence nor spoil.

SAMSON Among the daughters of the Philistines
I chose a wife, which argued me no foe,
And in your city held my nuptial feast;
But your ill-meaning politician lords,
Under pretence of bridal friends and guests,
Appointed to await me thirty spies,
Who, threatening cruel death, constrained the bride
To wring from me, and tell to them, my secret,
That solved the riddle which I had proposed.
When I perceived all set on enmity,
As on my enemies, wherever chanced,
I used hostility, and took their spoil,
To pay my underminers in their coin.
My nation was subjected to your lords!
It was the force of conquest; force with force
Is well ejected when the conquered can.
But I, a private person, whom my country
As a league-breaker gave up bound, presumed
Single rebellion, and did hostile acts!
I was no private, but a person raised,
With strength sufficient, and command from Heaven,
To free my country. If their servile minds
Me, their deliverer sent, would not receive,
But to their masters gave me up for nought,
The unworthier they; whence to this day they serve.
I was to do my part from Heaven assigned,
And had performed it if my known offence
Had not disabled me, not all your force.
These shifts refuted, answer thy appellant,
Though by his blindness maimed for high attempts,
Who now defies thee thrice to single fight,

As a petty enterprise of small enforce.
HARAPHA With thee, a man condemned, a slave enrolled,
Due by the law to capital punishment?
To fight with thee no man of arms will deign.
SAMSON Cam'st thou for this, vain boaster, to survey me,
To descant on my strength, and give thy verdit?
Come nearer; part not hence so slight informed;
But take good heed my hand survey not thee.
HARAPHA O Baal-zebub! can my ears unused
Hear these dishonours, and not render death?
SAMSON No man withholds thee; nothing from thy hand
Fear I incurable; bring up thy van;
My heels are fettered, but my fist is free.
HARAPHA This insolence other kind of answer fits.
SAMSON Go, baffled coward, lest I run upon thee,
Though in these chains, bulk without spirit vast,
And with one buffet lay thy structure low,
Or swing thee in the air, then dash thee down,
To the hazard of thy brains and shattered sides.
HARAPHA By Astaroth, ere long thou shalt lament
These braveries, in irons loaden on thee.
CHORUS His giantship is gone somewhat crest-fallen,
Stalking with less unconscionable strides,
And lower looks, but in a sultry chafe.
SAMSON I dread him not, nor all his giant brood,
Though fame divulge him father of five sons,
All of gigantic size, Goliah chief.
CHORUS He will directly to the lords, I fear,
And with malicious counsel stir them up
Some way or other yet further to afflict thee.
SAMSON He must allege some cause, and offered fight
Will not dare mention, lest a question rise
Whether he durst accept the offer or not;
And that he durst not plain enough appeared.
Much more affliction than already felt
They cannot well impose, nor I sustain,

If they intend advantage of my labours,
The work of many hands, which earns my keeping,
With no small profit daily to my owners.
But come what will; my deadliest foe will prove
My speediest friend, by death to rid me hence;
The worst that he can give to me the best.
Yet so it may fall out, because their end
Is hate, not help to me, it may with mine
Draw their own ruin who attempt the deed.
CHORUS O, how comely it is, and how reviving
To the spirits of just men long oppressed,
When God into the hands of their deliverer
Puts invincible might,
To quell the mighty of the earth, the oppressor,
The brute and boisterous force of violent men,
Hardy and industrious to support
Tyrannic power, but raging to pursue
The righteous, and all such as honour truth!
He all their ammunition
And feats of war defeats,
With plain heroic magnitude of mind
And celestial vigour armed;
Their armouries and magazines contemns,
Renders them useless, while
With winged expedition
Swift as the lightning glance he executes
His errand on the wicked, who, surprised,
Lose their defence, distracted and amazed.
  But patience is more oft the exercise
Of saints, the trial of their fortitude,
Making them each his own deliverer.
And victor over all
That tyranny or fortune can inflict.
Either of these is in thy lot,
Samson, with might endued
Above the sons of men; but sight bereaved

May chance to number thee with those
Whom patience finally must crown.
This Idol's day hath been to thee no day of rest,
Labouring thy mind
More than the working day thy hands.
And yet, perhaps, more trouble is behind;
For I descry this way
Some other tending; in his hand
A sceptre or quaint staff he bears,
Comes on amain, speed in his look.
By his habit I discern him now
A public officer, and now at hand.
His message will be short and voluble.

OFFICER Ebrews, the prisoner Samson here I seek.

CHORUS His manacles remark him; there he sits.

OFFICER Samson, to thee our lords thus bid me say:
This day to Dagon is a solemn feast,
With sacrifices, triumph, pomp, and games;
Thy strength they know surpassing human rate,
And now some public proof thereof require
To honour this great feast, and great assembly.
Rise, therefore, with all speed, and come along,
Where I will see thee heartened and fresh clad,
To appear as fits before the illustrious lords.

SAMSON Thou know'st I am an Ebrew; therefore tell them
Our law forbids at their religious rites
My presence; for that cause I cannot come.

OFFICER This answer, be assured, will not content them.

SAMSON Have they not sword-players, and every sort
Of gymnic artists, wrestlers, riders, runners,
Jugglers and dancers, antics, mummers, mimics,
But they must pick me out, with shackles tired,
And over-laboured at their public mill,
To make them sport with blind activity?
Do they not seek occasion of new quarrels,
On my refusal, to distress me more,

Or make a game of my calamities?
Return the way thou cam'st; I will not come.
OFFICER Regard thyself; this will offend them highly.
SAMSON Myself! my conscience, and internal peace.
Can they think me so broken, so debased
With corporal servitude, that my mind ever
Will condescend to such absurd commands?
Although their drudge, to be their fool or jester,
And, in my midst of sorrow and heart-grief,
To show them feats, and play before their god—
The worst of all indignities, yet on me
Joined with extreme contempt! I will not come.
OFFICER My message was imposed on me with speed,
Brooks no delay: is this thy resolution?
SAMSON So take it with what speed thy message needs.
OFFICER I am sorry what this stoutness will produce.
SAMSON Perhaps thou shalt have cause to sorrow indeed.
CHORUS Consider, Samson; matters now are strained
Up to the highth, whether to hold or break.
He's gone, and who knows how he may report
Thy words by adding fuel to the flame?
Expect another message, more imperious,
More lordly thundering than thou well wilt bear.
SAMSON Shall I abuse this consecrated gift
Of strength, again returning with my hair
After my great transgression—so requite
Favour renewed, and add a greater sin
By prostituting holy things to idols,
A Nazarite, in place abominable,
Vaunting my strength in honour to their Dagon?
Besides how vile, contemptible, ridiculous,
What act more execrably unclean, profane?
CHORUS Yet with this strength thou serv'st the Philistines,
Idolatrous, uncircumcised, unclean.
SAMSON Not in their idol-worship, but by labour
Honest and lawful to deserve my food

Of those who have me in their civil power.
CHORUS Where the heart joins not, outward acts defile not.
SAMSON Where outward force constrains, the sentence holds:
But who constrains me to the temple of Dagon,
Not dragging? The Philistian lords command:
Commands are no contraints. If I obey them,
I do it freely, venturing to displease
God for the fear of man, and man prefer,
Set God behind; which, in his jealousy,
Shall never, unrepented, find forgiveness.
Yet that he may dispense with me, or thee,
Present in temples at idolatrous rites
For some important cause, thou need'st not doubt.
CHORUS How thou wilt here come off surmounts my reach.
SAMSON Be of good courage; I begin to feel
Some rousing motions in me, which dispose
To something extraordinary my thoughts.
I with this messenger will go along—
Nothing to do, be sure, that may dishonour
Our Law, or stain my vow of Nazarite.
If there be aught of presage in the mind,
This day will be remarkable in my life
By some great act, or of my days the last.
CHORUS In time thou hast resolved: the man returns.
OFFICER Samson, this second message from our lords
To thee I am bid say: Art thou our slave,
Our captive, at the public mill our drudge,
And dar'st thou, at our sending and command,
Dispute thy coming? Come without delay;
Or we shall find such engines to assail
And hamper thee, as thou shalt come of force,
Though thou wert firmlier fastened than a rock.
SAMSON I could be well content to try their art,
Which to no few of them would prove pernicious,
Yet, knowing their advantages too many,
Because they shall not trail me through their streets

Like a wild beast, I am content to go.
Masters' commands come with a power resistless
To such as owe them absolute subjection;
And for a life who will not change his purpose?
(So mutable are all the ways of men!)
Yet this be sure, in nothing to comply
Scandalous or forbidden in our Law.

OFFICER I praise thy resolution. Doff these links:
By this compliance thou wilt win the lords
To favour, and perhaps to set thee free.

SAMSON Brethren, farewell. Your company along
I will not wish, lest it perhaps offend them
To see me girt with friends; and how the sight
Of me, as of a common enemy,
So dreaded once, may now exasperate them
I know not. Lords are lordliest in their wine;
And the well-feasted priest then soonest fired
With zeal, if aught religion seem concerned;
No less the people, on their holy-days,
Impetuous, insolent, unquenchable.
Happen what may, of me expect to hear
Nothing dishonourable, impure, unworthy
Our God, our Law, my nation, or myself;
The last of me or no I cannot warrant.

CHORUS Go, and the Holy One
Of Israel by thy guide
To what may serve his glory best, and spread his name
Great among the Heathen round;
Send thee the Angel of thy birth, to stand
Fast by thy side, who from thy father's field
Rode up in flames after his message told
Of thy conception, and be now a shield
Of fire; that Spirit that first rushed on thee
In the camp of Dan,
Be efficacious in thee now at need!
For never was from Heaven imparted

Measure of strength so great to mortal seed,
As in thy wondrous actions hath been seen.
But wherefore comes old Manoa in such haste
With youthful steps? Much livelier than erewhile
He seems; supposing here to find his son,
Or of him bringing to us some glad news?

MANOA Peace with you, brethren! My inducement hither
Was not at present here to find my son,
By order of the lords new parted hence
To come and play before them at their feast.
I heard all as I came; the city rings,
And numbers thither flock: I had no will,
Lest I should see him forced to things unseemly.
But that which moved my coming now was chiefly
To give ye part with me what hope I have
With good success to work his liberty.

CHORUS That hope would much rejoice us to partake
With thee. Say, reverend sire; we thirst to hear.

MANOA I have attempted, one by one, the lords,
Either at home, or through the high street passing,
With supplication prone and father's tears,
To accept of ransom for my son, their prisoner.
Some much averse I found, and wondrous harsh,
Contemptuous, proud, set on revenge and spite;
That part most reverenced Dagon and his priests:
Others more moderate seeming, but their aim
Private reward, for which both God and State
They easily would set to sale: a third
More generous far and civil, who confessed
They had enough revenged, having reduced
Their foe to misery beneath their fears;
The rest was magnanimity to remit,
If some convenient ransom were proposed.
What noise or shout was that? It tore the sky.

CHORUS Doubtless the people shouting to behold
Their once great dread, captive and blind before them,

Or at some proof of strength before them shown.
MANOA His ransom, if my whole inheritance
May compass it, shall willingly be paid
And numbered down. Much rather I shall choose
To live the poorest in my tribe, than richest
And he in that calamitous prison left.
No, I am fixed not to part hence without him.
For his redemption all my patrimony,
If need be, I am ready to forgo
And quit. Not wanting him, I shall want nothing.
CHORUS Fathers are wont to lay up for their sons;
Thou for thy son are bent to lay out all:
Sons wont to nurse their parents in old age;
Thou in old age car'st how to nurse thy son,
Made older than thy age through eye-sight lost.
MANOA It shall be my delight to tend his eyes,
And view him sitting in his house, ennobled
With all those high exploits by him achieved,
And on his shoulders waving down those locks
That of a nation armed the strength contained.
And I persuade me God hath not permitted
His strength again to grow up with his hair
Garrisoned round about him like a camp
Of faithful soldiery, were not his purpose
To use him further yet in some great service—
Not to sit idle with so great a gift
Useless, and thence ridiculous, about him.
And, since his strength with eye-sight was not lost,
God will restore him eye-sight to his strength.
CHORUS Thy hopes are not ill founded, nor seem vain,
Of his delivery, and thy joy thereon
Conceived, agreeable to a father's love;
In both which we, as next, participate.
MANOA I know your friendly minds, and . . . O, what noise!
Mercy of Heaven! What hideous noise was that?
Horribly loud, unlike the former shout.

CHORUS Noise call you it, or universal groan,
As if the whole inhabitation perished?
Blood, death, and deathful deeds, are in that noise,
Ruin, destruction at the utmost point.
MANOA Of ruin indeed methought I heard the noise.
Oh! it continues; they have slain my son.
CHORUS Thy son is rather slaying them: that outcry
From slaughter of one foe could not ascend.
MANOA Some dismal accident it needs must be.
What shall we do—stay here, or run and see?
CHORUS Best keep together here, lest, running thither,
We unawares run into danger's mouth.
This evil on the Philistines is fallen:
From whom could else a general cry be heard?
The sufferers, then, will scarce molest us here;
From other hands we need not much to fear.
What if, his eye-sight (for to Israel's God
Nothing is hard) by miracle restored,
He now be dealing dole among his foes,
And over heaps of slaughtered walk his way?
MANOA That were a joy presumptuous to be thought.
CHORUS Yet God hath wrought things as incredible
For his people of old; what hinders now?
MANOA He can, I know, but doubt to think he will;
Yet hope would fain subscribe, and tempts belief.
A little stay will bring some notice hither.
CHORUS Of good or bad so great, of bad the sooner;
For evil news rides post, while good news baits.
And to our wish I see one hither speeding—
An Ebrew, as I guess, and of our tribe.
MESSENGER O, whither shall I run, or which way fly
The sight of this so horrid spectacle,
Which erst my eyes beheld, and yet behold?
For dire imagination still pursues me.
But providence or instinct of nature seems,
Or reason, though disturbed and scarce consulted,

To have guided me aright, I know not how,
To thee first, reverend Manoa, and to these
My countrymen, whom here I knew remaining,
As at some distance from the place of horror,
So in the sad event too much concerned.

MANOA The accident was loud, and here before thee
With rueful cry; yet what it was we hear not.
No preface needs; thou seest we long to know.

MESSENGER It would burst forth; but I recover breath,
And sense distract, to know well what I utter.

MANOA Tell us the sum; the circumstance defer.

MESSENGER Gaza yet stands; but all her sons are fallen,
All in a moment overwhelmed and fallen.

MANOA Sad! but thou know'st to Israelites not saddest
The desolation of a hostile city.

MESSENGER Feed on that first; there may in grief be surfeit.

MANOA Relate by whom.

MESSENGER By Samson.

MANOA That still lessens
The sorrow, and converts it nigh to joy.

MESSENGER Ah! Manoa, I refrain too suddenly
To utter what will come at last too soon,
Lest evil tidings, with too rude irruption
Hitting thy aged ear, should pierce too deep.

MANOA Suspense in news is torture; speak them out.

MESSENGER Then take the worst in brief: Samson is dead.

MANOA The worst indeed! O, all my hope's defeated
To free him hence! but Death, who sets all free,
Hath paid his ransom now and full discharge.
What windy joy this day had I conceived,
Hopeful of his delivery, which now proves
Abortive as the first-born bloom of spring
Nipt with the lagging rear of winter's frost!
Yet, ere I give the reins to grief, say first
How died he; death to life is crown or shame.
All by him fell, thou say'st; by whom fell he?

What glorious hand gave Samson his death's wound?
MESSENGER Unwounded of his enemies he fell.
MANOA Wearied with slaughter, then, or how? explain.
MESSENGER By his own hands.
MANOA Self-violence! What cause
Brought him so soon at variance with himself
Among his foes?
MESSENGER Inevitable cause—
At once both to destroy and be destroyed.
The edifice, where all were met to see him,
Upon their heads and on his own he pulled.
MANOA O lastly over-strong against thyself!
A dreadful way thou took'st to thy revenge.
More than enough we know; but, while things yet
Are in confusion, give us, if thou canst,
Eye-witness of what first or last was done,
Relation more particular and distinct.
MESSENGER Occasions drew me early to this city;
And, as the gates I entered with sun-rise,
The morning trumpets festival proclaimed
Through each high street. Little I had dispatched,
When all abroad was rumored that this day
Samson should be brought forth, to show the people
Proof of his mighty strength in feats and games.
I sorrowed at his captive state, but minded
Not to be absent at that spectacle.
The building was a spacious theatre,
Half round on two main pillars vaulted high,
With seats where all the lords, and each degree
Of sort, might sit in order to behold;
The other side was open, where the throng
On banks and scaffolds under sky might stand:
I among these aloof obscurely stood.
The feast and noon grew high, and sacrifice
Had filled their hearts with mirth, high cheer, and wine,
When to their sports they turned. Immediately

Was Samson as a public servant brought,
In their state livery clad: before him pipes
And timbrels; on each side went armed guards;
Both horse and foot before him and behind,
Archers and slingers, cataphracts and spears.
At sight of him the people with a shout
Rifted the air, clamouring their god with praise,
Who had made their dreadful enemy their thrall.
He patient, but undaunted, where they led him,
Came to the place; and what was set before him,
Which without help of eye might be assayed,
To heave, pull, draw, or break, he still performed
All with incredible, stupendous force,
None daring to appear antagonist.
At length, for intermission sake, they led him
Between the pillars; he his guide requested
(For so from such as nearer stood we heard),
As over-tired, to let him lean a while
With both his arms on those two massy pillars,
That to the arched roof gave main support.
He unsuspicious led him; which when Samson
Felt in his arms, with head a while inclined,
And eyes fast fixed, he stood, as one who prayed,
Or some great matter in his mind revolved:
At last, with head erect, thus cried aloud:—
"Hitherto, Lords, what your commands imposed
I have performed, as reason was, obeying,
Not without wonder or delight beheld;
Now, of my own accord, such other trial
I mean to show you of my strength yet greater
As with amaze shall strike all who behold."
This uttered, straining all his nerves, he bowed;
As with the force of winds and waters pent
When mountains tremble, those two massy pillars
With horrible convulsion to and fro
He tugged, he shook, till down they came, and drew

The whole roof after them with burst of thunder
Upon the heads of all who sat beneath,
Lords, ladies, captains, counsellors, or priests,
Their choice nobility and flower, not only
Of this, but each Philistian city round,
Met from all parts to solemnize this feast.
Samson, with these immixed, inevitably
Pulled down the same destruction on himself;
The vulgar only scaped, who stood without.

CHORUS O dearly bought revenge, yet glorious!
Living or dying thou hast fulfilled
The work for which thou wast foretold
To Israel, and now liest victorious
Among thy slain self-killed;
Not willingly, but tangled in the fold
Of dire Necessity, whose law in death conjoined
Thee with thy slaughtered foes, in number more
Than all thy life had slain before.

SEMICHORUS While their hearts were jocund and sublime,
Drunk with idolatry, drunk with wine
And fat regorged of bulls and goats,
Chaunting their idol, and preferring
Before our living Dread, who dwells
In Silo, his bright sanctuary,
Among them he a spirit of phrenzy sent,
Who hurt their minds,
And urged them on with mad desire
To call in haste for their destroyer.
They, only set on sport and play,
Unweetingly importuned
Their own destruction to come speedy upon them.
So fond are mortal men,
Fallen into wrath divine,
As their own ruin on themselves to invite,
Insensate left, or to sense reprobate,
And with blindness internal struck.

SEMICHORUS But he, though blind of sight,
Despised, and thought extinguished quite,
With inward eyes illuminated,
His fiery virtue roused
From under ashes into sudden flame,
And as an evening dragon came,
Assailant on the perched roosts
And nests in order ranged
Of tame villatic fowl, but as an eagle
His cloudless thunder bolted on their heads.
So Virtue, given for lost,
Depressed and overthrown, as seemed,
Like that self-begotten bird
In the Arabian woods embost,
That no second knows nor third,
And lay erewhile a holocaust,
From out her ashy womb now teemed,
Revives, reflourishes, then vigorous most
When most unactive deemed;
And, though her body die, her fame survives,
A secular bird, ages of lives.

MANOA Come, come; no time for lamentation now,
Nor much more cause. Samson hath quit himself
Like Samson, and heroicly hath finished
A life heroic, on his enemies
Fully revenged—hath left them years of mourning,
And lamentation to the sons of Caphtor
Through all Philistian bounds; to Israel
Honour hath left and freedom, let but them
Find courage to lay hold on this occasion;
To himself and father's house eternal fame;
And, which is best and happiest yet, all this
With God not parted from him, as was feared,
But favouring and assisting to the end.
Nothing is here for tears, nothing to wail
Or knock the breast; no weakness, no contempt,

Dispraise, or blame; nothing but well and fair,
And what may quiet us in a death so noble.
Let us go find the body where it lies
Soaked in his enemies' blood, and from the stream
With lavers pure, and cleansing herbs, wash off
The clotted gore. I, with what speed the while
(Gaza is not in plight to say us nay),
Will send for all my kindred, all my friends,
To fetch him hence, and solemnly attend,
With silent obsequy and funeral train,
Home to his father's house. There will I build him
A monument, and plant it round with shade
Of laurel ever green and branching palm,
With all his trophies hung, and acts enrolled
In copious legend, or sweet lyric song.
Thither shall all the valiant youth resort,
And from his memory inflame their breasts
To matchless valour and adventures high;
The virgins also shall, on feastful days,
Visit his tomb with flowers, only bewailing
His lot unfortunate in nuptial choice,
From whence captivity and loss of eyes.

CHORUS All is best, though we oft doubt
What the unsearchable dispose
Of Highest Wisdom brings about,
And ever best found in the close.
Oft He seems to hide his face,
But unexpectedly returns,
And to his faithful champion hath in place
Bore witness gloriously; whence Gaza mourns,
And all that band them to resist
His uncontrollable intent.
His servants He, with new acquist
Of true experience from this great event,
With peace and consolation hath dismissed,
And calm of mind, all passion spent.

PART II

ANTECEDENTS

RELEVANT PORTIONS FROM THE BIBLE

The Scriptural sources of the Samson story are to be found in the Old Testament book Judges, chapters 13-16, and in the New Testament Epistle to the Hebrews, 11:32-34. The text presented here is that of the King James version (1611), with which Milton must have been familiar (although he doubtlessly was more familiar with the Geneva version [1557, 1560]).

One peculiarity of the King James version of the Bible is that the Hebrew tetragrammaton—the sacred name of Jehovah—was always printed in capital letters (LORD) *to distinguish it from the name Elohim (most often translated* God *but sometimes* Lord).

JUDGES 13–16

13:1 And the children of Israel did evil again in the sight of the
LORD; and the LORD delivered them into the hand of the Philistines forty years.
2 ¶ And there was a certain man of Zorah, of the family of the
Danites, whose name was Manoah; and his wife was barren, and
bare not.
3 And the angel of the LORD appeared unto the woman, and
said unto her, Behold now, thou art barren, and bearest not: but
thou shalt conceive, and bear a son.

4 Now therefore beware, I pray thee, and drink not wine nor
strong drink, and eat not any unclean thing:
5 For, lo, thou shalt conceive, and bear a son; and no razor
shall come on his head: for the child shall be a Nazarite unto God
from the womb; and he shall begin to deliver Israel out of the
hand of the Philistines.
6 ¶ Then the woman came and told her husband, saying, A
man of God came unto me, and his countenance was like the
countenance of an angel of God, very terrible: but I asked him
not whence he was, neither told he me his name:
7 But he said unto me, Behold, thou shalt conceive, and bear a
son; and now drink no wine nor strong drink, neither eat any unclean thing: for the child shall be a Nazarite to God from the
womb to the day of his death.
8 ¶ Then Manoah entreated the LORD, and said, O my Lord,
let the man of God which thou didst send come again unto us,
and teach us what we shall do unto the child that shall be born.
9 And God hearkened to the voice of Manoah; and the angel of
God came again unto the woman as she sat in the field: but Manoah her husband was not with her.
10 And the woman made haste, and ran, and shewed her husband, and said unto him, Behold, the man hath appeared unto
me, that came unto me the other day.
11 And Manoah arose, and went after his wife, and came to
the man, and said unto him, Art thou the man that spakest unto
the woman? And he said, I am.
12 And Manoah said, Now let thy words come to pass. How
shall we order the child, and how shall we do unto him?
13 And the angel of the LORD said unto Manoah, Of all that I
said unto the woman let her beware.
14 She may not eat of any thing that cometh of the vine, neither let her drink wine or strong drink, nor eat any unclean thing:
all that I commanded her let her observe.
15 ¶ And Manoah said unto the angel of the LORD, I pray thee,
let us detain thee, until we shall have made ready a kid for thee.
16 And the angel of the LORD said unto Manoah, Though thou

detain me, I will not eat of thy bread: and if thou wilt offer a
burnt offering, thou must offer it unto the LORD. For Manoah
knew not that he was an angel of the LORD.
17 And Manoah said unto the angel of the LORD, What is thy
name, that when thy sayings come to pass we may do thee
honour?
18 And the angel of the LORD said unto him, Why askest thou
thus after my name, seeing it is secret?
19 So Manoah took a kid with a meat offering, and offered it
upon a rock unto the LORD: and the angel did wondrously; and
Manoah and his wife looked on.
20 For it came to pass, when the flame went up toward heaven
from off the altar, that the angel of the LORD ascended in the
flame of the altar. And Manoah and his wife looked on it, and fell
on their faces to the ground.
21 But the angel of the LORD did no more appear to Manoah
and to his wife. Then Manoah knew that he was an angel of the
LORD.
22 And Manoah said unto his wife, We shall surely die, because
we have seen God.
23 But his wife said unto him, If the LORD were pleased to kill
us, he would not have received a burnt offering and a meat offering at our hands, neither would he have shewed us all these
things, nor would as at this time have told us such things as these.
24 ¶ And the woman bare a son, and called his name Samson:
and the child grew, and the LORD blessed him.
25 And the spirit of the LORD began to move him at times in
the camp of Dan between Zorah and Eshtaol.

14:1 And Samson went down to Timnath, and saw a woman in
Timnath of the daughters of the Philistines.
2 And he came up, and told his father and his mother, and
said, I have seen a woman in Timnath of the daughters of the
Philistines: now therefore get her for me to wife.
3 Then his father and his mother said unto him, Is there never
a woman among the daughters of thy brethren, or among all my

people, that thou goest to take a wife of the uncircumcised Philistines? And Samson said unto his father, Get her for me; for she pleaseth me well.

4 But his father and his mother knew not that it was of the LORD, that he sought an occasion against the Philistines: for at that time the Philistines had dominion over Israel.

5 ¶ Then went Samson down, and his father and his mother, to Timnath, and came to the vineyards of Timnath: and, behold, a young lion roared against him.

6 And the spirit of the LORD came mightily upon him, and he rent him as he would have rent a kid, and he had nothing in his hand: but he told not his father or his mother what he had done.

7 And he went down, and talked with the woman; and she pleased Samson well.

8 ¶ And after a time he returned to take her, and he turned aside to see the carcase of the lion: and, behold, there was a swarm of bees and honey in the carcase of the lion.

9 And he took thereof in his hands, and went on eating, and came to his father and mother, and he gave them, and they did eat: but he told not them that he had taken the honey out of the carcase of the lion.

10 ¶ So his father went down unto the woman: and Samson made there a feast; for so used the young men to do.

11 And it came to pass, when they saw him, that they brought thirty companions to be with him.

12 ¶ And Samson said unto them, I will now put forth a riddle unto you: if ye can certainly declare it me within the seven days of the feast, and find it out, then I will give you thirty sheets and thirty change of garments:

13 But if ye cannot declare it me, then shall ye give me thirty sheets and thirty change of garments. And they said unto him, Put forth thy riddle, that we may hear it.

14 And he said unto them, Out of the eater came forth meat, and out of the strong came forth sweetness. And they could not in three days expound the riddle.

15 And it came to pass on the seventh day, that they said unto Samson's wife, Entice thy husband, that he may declare unto us the riddle, lest we burn thee and thy father's house with fire: have ye called us to take that we have? is it not so?

16 And Samson's wife wept before him, and said, Thou dost but hate me, and lovest me not: thou hast put forth a riddle unto the children of my people, and hast not told it me. And he said unto her, Behold, I have not told it my father nor my mother, and shall I tell it thee?

17 And she wept before him the seven days, while their feast lasted: and it came to pass on the seventh day, that he told her, because she lay sore upon him: and she told the riddle to the children of her people.

18 And the men of the city said unto him on the seventh day before the sun went down, What is sweeter than honey? and what is stronger than a lion? And he said unto them, If ye had not plowed with my heifer, ye had not found out my riddle.

19 ¶ And the spirit of the LORD came upon him, and he went down to Ashkelon, and slew thirty men of them, and took their spoil, and gave change of garments unto them which expounded the riddle. And his anger was kindled, and he went up to his father's house.

20 But Samson's wife was given to his companion, whom he had used as his friend.

15:1 But it came to pass within a while after, in the time of wheat harvest, that Samson visited his wife with a kid; and he said, I will go in to my wife into the chamber. But her father would not suffer him to go in.

2 And her father said, I verily thought that thou hadst utterly hated her; therefore I gave her to thy companion: is not her younger sister fairer than she? take her, I pray thee, instead of her.

3 ¶ And Samson said concerning them, Now shall I be more blameless than the Philistines, though I do them a displeasure.

4 And Samson went and caught three hundred foxes, and took firebrands, and turned tail to tail, and put a firebrand in the midst between two tails.

5 And when he had set the brands on fire, he let them go into the standing corn of the Philistines, and burnt up both the shocks, and also the standing corn, with the vineyards and olives.

6 ¶ Then the Philistines said, Who hath done this? And they answered, Samson, the son in law of the Timnite, because he had taken his wife, and given her to his companion. And the Philistines came up, and burnt her and her father with fire.

7 ¶ And Samson said unto them, Though ye have done this, yet will I be avenged of you, and after that I will cease.

8 And he smote them hip and thigh with a great slaughter: and he went down and dwelt in the top of the rock Etam.

9 ¶ Then the Philistines went up, and pitched in Judah, and spread themselves in Lehi.

10 And the men of Judah said, Why are ye come up against us? And they answered, To bind Samson are we come up, to do to him as he hath done to us.

11 Then three thousand men of Judah went to the top of the rock Etam, and said to Samson, Knowest thou not that the Philistines are rulers over us? what is this that thou hast done unto us? And he said unto them, As they did unto me, so have I done unto them.

12 And they said unto him, We are come down to bind thee, that we may deliver thee into the hand of the Philistines. And Samson said unto them, Swear unto me, that ye will not fall upon me yourselves.

13 And they spake unto him, saying, No; but we will bind thee fast, and deliver thee into their hand: but surely we will not kill thee. And they bound him with two new cords, and brought him up from the rock.

14 ¶ And when he came unto Lehi, the Philistines shouted against him: and the spirit of the LORD came mightily upon him, and the cords that were upon his arms became as flax that was burnt with fire, and his bands loosed from off his hands.

15 And he found a new jawbone of an ass, and put forth his hand, and took it, and slew a thousand men therewith.

16 And Samson said, With the jawbone of an ass, heaps upon heaps, with the jaw of an ass have I slain a thousand men.

17 And it came to pass, when he had made an end of speaking, that he cast away the jawbone out of his hand, and called that place Ramath-lehi.

18 ¶ And he was sore athirst, and called on the LORD, and said, Thou hast given this great deliverance into the hand of thy servant: and now shall I die for thirst, and fall into the hand of the uncircumcised?

19 But God clave an hollow place that was in the jaw, and there came water thereout; and when he had drunk, his spirit came again, and he revived: wherefore he called the name thereof En-hakkore, which is in Lehi unto this day.

20 And he judged Israel in the days of the Philistines twenty years.

16:1 Then went Samson to Gaza, and saw there an harlot, and went in unto her.

2 And it was told the Gazites, saying, Samson is come hither. And they compassed him in, and laid wait for him all night in the gate of the city, and were quiet all the night, saying, In the morning, when it is day, we shall kill him.

3 And Samson lay till midnight, and arose at midnight, and took the doors of the gate of the city, and the two posts, and went away with them, bar and all, and put them upon his shoulders, and carried them up to the top of an hill that is before Hebron.

4 ¶ And it came to pass afterward, that he loved a woman in the valley of Sorek, whose name was Delilah.

5 And the lords of the Philistines came up unto her, and said unto her, Entice him, and see wherein his great strength lieth, and by what means we may prevail against him, that we may bind him to afflict him: and we will give thee every one of us eleven hundred pieces of silver.

6 ¶ And Delilah said to Samson, Tell me, I pray thee, wherein thy great strength lieth, and wherewith thou mightest be bound to afflict thee.

7 And Samson said unto her, If they bind me with seven green withs that were never dried, then shall I be weak, and be as another man.

8 Then the lords of the Philistines brought up to her seven green withs which had not been dried, and she bound him with them.

9 Now there were men lying in wait, abiding with her in the chamber. And she said unto him, The Philistines be upon thee, Samson. And he brake the withs, as a thread of tow is broken when it toucheth the fire. So his strength was not known.

10 And Delilah said unto Samson, Behold, thou hast mocked me, and told me lies: now tell me, I pray thee, wherewith thou mightest be bound.

11 And he said unto her, If they bind me fast with new ropes that never were occupied, then shall I be weak, and be as another man.

12 Delilah therefore took new ropes, and bound him therewith, and said unto him, The Philistines be upon thee, Samson. And there were liers in wait abiding in the chamber. And he brake them from off his arms like a thread.

13 And Delilah said unto Samson, Hitherto thou hast mocked me, and told me lies: tell me wherewith thou mightest be bound. And he said unto her, If thou weavest the seven locks of my head with the web.

14 And she fastened it with the pin, and said unto him, The Philistines be upon thee, Samson. And he awaked out of his sleep, and went away with the pin of the beam, and with the web.

15 ¶ And she said unto him, How canst thou say, I love thee, when thine heart is not with me? thou hast mocked me these three times, and hast not told me wherein thy great strength lieth.

16 And it came to pass, when she pressed him daily with her words, and urged him, so that his soul was vexed unto death;

17 That he told her all his heart, and said unto her, There hath
not come a razor upon mine head; for I have been a Nazarite
unto God from my mother's womb: if I be shaven, then my
strength will go from me, and I shall become weak, and be like
any other man.
18 And when Delilah saw that he had told her all his heart, she
sent and called for the lords of the Philistines, saying, Come up
this once, for he hath shewed me all his heart. Then the lords of
the Philistines came up unto her, and brought money in their
hand.
19 And she made him sleep upon her knees; and she called for
a man, and she caused him to shave off the seven locks of his
head; and she began to afflict him, and his strength went from
him.
20 And she said, The Philistines be upon thee, Samson. And he
awoke out of his sleep, and said, I will go out as at other times
before, and shake myself. And he wist not that the LORD was de-
parted from him.
21 ¶ But the Philistines took him, and put out his eyes, and
brought him down to Gaza, and bound him with fetters of brass;
and he did grind in the prison house.
22 Howbeit the hair of his head began to grow again after he
was shaven.
23 Then the lords of the Philistines gathered them together for
to offer a great sacrifice unto Dagon their god, and to rejoice: for
they said, Our god hath delivered Samson our enemy into our
hand.
24 And when the people saw him, they praised their god: for
they said, Our god hath delivered into our hands our enemy, and
the destroyer of our country, which slew many of us.
25 And it came to pass, when their hearts were merry, that
they said, Call for Samson, that he may make us sport. And they
called for Samson out of the prison house; and he made them
sport: and they set him between the pillars.
26 And Samson said unto the lad that held him by the hand,

Suffer me that I may feel the pillars whereupon the house standeth, that I may lean upon them.

27 Now the house was full of men and women; and all the lords of the Philistines were there; and there were upon the roof about three thousand men and women, that beheld while Samson made sport.

28 And Samson called unto the LORD, and said, O Lord GOD, remember me, I pray thee, and strengthen me, I pray thee, only this once, O God, that I may be at once avenged of the Philistines for my two eyes.

29 And Samson took hold of the two middle pillars upon which the house stood, and on which it was borne up, of the one with his right hand, and of the other with his left.

30 And Samson said, Let me die with the Philistines. And he bowed himself with all his might; and the house fell upon the lords, and upon all the people that were therein. So the dead which he slew at his death were more than they which he slew in his life.

31 Then his brethren and all the house of his father came down, and took him, and brought him up, and buried him between Zorah and Eshtaol in the buryingplace of Manoah his father. And he judged Israel twenty years.

HEBREWS 11

32 And what shall I more say? for the time would fail me to tell of Gedeon, and of Barak, and of Samson, and of Jephthæ; of David also, and Samuel, and of the prophets:

33 Who through faith subdued kingdoms, wrought righteousness, obtained promises, stopped the mouths of lions,

34 Quenched the violence of fire, escaped the edge of the sword, out of weakness were made strong, waxed valiant in fight, turned to flight the armies of the aliens.

JOSEPHUS

HISTORY OF SAMSON

Flavius Josephus (A.D. 37-95?) *is probably best known to us as the compiler of* Antiquities of the Jews, *a history of his people from creation to the war with Rome. The translation from which the Samson portion is here reprinted was made in 1737 by William Whiston (1667-1752), an English clergyman and mathematician. Many times reprinted, the edition here employed was published in Hartford, Connecticut, in 1909, in* The Works of Flavius Josephus *(pp. 170-173).*

Book V, Chapter VIII

After Abdon was dead, the Philistines overcame the Israelites, and received tribute of them for forty years; from which distress they were delivered after this manner:—

There was one Manoah, a person of such great virtue that he had few men his equals, and without dispute the principal person of his country. He had a wife celebrated for her beauty, and excelling her contemporaries. He had no children; and, being uneasy at his want of posterity, he entreated God to give them seed of their own body to succeed them; and with that intent he came constantly into the suburbs, together with his wife; which suburbs were in the Great Plain. Now, he was fond of his wife to a degree of madness, and on that account was unmeasurably jealous of her. Now, when his wife was once alone, an apparition was seen by her: it was an angel of God, and resembled a young man, beautiful and tall, and brought her the good news that she should have a son, born of God's providence, who should be a goodly child, of great strength; by whom, when he had grown up to man's estate, the Philistines should be afflicted. He exhorted her also not to poll his hair, and that he should avoid all kinds of strong drink, (for so had God commanded,) and be entirely contented with water. So the angel, when he had delivered that message, went his way, his coming having been by the will of God.

Now the wife informed her husband when he came home of what the angel had said, and showed so great an admiration of the beauty and tallness of the young man that had appeared to her, that her husband was astonished, and out of himself for jealousy, and such suspicions as are excited by that passion; but she was desirous of having her husband's unreasonable sorrow taken away; accordingly, she entreated God to send the angel again, that he might be seen by her husband. So the angel came again, by the favour of God, while they were in the suburbs, and appeared to her when she was alone without her husband. She desired the angel to stay so long till she might bring her husband; and that request being granted, she went to call Manoah. When he saw the angel, he was not yet free from his suspicion, and he desired him to inform him of all that he told his wife; but when he said it was sufficient that she alone knew what he had said, he then requested of him to tell who he was, that when the child was born, they might return him thanks, and give him a present. He replied that he did not want any present, for that he did not bring them the good news of the birth of a son out of the want of any thing; and when Manoah had entreated him to stay, and partake of his hospitality, he did not give his consent. However, he was persuaded, at the earnest request of Manoah, to stay so long as while he brought him one mark of his hospitality; so he slew a kid of the goats, and bade his wife boil it. When all was ready, the angel enjoined him to set the loaves and the flesh, but without the vessels, upon the rock; which, when they had done, he touched the flesh with the rod which he had in his hand, which, upon the breaking out of a flame, was consumed, together with the loaves; and the angel ascended openly, in their sight, up to heaven, by means of the smoke, as by a vehicle. Now Manoah was afraid that some danger would come to them from this sight of God; but his wife bade him be of good courage, for that God appeared to them for their benefit.

So the woman proved with child, and was careful to observe the injunctions that were given her; and they called the child, when he was born, Samson, which name signifies one that is "strong." So the child grew apace; and it appeared evidently that he would be a prophet,[1] both by the moderation of his diet, and the permission of his hair to grow.

Now when he once came with his parents to Timnath, a city of the Philistines, when there was a great festival, he fell in love with a maid of that country, and he desired of his parents that they would procure him the damsel for his wife: but they refused so to do, because she was not of the stock of Israel; yet because this marriage was of God, who intended to convert it to the benefit of the Hebrews, he overpersuaded them to procure her to be espoused to him; and as he was continually coming to his parents, he met a lion, and though he was naked, he received his onset, and strangled him with his hands, and cast the wild beast into a woody piece of ground on the inside of the road.

And when he was going another time to the damsel, he lit upon a swarm of bees making their combs in the breast of that lion; and taking three honey-combs away, he gave them, together with the rest of his presents, to the damsel. Now the people of Timnath, out of a dread of the young man's strength, gave him, during the time of the wedding-feast, (for he then feasted them all,) thirty of the most stout of their youth, in pretence to be his com-

[1] Here, by a "prophet," Josephus seems only to mean one that was born by a particular providence, lived after the manner of a Nazarite devoted to God, and was to have an extraordinary commission and strength from God for the judging and avenging his people Israel, without any proper prophetic revelations at all.

panions, but in reality to be a guard upon him, that he might not attempt to give them any disturbance. Now as they were drinking merrily and playing, Samson said, as it was usual at such times, "Come, if I propose you a riddle, and you can expound it in seven days' time, I will give you every one a linen shirt and a garment, as the reward of your wisdom." So they being very ambitious to obtain the glory of wisdom, together with the gains, desired him to propose his riddle: he said, "That a devourer produced sweet food out of itself, though itself was very disagreeable:" and when they were not able, in three days' time, to find out the meaning of the riddle, they desired the damsel to discover it by the means of her husband, and tell it them; and they threatened to burn her if she did not tell it them. So when the damsel entreated Samson to tell it her, he at first refused to do it; but when she lay hard at him, and fell into tears, and made his refusal to tell it a sign of his unkindness to her, he informed her of his slaughter of a lion, and how he found bees in his breast, and carried away three honey-combs, and brought them to her. Thus he, suspecting nothing of deceit, informed her of all, and she revealed it to those that desired to know it. Then on the seventh day, whereon they were to expound the riddle proposed to them, they met together before sun-setting, and said, "Nothing is more disagreeable than a lion to those that light on it; and nothing is sweeter than honey to those that make use of it." To which Samson made this rejoinder: "Nothing is more deceitful than a woman, for such was the person that discovered my interpretation to you." Accordingly he gave them the presents he had promised them, making such Askelonites as met him upon the road his prey, who were themselves Philistines also. But he divorced this his wife; and the girl despised his anger, and was married to his companion, who made the former match between them.

At this injurious treatment Samson was so provoked, that he resolved to punish all the Philistines, as well as her: so it being then summer time, and the fruits of the land being almost ripe enough for reaping, he caught 300 foxes, and joining lighted torches to their tails, he sent them into the fields of the Philistines, by which means the fruits of the fields perished. Now when the Philistines knew that this was Samson's doing, and knew also for what cause he did it, they sent their rulers to Timnath, and burnt his former wife, and her relations, considering they had been the occasion of their misfortunes.

Now when Samson had slain many of the Philistines in the plain country, he dwelt at Etam, which is a strong rock of the tribe of Judah; for the Philistines at that time made an expedition against that tribe: but the people of Judah said that they did not act justly with them, in inflicting punishments upon them while they paid their tribute, and this only on account of Samson's offences. They answered, that in case they would not be blamed themselves, they must deliver up Samson, and put him into their power. So they being desirous not to be blamed themselves, came to the rock with 3000 armed men, and complained to Samson of the bold insults he had made upon the Philistines, who were men able to bring calamity upon the whole nation of the Hebrews; and they told him they were come to take him, and to deliver him up to them, and put him into their power; so they desired him to bear this willingly. Accordingly, when he had received assurances from them upon oath, that they would do him no other harm than only to deliver him into his enemies' hands, he came down from the rock, and put himself into the power of his countrymen. Then did they bind him with two cords, and lead him on, in order to deliver him to the Philistines; and when they came to a certain place, which is now called the "Jaw-bone," on account of the great action there performed by Samson, though of old it had no particular name at all, the Philistines, who had pitched their camp not far off, came to meet them with joy and shouting, as having done a great thing, and gained what they desired; but Samson broke his bonds asunder, and catching up the jaw-bone of an ass that lay at his feet, fell upon his enemies, and smiting them with the jaw-bone, slew 1000 of them, and put the rest to flight and to great disorder.

Upon this slaughter Samson was too proud of what he had performed, and said that this did not come to pass by the assistance of God, but that his success was to be ascribed to his own courage; and vaunted himself, that it was out of a dread of him that some of his enemies fell, and the rest ran away upon his use of the jaw-bone; but when a great thirst came upon him, he considered that human courage is nothing, and bare his testimony that all is to be ascribed to God, and besought him that he would not be angry at any thing he had said, nor give him up into the hands of his enemies, but afford him help under his affliction, and deliver him from the misfortune he was under. Accordingly, God was moved with his entreaties, and raised him up a plentiful fountain of sweet water at a certain rock; whence it was that Samson called the place the "Jaw-bone," and so it is called to this day.

After this fight, Samson held the Philistines in contempt, and came to Gaza, and took up his lodgings in a certain inn. When the rulers of Gaza were informed of his coming thither, they seized upon the gates, and placed men in ambush about them, that he might not escape without being perceived; but Samson, who was acquainted with their contrivances against him, arose about midnight, and ran by force upon the gates, with their posts and beams, and the rest of their wooden furniture, and carried them away on his shoulders, and bare them to the mountain that is over Hebron, and there laid them down.

However, he at length transgressed the laws of his country, and altered his own regular way of living, and imitated the strange customs of foreigners, which thing was the beginning of his miseries; for he fell in love with a woman that was an harlot among the Philistines; her name was Delilah, and he lived with her. So those that administered the public affairs of the Philistines came to her, and with promises induced her to get out of Samson what was the cause of that strength by which he became unconquerable to his enemies. Accordingly, when they were drinking, and had the like conversation together, she pretended to admire the actions he had done, and contrived to get out of him by subtilty, by what means he so much excelled others in strength. Samson, in order to delude Delilah, for he had not yet lost his senses, replied that if he was bound with seven green withes of a vine, such as might still be wreathed, he should be weaker than any other man. The woman said no more then, but told this to the rulers of the Philistines, and hid certain of the soldiers in ambush within the house; and when he was disordered in drink and asleep, she bound him as fast as possible with the withes; and then upon her awakening him, she told him some of the people were upon him; but he broke the withes, and endeavoured to defend himself, as though some of the people were upon him. Now this woman, in the constant conversation Samson had with her, pretended that she took it very ill that he had such little confidence in her affections to him, that he would not tell her what she desired, as if she would not conceal what she knew it was for his interest to have concealed. However, he deluded her again, and told her, that if they bound him with seven cords, he should lose his strength. And when upon doing this, she gained nothing, he told her the third time, that his hair should be woven into a web; but when, upon doing this, the truth was not yet discovered, at length Samson, upon Delilah's prayer, (for he was doomed to fall into some affliction,) was desirous to please her, and told her that God took care of him, and that he was born by his providence, and that "thence it is that I suffer my hair to grow, God having charged me never to poll my head, and thence my strength is according to the increase and continuance of my hair." When she had learned thus much, and had deprived him of his hair, she delivered him up to his enemies, when he was not strong enough to defend himself from their attempts upon him; so they put out his eyes, and bound him, and had him led about among them.

But in process of time, Samson's hair grew again. And there was a public festival among the Philistines, when the rulers and those of the most eminent character were feasting together (now the room wherein they were had its roof supported by two pillars;) so they sent for Samson, and he was brought to their feast, that they might insult him in their cups. Hereupon he, thinking it one of the greatest misfortunes, if he should not be able to revenge himself when he was thus insulted, persuaded the boy that led him by the hand, that he was weary and wanted to rest himself, and desired he would bring him near the pillars; and as soon as he came to them, he rushed with force against them, and overthrew the house, by overthrowing its pillars, with 3000 men in it, who were all slain, and Samson with them.[2] And such was the end of this man, when he had ruled over the Israelites twenty years. And indeed this man deserves to be admired for his courage and strength, and magnanimity at his death, and that his wrath against his enemies went so far as to die himself with them. But as for his being ensnared by a woman, that is to be ascribed to human nature, which is too weak to resist the temptations to that sin; but we ought to bear him witness, that in all other respects he was of extraordinary virtue. But his kindred took away his body, and buried it in Sarasat, his own country, with the rest of his family.

[2] Pliny mentions two theatres built at Rome, which were large enough to contain the whole Roman people, and yet of so singular a construction as to depend on a single hinge or pivot. And in Tacitus we read of great destruction being made by the fall of a theatre similar to this occasioned by Samson. Sir Christopher Wren thus describes what he considers to have been the form of this temple, thus miraculously destroyed by Samson:—"I conceive it was an oval amphitheatre, the scene in the middle, where a vast roof of cedar beams, resting round on the walls, centred all upon one short architrave, that united two cedar pillars in the middle. Now if Samson, by his miraculous strength, pressing upon these pillars, moved them from their bases the whole roof must of necessity fall."

FROM CURSOR MUNDI

Cursor Mundi, *meaning Cursor of the World, is a Northumbrian poem of the fourteenth century which has survived in four manuscript versions. Note how closely the Samson portion of* Cursor Mundi *below adheres to some details in the account of Josephus.*

The version printed here is the text of Cotton MS. Vespasian A iii in the British Museum with a portion (ll. 7137-7145) from the Fairfax MS. 14 in the Bodleian Library, Oxford. Four versions are given in the Early English Text Society edition by Richard Morris (London, 1874-1893), from which the portions here are reprinted. Italicized letters indicate appropriate editorial expansions of abbreviations in the primary texts. Two Old English letters are employed: þ = th; ȝ (ll. 7138, 7139, 7141) = y. Footnotes have been renumbered to run in series.

¶ Eftter him, þis ilk labdon,
þair dempster was sir sampson,
þat was sa bald and wight and st*ra*ng;
Barnles was his moder lang,
And in hir heild, thoru g*ra*ce o dright,
An angel has þis barn ham hight
þat thoru his hare þ*at* was wight,
þ*at* he had tuenti mens might.

Vnder philistiens þan war
þe Iuus halden þat si-quar.
¶ Sampson soght chesun o strijf,
O philistiens he wal[d] ha wijf,
Apon a dai he went and sagh
A fair wom*m*an was o þair lagh,
He tald his frendes son on-nan
þ*at* he had chosen suilk a wom*m*an,
And tok þam wit him for to p*ro*ue,
For to gette hir til his be-houe,
If hir freindes him wald hir yate.
Als he went walkand be þe gatte,
A lion quilpe þ*at* ran ou*er*-thuert,
Rampand to sampson he stert,
Sampson slogh þat leon kene,
Godds g*ra*ce was in him sene.
Que*n* þat he had his errand dune,
Again homward he went als sune,
And bot a littel term was gan,
Yod he to take him his lemman.
And als he went þat gat again,
In leon muth he fand, was slain,
A bike o bees þar-in be-bredd,
And wit þe hony he him fedd;
His wijf fader and mod*er* he gaue
O þis hony at ete þe laue,
Bot noght he did þam vnderstand,
Hugat he þat hony faand.
At þat fest war he was stadd,
A redel þam vndo he badd,
And hight þaa men to giue þair mede,
If þai cuth right þat redel rede;
þat ilk mede þai suld him hight,
If þai ne it rede in seuen night.
'Of þe etand þe mete vt sprang,
And þe suete vte o þe strang.'

þis it was q*ue*n þai had soght,
And stodid thre dais, al for noght,
þai bisoght his wijf þat sco
Suld gar him til hir it vndo.
Vn-to þat birde was biddand bald,
Sampson al þe soth hir tald,
And sco til all þat hir was kidd
Til þas oþer sco it vndidd,—
And þat was mikel vnleute,
To tell hir husband pr*i*uete.
¶ Sampson ham calde þe seyue*n*t day
con ȝe he saide þe ridil say.
ȝe þai saide ellis ware we mad.
to sampson þai þe ridil rad.
hony is squete wiþ riȝt resoun.
and quat is stranger þen a lyou*n*.
¶ Soþ he saide haue ho maugre.
þat has vndone my pr*i*uate.
Sampson was wrath, his wijf for-soke,
And sco on-oþer husband toke.
¶ *Que*n sampson þar-of hard sai,
"Nu," he said, "forth fra þis dai
Agh i for to haue na wite,
To do philistens despite."
Thre hundreth fox he samu*n* knitt,
(I wat noght hu he on þam hitte)
Vn-to þair tails fir he band,
Foluand ilk fox a brand,
And in þe philistiens land,
Thoru þe feldes alsua re*n*nand,
[When corn was[1]] ripe he late þam rin,
And sua þair corns did he brin,
þair oliues, wit þair vintres,
þe foxs brint al wit þat bles.
¶ þe philistiens þan went þam vte,

[[1] *in later hand*]

And soght þan sampson al abute,
þe Iuus was þan þair vnder-lute,
Sampson bunden þai yald for dute,
þe philistiens, wit-vten les,
Ran on sampson in a res;
Bot sampson, þat was selcuth smert,
Vte o þair handes son he stert,
And gaue a-braid sa fers and fast,
þat all þe bandes of him brast.
Thoru chance he fand an assban,—
For oþer wepen had he nan,—
O þat heþen folk he feld
A thusand þat wit tal was teld.
Siþen he went vntil a tun,
Til a wijf þat was commun,
Biside hir al þe night he lai:
þe philistiens quen þai herd sai,
þai vmbisett þat tun a-bute,
þat if sampson went oþer vte
On nighter-tale, or in morning,
To derfly ded þai suld him bring.
Bot sampson, þat was selcuth wight,
Vp he ras midward þe night,
And bar þe yates o þe tun,
And laid þam on a hei dun.
¶ Siþen he ches a wijf to wale,
Dalidam, him broght in bale.
þe philistiens, sa ful o strijf,
þai hight to dalida his wijf
Gyftes gret al for to frain
Quar was sampson might and mayn.
Sua lang sco frain him, þat bald,
þat suilk a gabing he hir tald,
"Wit seuen sinous wa sa me band,
I tint my strenth o fote and hand."
His faas stilli sco badd ta kepe,

And band him quils he was on-slepe,
And þan opon his faas sco cald,
To do wit him wat þai wald.
Bot sampson wakken[d] of his slape,
O bandes let he-self him scape,
His bandes al he brac in tua,
Als þai had ben made bot on stra.
Bot yitt his wijf wald noght fin
Thoru egging of his wiþerwin,
Til sco þe soth had gert him sai,
In quat stede al his strencth lai.
"Q*ua*r es þi strencth, leif?" said sco, "quare?"
"It es," he said, "al in mi hare;
War mi hare schorn, i war noght þan
Strang*er* þan a-noþer man."
¶ Nu has sampson bikend his liif
In will to weld, al of his wijf,
Was neu*er* als now sampson in wath,
His liue, his ded, now has sco bath,
Bath in hir will now has he don,
þ*at* sal on him be sene ful son.
[2]Sampson, þi first wijf lerd þe witte,
If þat þou cuth haf halden it!
þis wijf alsua, þat þou has now,
If þou[3] ne war sua lightli to tru!
Sare man aght to dred þe brand
þ*at* brint him forwit in his hand,
Bot herd it es to stand again
þe wijf þ*at* fines noght to frain,
For noiþer for luue dredes, ne au,
Dos man his priuetes to scau;
Or drunkennes oftmai bitide
Dos man his consail to vn-hide,

[[2] The next four lines are partially corrected to be read in the third person.]

[[3] *The later hand reads* hoo.]

þ*at* oft in faand man findes sua,
Man priueest es mast man faa,
Ne þare es nan sa gret mai greif
Als trait*ur* dern and priue theif.
Als sua sco, dame dalida,
Of al wicke ai worth hir waa?
Hir lau*er*d consail all to þaa
Sco tald þ*at* heild him mast for faa.
Hir time sco soght, bad þam be nere,
Quils sampson slepped, sco laght a schere,
His hare sco kerf, wa worth hir hend!
And till his foos sco him be-kend.
Al moght þai þan do q*uat* þai mint,
For thoru his fax his force was tint,
And did him selcuth mikel lath,
þai blinded him and p*ri*sund bath.
And q*ue*n he was don in prisun,
A man son o þ*at* ilk nacion
Gun dalidam hijs wijf at wedd;
Sampson was to þe bridal ledd,
For he was sle on harpingleu.
Wit þis his [hare[4]] was waxen neu;
Bi a piler was he þar sett,
To gleu þaa gomes at þair mete.
Quils þai war blithes[t] at þ*at* fest,
Sampson cuth well*e* of ald gest.
Wexen was su*m*del his hare;
þe post þ*at* al þ*at* huse vpbare
Wit bath his handes he it scok,
Sua fast þat al þe hus quok,
þat hus he feld, gaf naman grith,
And slogh his faas, him-self þar with.

[[4] *The later hand reads* hore.]

GEOFFREY CHAUCER

FROM THE MONK'S TALE

Geoffrey Chaucer (1340?-1400) gave to the monk included among the Canterbury pilgrims the appropriate tale De Casibus Virorum Illustrium (On the Reversals of Fortune of Illustrious Men). *The monk's "ensamples trewe and olde" included Lucifer, Adam, Hercules, Nebuchadnezzar, Belshazzar, Zenobia, Nero, Alexander, Julius Caesar, and, among others, of course Samson. Samson's story occupies the fourth through the thirteenth stanzas of "The Monk's Tale." The version printed here is that of Walter William Skeat (1835-1912), first published in the Oxford Edition of Chaucer's works (6 vols., 1894), IV, 245-247.*

SAMPSON.

Lo Sampson, which that was annunciat
By thangel, longe er his nativitee,
And was to god almighty consecrat,
And stood in noblesse, whyl he mighte see.
Was never swich another as was he,
To speke of strengthe, and therwith hardinesse;
But to his wyves tolde he his secree,
Through which he slow him-self, for wrecchednesse.

Sampson, this noble almighty champioun,
Withouten wepen save his hondes tweye,
He slow and al to-rente the leoun,

Toward his wedding walking by the weye.
His false wyf coude him so plese and preye
Til she his conseil knew, and she untrewe
Un-to his foos his conseil gan biwreye,
And him forsook, and took another newe.

Three hundred foxes took Sampson for ire,
And alle hir tayles he togider bond,
And sette the foxes tayles alle on fire,
For he on every tayl had knit a brond;
And they brende alle the cornes in that lond,
And alle hir oliveres and vynes eek.
A thousand men he slow eek with his hond,
And had no wepen but an asses cheek.

Whan they were slayn, so thursted him that he
Was wel ny lorn, for which he gan to preye
That god wolde on his peyne han som pitee,
And sende him drinke, or elles moste he deye;
And of this asses cheke, that was dreye,
Out of a wang-tooth sprang anon a welle,
Of which he drank y-nogh, shortly to seye,
Thus heelp him god, as *Iudicum*[1] can telle.

By verray force, at Gazan, on a night,
Maugree Philistiens of that citee,
The gates of the toun he hath up-plight,
And on his bak y-caried hem hath he
Hye on an hille, that men mighte hem see.
O noble almighty Sampson, leef and dere,
Had thou nat told to wommen thy secree,
In al this worlde ne hadde been thy pere!

This Sampson never sicer drank ne wyn,
Ne on his heed cam rasour noon ne shere,
By precept of the messager divyn,
For alle his strengthes in his heres were;
And fully twenty winter, yeer by yere,

[1] Latin, the *Book of Judges [Editor's Note]*.

He hadde of Israel the governaunce.
But sone shal he wepen many a tere,
For wommen shal him bringen to meschaunce!

Un-to his lemman Dalida he tolde
That in his heres al his strengthe lay,
And falsly to his fo-men she him solde.
And sleping in hir barme up-on a day
She made to clippe or shere his heer awey,
And made his fo-men al his craft espyen;
And whan that they him fonde in this array,
They bounde him faste, and putten out his yën.

But er his heer were clipped or y-shave,
Ther was no bond with which men might him binde;
But now is he in prisoun in a cave,
Wher-as they made him at the querne grinde.
O noble Sampson, strongest of mankinde,
O whylom Iuge in glorie and in richesse,
Now maystow wepen with thyn yën blinde,
Sith thou fro wele art falle in wrecchednesse.

Thende of this caytif was as I shal seye;
His fo-men made a feste upon a day,
And made him as hir fool bifore hem pleye,
And this was in a temple of greet array.
But atte last he made a foul affray;
For he two pilers shook, and made hem falle,
And doun fil temple and al, and ther it lay,
And slow him-self, and eek his fo-men alle.

This is to seyn, the princess everichoon,
And eek three thousand bodies wer ther slayn
With falling of the grete temple of stoon.
Of Sampson now wol I na-more seyn.
Beth war by this ensample old and playn
That no men telle hir conseil til hir wyves
Of swich thing as they wolde han secree fayn,
If that it touche hir limmes or hir lyves.

JOHN LYDGATE

FROM FALL OF PRINCES

Written in the form of a dream or vision, the almost 37,000 lines of Fall of Princes *by John Lydgate (c.1370-c.1450), a monk of Bury St. Edmunds, constitute a paraphrase of a French translation of Boccaccio's Latin poem* De Casibus Virorum Illustrium *(the source also of Chaucer's "Monk's Tale"). The version following is reprinted from the Early English Text Society edition by Henry Bergen (London, 1924-1927; I, 179-184 [ll. 6336-6510]). Italicized letters indicate appropriate editorial expansions of abbreviations in the primary text. Footnotes and marginal notes have been omitted.*

[Off mighty Sampson whiche tolde his counsaile to Dalida whereby he was deceived.]

Who was mor myhti or stro*n*g tha*n* Sampson?
Non mor delyuer, þe Bible berth witnesse:
Withoute wepne he slouh a fers leou*n*,
And for his enmyes to hym dede expresse
His vnkouth problem, anon he gan hym dresse
Geyn Philistes, and slouh off hem thretti,
To paie his promys spoiled hem bi and bi.

His problem was, the text thus rehersyng,
Afftir the lettir in veray sothfastnesse:

"Ther cam out mete off a thyng etyng,
And fro the stronge ther wente out suetnesse."
But his wiff, off froward doubilnesse,
Which euer wrouhte to his disauail,
Off worthi Sampson tolde the cou*n*sail:

"What is mor strong than is a leou*n*,
Or mor soote than hony in tastyng?"—
But women haue this condiciou*n*,
Off secre thynges whan thei haue knowlechyng,
Thei bollyn inward, ther hertis ay fretyng:
Outher thei musten deien or discure,
So brotil is off custum ther nature.

This was the cas: the leou*n* that was ded,
Ageyn the son*n*e gapyng lay vpriht;
A swarm off been entred in his hed,
Off whom ther cam hony anon riht.
And whan Sampson theroff hadde a siht,
He fantasied in his opynyou*n*
Ful secreli this proposiciou*n*,

As ye han herd, and gan it foorth purpose,
That Philistes to hym it sholde expowne,
Vnder a peyne the trouthe to hym onclose.
But with his wiff thei preueli gan rowne;
And she on Sampson gan compleyne & frowne,
And feynyngli so longe vpon hym weepe,
That he nat coude his cou*n*sail from hir keepe.

Which whan she kneuh, she made no tarieng,
But pleyn and hool she gan it to declare.
Such double trust is in ther wepyng;
To keepe ther tu*n*ges wom*m*en ca*n* nat spare.
Such wepying wyues, euel mut thei fare!
And all husbondis, I pray God yiue hem sorwe,
That to hem tell ther cou*n*seil eue or morwe.

She told hem hool, she tolde it hem nat halff;
And Sampson than*n*e gan vpon hem smyle,
"Yiff ye nat hadde herd it in my calff,
Ye sholde nat a fou*n*de it a gret while."
Who may be seur, wher women list begile! —
Thouh bookis Sampson off strengthe so comende,
Yit durste he nat ageyn his wiff offende.

This myhti Sampson dede also his peyne,
Thre hu*n*dred foxis onys that he fond,
He took her tailes, knet hem tweyne & tweyne,
And amyd euerich he sette a feer-brond;
And as thei ran in Philistes lond,
So furiousli vp and dou*n* thei wente,
That thei her frutis & ther vynes brente.

Eek be tresou*n* whan he was onys bou*n*de
With newe cordis as he lay and sleep,
Ther ca*m* thr*e* thousand, which that Sampson fou*n*de,
Tamoordred hym, or that he took keep:
He brak his bondis, and vp anon he leep,
Off an asse [he] cauhte a chaule-bon,
And a thousand he slouh off hem anon.

He gan to feynte & hadde a sodeyn lust
For to drynke, fadid face and cheer;
And God sente hym to stau*n*che with his thrust
From thassis toth watir cristal cleer,
Which that sprang out large as a ryuer,
Refresshid his sperit, which afforn gan dull,
Til that he hadde off watir dru*n*ke his full.

Afftir he wente to Gazam the cite,
Mong all his enmyes, that were off gret myht,
To his plesau*n*ce where he dede see
A ful fair woman, lay with hire al nyht,
And on the morwe, longe or it was lyht,

Maugre the wach, vpon his shuldres squar
The gatis stronge vp to an hill he bar.

And in a vale which callid was Soret
Ful hoote he loued Dalida the faire,
On whom his herte was ful sore set,
She koude hir feyne so meek & debonaire,
Make hym such cheer whan that hym list repaire.
But I dar calle hir Dalida the double,
Cheeff roote & cause off al his mortal trouble.

He neuer drank wynes whiht nor red,
Off Nazarees such is the goueraunce;
Rasour nor sheer touchid neuer his hed,
For in long growyng stondeth ther plesaunce.
And this Sampson, most myhti off substaunce,
Hadde al his force be influence off heuene,
B[y] heris wexyng, that were in noumbre seuene.

It was ful secre in euery manys siht,
Among peeple told for an vnkouth thyng,
Whereoff Sampson hadde so gret myht,
Outward shewed bi force off his werkyng.
But Dalida with hir flateryng
Wolde neuer stynte, enqueryng euer among,
Til that she kneuh wherbi he was so strong.

She lich a serpent daryng vnder floures,
Or lik a werm that wrotith on a tre,
Or lich an addere off manyfold coloures,
Riht fressh apperyng and fair vpon to see:
For shrowdid was hir mutabilite
With lowliheed[e] and a fair pretense
Off trewe menyng vnder fals apparence.

He mente trouthe, & she was variable,
He was feithful, and she was ontrewe,
He was stedfast, and she was onstable,

His trust ay oon; she loued thynges newe:
She wered colour*es* off many dyuers hewe,
In stede off bleu, which stedfast is and cleene;
She loued chau*n*ges off many dyuers greene.

But to the purpos for to condescende,
Whan she off Sampson kneuh al the preuite,
Hir falsheed shortli for to comprehende,
She made hym slepe ful sofftli on hir kne;
And a sharp rasour afftir that took she,
Shoof off his her, large and off gret lengthe,
Wherbi, allas, he loste al his strengthe.

Damage is [in?] erthe is non so greuous,
As an enmy which that is secre,
Nor pestilence non so pereilous
As falsnesse where he is preue,
And speciali in femynyte;
For yiff wyues be fou*n*den variable,
Wher shal husbondis fynden other stable?

Thus Sampson was be Dalida deceyued,
She coude so weel flatre, forge and feyne,—
Which Philistes, whan thei ha[ue] conceyued,
Onwarli bond hym in a mythi cheyne,
Cast hym in priso*u*n, put out his eyen tweyne,
And off despiht, afftir, as I fynde,
At ther queernys maad hym for to grynde.

Thei made a feste statli and solempne,
Whan thei hadde al this treso*u*n wrouht;
And to rebuke hym, scorne hym & condempne,
Blynde Sampson was aforn hem brouht:
Which thyng ful sore greued hym in his thouht,
Caste he wolde in his preue mynde
Tauenge his blyndnesse sum maner weie fynde.

And whan he hadde thus bethouht hym longe,
He made a child hym preueli to leede

To tweyne postis, large, squar and stronge,
Enbraced hem, or any man took heede,
And gan to shake hem, withoute feer or dreede,
So sturdili among his fomen all,
That the temple is vpon hem fall.

Thus he was auengid on his foon,
Which that falsli dede ageyn hym stryue,
Slouh in his deieng, God wot, many on
Mo than he dede euer afforn his lyue.
And he was also, the date to descryue,
In Israel, the Bible is myn auctour,
Twenti yeer ther iuge and gouernour.

[LENVOY.]

This t*r*agedie yeueth in euidence
To whom men shal their cou*n*seil out discure;
For rakell tu*n*ges, for lak off prouidence,
Ha[ue] do gret harm to many a creature:
Whan harm is doon, ful hard is to recure.
Beth war be Sampson, y*our* cou*n*sail weel to keepe,
Thouh Dalida compleyne, crie and weepe.

Whilom Sampson, for manhod & prudence,
Hadde Israel in gouernau*n*ce and cure,
Dau*n*ted leou*n*s thoruh his magnyficence,
Made on a thousand a disconfiture;
But his moste pereilous auenture,
Was whan he lay with Dalida to slepe,
Which falsli coude compleyne, crie and weepe.

Ye noble Pryncis, conceyueth the sentence
Off this story, remembrid in scripture,
How that Sampson off wilful necligence
Was shaue & shorn, diffacid his figure;
Keep your conceitis vnder couerture,
Suffre no nyhtwerm withy*n*ne *your* cou*n*sail kreepe,
Thouh Dalida compleyne, crie and weepe!

MILTON'S OTHER REFERENCES TO SAMSON

In half a dozen other places besides Samson Agonistes, *Milton made use of the Samson story. The range covers mere jottings for plans for tragedies, allegorical interpretations for political argument, simple allusion, citation of Scripture story for "proof," and an interesting telescoping of Biblical allusion and classical mythological reference in his great epic poem. Given below with the sources and dates are Milton's other references to Samson.*

FROM OUTLINES FOR TRAGEDIES ON OLD TESTAMENT THEMES IN THE TRINITY MS., c.1640

Samson pursophorus or Hybristes, or Samson marriing or in Ramath Lechi. Jud. 15.

Dagonalia. Jud. 16.

FROM THE REASON OF CHURCH GOVERNMENT URGED AGAINST PRELATY, 1641

I cannot better liken the state and person of a king than to that mighty Nazarite Samson; who being disciplined from his birth in the precepts and the practice of temperance and sobriety, without the strong drink of injurious and excessive desires, grows up to a noble strength and perfection with those his illustrious and sunny locks, the laws, waving and curling about his godlike shoulders. And while he keeps them about him undiminished and unshorn, he may with the jawbone of an ass, that is, with the word of his meanest officer, suppress and put to confusion thousands of those that rise against his just power. But laying down his head among the strumpet flatteries of prelates, while he sleeps and thinks no harm, they wickedly shaving off all those bright and weighty tresses of his law, and just prerogatives, which were his ornament and strength, deliver him over to indirect and violent counsels, which, as those Philistines, put out the fair and far-sighted eyes of his natural discerning, and make him grind in the prisonhouse of their sinister ends and practices upon him: till he, knowing this prelatical rasor to have bereft him of his wonted might, nourish again his puissant hair, the golden beams of law and right; and they sternly shook, thunder with ruin upon the heads of those his evil counsellors, but not without great affliction to himself. This is the sum of their loyal service to kings; yet these are the men that still cry, The king, the king, the Lord's anointed! (J. A. St. John, ed., *The Prose Works of John Milton,* 5 vols. [London: Henry G. Bohn, 1848], II, 506-507.)

FROM AREOPAGITICA, 1644

Methinks I see in my mind a noble and puissant nation rousing herself like a strong man after sleep, and shaking her invincible locks: . . . (Bohn Edition, II, 94.)

FROM ICONOCLASTES, 1649

And if the parliament so thought not, but desired him to follow their advice and deliberation in things of public concernment, he accounts it the same proposition as if Samson had been moved "to the putting out his eyes, that the Philistines might abuse him." (Bohn Edition, I, 400.)

The words of a king, as they are full of power, in the authority and strength of law, so, like Samson, without the strength of that Nazarite's lock, they have no more power in them than the words of another man. (Bohn Edition, I, 457.)

FROM A FIRST DEFENCE, 1651

Samson, that renowned champion of the Hebrews, though his countrymen blamed him for it, "Dost thou not know," say they, "that the Philistines have dominion over us?" Yet against those Philistines, under whose dominion he was, he himself undertook a war in his own person, without any other help; and whether he acted in pursuance of a command from Heaven, or was prompted by his own valour only, or whatsoever inducement he had, he did not put to death one, but many, that tyrannized over his country, having first called upon God by prayer, and implored his assistance. So that Samson counted it no act of impiety, but quite contrary, to kill those that enslaved his country, though they had dominion over himself too; and though the greater part of his countrymen submitted to their tyranny. (Bohn Edition, I, 90.)

FROM PARADISE LOST, 1674

So rose the *Danite* strong
Herculean Samson from the Harlot-lap
Of *Philistean Dalilah,* and wak'd
Shorn of his strength . . . (IX, 1059-1062)

PART III

CRITICISM

SAMUEL JOHNSON

FROM THE RAMBLER

Samuel Johnson (1709-1784) was the literary dictator of his age. Poet, dramatist, biographer, essayist, novelist, lexicographer, he employed words in a variety of genres to express his cogent and often prejudiced criticism. Reluctant to praise Milton, from whom he differed in many allegiances, he is responsible for one of the best-known critiques of the dramatic structure of Samson Agonistes. *The passages that follow are two consecutive essays written for* The Rambler *in July 1751; they are taken from the edition of* The Works of Samuel Johnson, *6 vols. (Philadelphia, 1825), III, 273-282.*

No. 139. Tuesday, July 16, 1751.

Sit quod vis simplex duntaxat et unum. Horace

Let every piece be simple and be one.

It is required by Aristotle to the perfection of a tragedy, and is equally necessary to every other species of regular composition, that it should have a beginning, a middle, and an end. "The beginning," says he, "is that which hath nothing necessarily previous, but to which that which follows is naturally consequent; the end, on the contrary, is that which by necessity, or at least according to the common course of things, succeeds something else, but which implies nothing consequent to itself; the middle is connected on one side to something that naturally goes before, and on the other to something that naturally follows it."

Such is the rule laid down by this great critic, for the disposition of the different parts of a well constituted fable. It must begin, where it may be made intelligible without introduction; and end, where the mind is left in repose, without expectation of any farther event. The intermediate passages must join the last effect to the first cause, by a regular and unbroken concatenation; nothing must be therefore inserted which does not apparently arise from something foregoing, and properly make way for something that succeeds it.

This precept is to be understood in its rigour only with respect to great and essential events, and cannot be extended in the same force to minuter circumstances and arbitrary decorations, which yet are more happy, as they contribute more to the main design; for it is always a proof of extensive thought and accurate circumspection, to promote various purposes by the same act; and the idea of an ornament admits use, though it seems to exclude necessity.

Whoever purposes, as it is expressed by Milton, "to build the lofty rhyme," must acquaint himself with this law of poetical architecture, and take care that his edifice be solid as well as beautiful; that nothing stand single or independent, so as that it may be taken away without injuring the rest; but that, from the foundation to the pinnacles, one part rest firm upon another.

This regular and consequential distribution is, among common authors, frequently neglected; but the failures of those, whose example can have no influence, may be safely overlooked, nor is it of much use to recall obscure and unregarded names to memory for the sake of sporting with their infamy. But if there be any writer whose genius can embellish impropriety, and whose authority can make errour venerable, his works are the proper objects of critical inquisition. To expunge faults where there are no excellencies, is a task equally useless with that of the chemist, who employs the arts of separation and refinement upon ore in which no precious metal is contained to reward his operations.

The tragedy of Samson Agonistes has been celebrated as the second work of the great author of Paradise Lost, and opposed, with all the confidence of triumph, to the dramatic performances of other nations. It contains indeed just sentiments, maxims of wisdom, and oracles of piety, and many passages written with the ancient spirit of choral poetry, in which there is a just and pleasing mixture of Seneca's moral declamation, with the wild enthusiasm of the Greek writers. It is therefore worthy of examination, whether a performance thus illuminated with genius, and enriched with learning, is composed according to the indispensable laws of Aristotelian criticism: and, omitting at present all other considerations, whether it exhibits a beginning, a middle, and an end.

The beginning is undoubtedly beautiful and proper, opening with a graceful abruptness, and proceeding naturally to a mournful recital of facts necessary to be known:

SAMSON A little onward lend thy guiding hand
To these dark steps, a little farther on;
For yonder bank hath choice of sun and shade;
There I am wont to sit when any chance
Relieves me from my task of servile toil,
Daily in the common prison else enjoin'd me . . .
O wherefore was my birth from heav'n foretold
Twice by an angel . . . ?
Why was my breeding order'd and prescrib'd,
As of a person separate to God,
Design'd for great exploits; if I must die
Betray'd, captiv'd, and both my eyes put out . . . ?
Whom have I to complain of but myself?
Who this high gift of strength, committed to me,
In what part lodg'd, how easily bereft me,
Under the seal of silence could not keep,
But weakly to a woman must reveal it.

His soliloquy is interrupted by a chorus or company of men of his own tribe, who condole his miseries, extenuate his fault, and conclude with a solemn vindication of divine justice. So that at the conclusion of the first act there is no design laid, no discovery made, nor any disposition formed towards the subsequent event.

In the second act, Manoah, the father of Samson, comes to seek his son, and, being shown him by the chorus, breaks out into lamentations of his misery, and comparisons of his present with his former state, representating to him the ignominy which his religion suffers, by the festival this day celebrated in honour of Dagon, to whom the idolaters ascribed his overthrow:

. . . Thou bear'st
Enough, and more, the burthen of that fault;
Bitterly hast thou paid and still art paying
That rigid score. A worse thing yet remains,
This day the Philistines a pop'lar feast
Here celebrate in Gaza; and proclaim
Great pomp and sacrifice, and praises loud
To Dagon as their God, who hath deliver'd
Thee, Samson, bound and blind, into their hands,
Them out of thine, who slew'st them many a slain.

Samson, touched with this reproach, makes a reply equally penitential and pious, which his father considers as the effusion of prophetic confidence.

SAMSON . . . God, be sure,
Will not connive or linger thus provok'd,
But will arise and his great name assert:
Dagon must stoop, and shall ere long receive
Such a discomfit, as shall quite despoil him
Of all these boasted trophies won on me. . . .

MANOAH With cause this hope relieves thee, and these words
I as a prophecy receive; for God,
Nothing more certain, will not long defer
To vindicate the glory of his name. . . .

This part of the dialogue, as it might tend to animate or exasperate Samson, cannot, I think, be censured as wholly superfluous; but the succeeding dispute, in which Samson contends to die, and which his father breaks off, that he may go to solicit his release, is only valuable for its own beauties, and has no tendency to introduce any thing that follows it.

The next event of the drama is the arrival of Delilah, with all her graces, artifices, and allurements. This produces a dialogue, in a very high degree elegant and instructive, from which she retires, after she has exhausted her persuasions, and is no more seen nor heard of; nor has her visit any effect but that of raising the character of Samson.

In the fourth act enters Harapha, the giant of Gath, whose name had never been mentioned before, and who has now no other motive of coming, than to see the man whose strength and actions are so loudly celebrated:

HARAPHA . . . Much I have heard
Of thy prodigious might, and feats perform'd
Incredible to me; in this displeas'd
That I was never present in the place
Of those encounters, where we might have tried
Each other's force in camp or listed fields:
And now am come to see of whom such noise
Hath walk'd about, and each limb to survey,
If thy appearance answer loud report.

Samson challenges him to the combat; and after an interchange of reproaches, elevated by repeated defiance on one side, and imbittered by contemptuous insults on the other, Harapha retires; we then hear it determined, by Samson and the chorus, that no consequence good or bad will proceed from their interview:

CHORUS He will directly to the lords, I fear,
And with malicious counsel stir them up
Some way or other farther to afflict thee.

SAMSON He must allege some cause, and offer'd fight
Will not dare mention, lest a question rise,
Whether he durst accept the offer or not;
And that he durst not, plain enough appear'd.

At last, in the fifth act, appears a messenger from the lords assembled at the festival of Dagon, with a summons by which Samson is required to come and entertain them with some proof of his strength. Samson, after a short expostulation, dismisses him with a firm and resolute refusal; but, during the absence of the messenger, having a while defended the propriety of his conduct, he at last declares himself moved by a secret impulse to comply, and utters some dark presages of a great event to be brought to pass by his agency, under the direction of Providence:

SAMSON Be of good courage; I begin to feel
Some rousing motions in me, which dispose
To something extraordinary my thoughts.
I with this messenger will go along,
Nothing to do, be sure, that may dishonour
Our law, or stain my vow of Nazarite.
If there be ought of presage in the mind,
This day will be remarkable in my life
By some great act, or of my days the last.

While Samson is conducted off by the messenger, his father returns with hopes of success in his solicitation, upon which he confers with the chorus till their dialogue is interrupted, first by a shout of triumph, and afterwards by screams of horrour and agony. As they stand deliberating where they shall be secure, a man who had been present at the show enters, and relates how Samson, having prevailed on his guide to suffer him to lean against the main pillars of the theatrical edifice, tore down the roof upon the spectators and himself:

. . . Those two massy pillars,
With horrible confusion, to and fro
He tugg'd, he shook, till down they came, and drew
The whole roof after them, with burst of thunder,
Upon the heads of all who sat beneath . . .
Samson, with these immixt, inevitably
Pull'd down the same destruction on himself.

This is undoubtedly a just and regular catastrophe, and the poem, therefore, has a beginning and an end which Aristotle himself could not have disapproved; but it must be allowed to want a middle, since nothing passes between the first act and the last, that either hastens or delays the death of Samson. The whole drama, if its superfluities were cut off, would scarcely fill a single act; yet this is the tragedy which ignorance has admired, and bigotry applauded.

No. 140. Saturday, July 20, 1751.

Quis tam Lucili fautor inepte est,
Ut non hoc fateatur. HORACE
What doating bigot, to his faults so blind,
As not to grant me this, can Milton find?

It is common, says Bacon, to desire the end without enduring the means. Every member of society feels and acknowledges the necessity of detecting crimes, yet scarce any degree of virtue or reputation is able to secure an informer from public hatred. The learned world has always admitted the usefulness of critical disquisitions, yet he that attempts to show, however modestly, the failures of a celebrated writer, shall surely irritate his admirers, and incur the imputation of envy, captiousness, and malignity.

With this danger full in my view, I shall proceed to examine the sentiments of Milton's tragedy, which, though much less liable to censure than the disposition of his plan, are, like those of other writers, sometimes exposed to just exceptions for want of care, or want of discernment.

Sentiments are proper and improper as they consist more or less with the character and circumstances of the person to whom they are attributed, with the rules of the composition, in which they are found, or with the settled and unalterable nature of things.

It is common among the tragic poets to introduce their persons alluding to events or opinions, of which they could not possibly have any knowledge. The barbarians of remote or newly discovered regions often display their skill in European learning. The god of love is mentioned in Tamerlane with all the familiarity of a Roman epigrammatist; and a late writer has put Harvey's doctrine of the circulation of the blood into the mouth of a Turkish statesman, who lived near two centuries before it was known even to philosophers or anatomists.

Milton's learning, which acquainted him with the manners of the ancient eastern nations, and his invention, which required no assistance from the common cant of poetry, have preserved him from frequent outrages of local or chronological propriety. Yet he has mentioned Chalybean Steel, of which it is not very likely that his chorus should have heard, and has made Alp the general name of a mountain, in a region where the Alps could scarcely be known:

No medicinal liquor can assuage,
Nor breath of cooling air from snowy Alp.

He has taught Samson the tales of Circe, and the Syrens, at which he apparently hints in his colloquy with Delilah:

. . . I know thy trains,
Tho' dearly to my cost, thy gins and toils;
Thy fair *enchanted cup,* and *warbling charms,*
No more on me have pow'r.

But the grossest errour of this kind is the solemn introduction of the Phœnix in the last scene; which is faulty, not only as it is incongruous to the personage to whom it is ascribed, but as it is so evidently contrary to reason and nature, that it ought never to be mentioned but as a fable in any serious poem:

. . . Virtue giv'n for lost,
Deprest, and overthrown, as seem'd
Like that self-begotten bird
In the Arabian woods embost
That no second knows, nor third,
And lay ere while a holocaust;
From out her ashy womb now teem'd
Revives, reflourishes, then vigorous most
When most unactive deem'd.
And tho' her body die, her fame survives,
A secular bird, ages of lives.

Another species of impropriety is the unsuitableness of thoughts to the general character of the poem. The seriousness and solemnity of tragedy necessarily reject all pointed or epigrammatical expressions, all remote conceits and opposition of ideas. Samson's complaint is therefore too elaborate to be natural:

As in the land of darkness, yet in light,
To live a life half dead, a living death,
And bury'd but, O yet more miserable!
Myself my sepulchre, a moving grave!
Bury'd, yet not exempt,
By privilege of death and burial,
From worst of other evils, pains and wrongs.

All allusions to low and trivial objects, with which contempt is usually associated, are doubtless unsuitable to a species of composition which ought to be always awful though not always magnificent. The remark therefore of the chorus on good and bad news seems to want elevation:

MANOAH A little stay will bring some notice hither.
CHORUS Of good or bad so great, of bad the sooner;
For evil news *rides post,* while good news *baits.*

But of all meanness, that has least to plead which is produced by mere verbal conceits, which, depending only upon sounds, lose their existence by the change of a syllable. Of this kind is the following dialogue:

CHORUS But had we best retire? I see a *storm.*
SAMSON Fair days have oft contracted wind and rain.
CHORUS But this another kind of tempest brings.
SAMSON Be less abstruse, my riddling days are past.
CHORUS Look now for no enchanting voice, nor fear
The bait of honied words; a rougher tongue
Draws hitherward, I know him by his stride,
The giant Harapha. . . .

And yet more despicable are the lines in which Manoah's paternal kindness is commended by the chorus:

Fathers are wont to *lay up* for their sons,
Thou for thy son are bent to *lay out* all;—

Samson's complaint of the inconveniencies of imprisonment is not wholly without verbal quaintness:

. . . I, a prisoner chain'd, scarce freely draw
The air, imprison'd also, close and damp.

From the sentiments we may properly descend to the consideration of the language, which, in imitation of the ancients, is through the whole dialogue remarkably simple and unadorned, seldom heightened by epithets, or varied by figures; yet sometimes metaphors find admission, even where their consistency is not accurately preserved. Thus Samson confounds loquacity with a shipwreck:

How could I once look up, or heave the head,
Who, like a foolish *pilot* have *shipwreck'd*
My *vessel* trusted to me from above,
Gloriously *rigg'd;* and for a word, a tear,
Fool, have *divulg'd* the *secret gift* of God
To a deceitful woman! . . .

And the chorus talks of adding fuel to flame in a report:

He's gone, and who knows how he may *report*
Thy *words,* by *adding fuel to the flame?*

The versification is in the dialogue much more smooth and harmonious than in the parts allotted to the chorus, which are often so harsh and dissonant, as scarce to preserve, whether the lines end with or without rhymes, any appearance of metrical regularity:

Or do my eyes misrepresent? Can this be he,
That heroic, that renown'd,
Irresistible Samson; whom unarm'd
No strength of man, or fiercest wild beast, could withstand;
Who tore the lion, as the lion tears the kid? . . .

Since I have thus pointed out the faults of Milton, critical integrity requires that I should endeavour to display his excellencies, though they will not easily be discovered in short quotations, because they consist in the justness of diffuse reasonings, or in the contexture and method of continued dialogues: this play having none of those descriptions, similes, or splendid sentences, with which other tragedies are so lavishly adorned.

Yet some passages may be selected which seem to deserve particular notice, either as containing sentiments of passion, representations of life, precepts of conduct, or sallies of imagination. It is not easy to give a stronger representation of the weariness of despondency, than in the words of Samson to his father:

> . . . I feel my genial spirits droop,
> My hopes all flat; nature within me seems
> In all her functions weary of herself;
> My race of glory run, and race of shame;
> And I shall shortly be with them that rest.

The reply of Sampson to the flattering Delilah affords a just and striking description of the stratagems and allurements of feminine hypocrisy:

> . . . These are thy wonted arts,
> And arts of every woman false like thee,
> To break all faith, all vows, deceive, betray,
> Then as repentant, to submit, beseech,
> And reconcilement move with feign'd remorse,
> Confess and promise wonders in her change;
> Not truly penitent, but chief to try
> Her husband, how far urg'd his patience bears,
> His virtue or weakness which way to assail;
> Then with more cautious and instructed skill
> Again transgresses, and again submits.

When Samson has refused to make himself a spectacle at the feast of Dagon, he first justifies his behaviour to the chorus, who charge him with having served the Philistines, by a very just distinction; and then destroys the common excuse of cowardice and servility, which always confound temptation with compulsion:

> CHORUS Yet with thy strength thou servest the Philistines.
> SAMSON Not in their idol worship, but by labour

Honest and lawful to deserve my food
Of those who have me in their civil power.
CHORUS Where the heart joins not, outward acts defile not.
SAMSON Where outward force constrains, the sentence holds.
But who constrains me to the temple of Dagon,
Not dragging? The Philistine lords command.
Commands are no constraints. If I obey them,
I do it freely, vent'ring to displease
God for the fear of man, and man prefer,
Set God behind.

The complaint of blindness which Samson pours out at the beginning of the tragedy is equally addressed to the passions and the fancy. The enumeration of his miseries is succeeded by a very pleasing train of poetical images, and concluded by such expostulations and wishes, as reason too often submits to learn from despair:

O first created beam, and thou great word
Let there be light, and light was over all;
Why am I thus bereav'd thy prime decree?
The sun to me is dark,
And silent as the moon,
When she deserts the night,
Hid in her vacant interlunar cave.
Since light so necessary is to life,
And almost life itself; if it be true,
That light is in the soul,
She all in ev'ry part: why was the sight
To such a tender ball as the eye confin'd,
So obvious and so easy to be quench'd.
And not, as feeling, through all parts diffus'd,
That she may look at will thro' ev'ry pore?

Such are the faults and such the beauties of Samson Agonistes, which I have shown with no other purpose than to promote the knowledge of true criticism. The everlasting verdure of Milton's laurels has nothing to fear from the blasts of malignity; nor can my attempt produce any other effect, than to strengthen their shoots by lopping their luxuriance.

RICHARD CUMBERLAND

PRELIMINARY OBSERVATIONS ON *SAMSON AGONISTES*

A moderate reply to Dr. Johnson's strictures on the structure of Samson Agonistes *was given by Richard Cumberland in* The Observer *(IV, No. cxi, London, 1788). The pertinent passage given here appears in Henry John Todd, ed.,* The Poetical Works of Milton, *4 vols. (London, 1842), III, 218-221.*

When I remarked that Jonson, in his comedy of *The Fox*, was a close copier of the ancients, it occurred to me to say something upon the celebrated drama of *Samson Agonistes;* which, though less beholden to the Greek poets in its dialogue than the comedy above-mentioned, is in all other particulars as complete an imitation of the Ancient Tragedy, as the distance of times and the difference of languages will admit of.

It is professedly *built according to ancient rule and example;* and the author, by taking Aristotle's definition of tragedy for his motto, fairly challenges the critick to examine and compare it by that test. His close adherence to the model of the Greek tragedy is in nothing more conspicuous than in the simplicity of his diction; in this particular he has curbed his fancy with so tight a hand, that, knowing as we do the fertile vein of his genius, we cannot but lament the fidelity of his imitation; for there is a harshness in the metre of his Chorus, which to a certain degree seems to border upon pedantry and affectation; he premises that *the measure is indeed of all sorts,* but I must take leave to observe that in some places it is no measure at all, or such at least as the ear will not patiently endure, nor which any recitation can make harmonious. By casting out of his composition the strophe and antistrophe, those stanzas which the Greeks appropriated to singing, or in one word by making his Chorus monostrophick, he has robbed it of that lyrick beauty, which he was capable of bestowing in the highest perfection; and why he should stop short in this particular, when he had otherwise gone so far in imitation, is not easy to guess; for surely it would have been quite as natural to suppose those stanzas, had he written any, might be sung, as that all the other parts, as the drama now stands with a Chorus of such irregular measure, might be recited or given in representation.

Now it is well known to every man conversant in the Greek theatre, how the Chorus, which in fact is the parent of the drama, came in process of improvement to be woven into the fable, and from being at first the whole grew in time to be only a part: The fable being simple, and the characters few, the striking part of the spectacle rested upon the singing and dancing of the interlude, if I may so call it, and to these the people were too long accustomed and too warmly attached, to allow of any reform for their exclusion; the tragick poet therefore never got rid of his Chorus, though the writers of the Middle Comedy contrived to dismiss theirs, and probably their fable being of a more lively character, their scenes were better able to stand without the support of musick and spectacle, than the mournful fable and more languid recitation of the tragedians. That the tragick authors laboured against the Chorus, will appear from their efforts to expel Bacchus and his Satyrs from the stage, in which they were long time opposed by the audience, and at last by certain ingenious expedients, which were a kind of compromise with the publick, effected their point: This in part was brought about by the introduction of a fuller scene and a more active fable, but the Chorus with its accompaniments kept its place; and the poet, who seldom ventured upon introducing more than three speakers on the scene at the same time, qualified the sterility of his business by giving to the Chorus a share of the dialogue, who, at the same time that they furnished the stage with numbers, were not counted among the speaking characters according to the rigour of the usage above-mentioned. A man must be an enthusiast for antiquity, who can find charms in the dialogue-part of a Greek chorus, and reconcile himself to their unnatural and chilling interruptions of the action and pathos of the scene: I am fully persuaded they came there upon motives of expediency only, and kept their post upon the plea of long possession, and the attractions of spectacle and musick: In short, nature was sacrificed to the display of art, and the heart gave up its feelings that the ear and eye might be gratified.

When Milton therefore takes the Chorus into his dialogue, excluding from his drama the lyrick strophe and antistrophe, he rejects what I conceive to be its only recommendation, and which an elegant contemporary in his imitations of the Greek tragedy is more properly attentive to; at the same time it cannot be denied that Milton's Chorus subscribes more to the dialogues, and harmonizes better with the business of the scene, than that of any Greek tragedy we can now refer to.

I would now proceed to the review of the performance itself, if it were not a discussion, which the author of *The Rambler* has very ably prevented me in; respect however to an authority so high in criticism must not prevent me from observing, that when he says—*This is the tragedy which ignorance has admired and bigotry applauded,* he makes it meritorious in any future critick to attempt at following him over the ground he has trod, for the purpose of discovering what those blemishes are, which he has found out by superior sagacity, and which others have so palpably overlooked, as to merit the disgraceful character of *ignorance and bigotry.*

The principal, and in effect the only, objection, which he states, is that *the poem wants a middle, since nothing passes between the first act and the last, that either hastens or delays the death of Samson.* This demands examination: The death of Samson I need not describe: it is a sudden, momentary, event; what can hasten or delay it, but the will of the person, who by an exertion of miraculous strength was to bury himself under the ruins of a structure, in which his enemies were assembled? To determine that will, depends upon the impulse of his own spirit, or it may be upon the inspiration of Heaven: If there be any incidents in the body of the drama, which lead to this determination, and indicate an impulse, either natural or preternatural, such must be called leading incidents; and those leading incidents will constitute a middle, or, in more diffuse terms, the middle business of the drama. Manoah in his interview with Samson, which the author of the Rambler denominates the second act of the tragedy, tells him

> This day the Philistines a popular feast
> Here celebrate in Gaza, and proclaim
> Great pomp, and sacrifice, and praises loud,
> To Dagon, as their god—

Here is information of a meeting of his enemies to celebrate their idolatrous triumphs; an incident of just provocation to the servant of the living God, an opportunity perhaps for vengeance, either human or divine; if it passes without notice from Samson, it is not to be styled an incident; if, on the contrary, he remarks upon it, it must be one—but Samson replies,

> Dagon must stoop, and shall ere long receive
> Such a discomfit, as shall quite despoil him
> Of all these boasted trophies won on me,
> And with confusion blank his worshippers.

Who will say the expectation is not here prepared for some catastrophe, we know not what, but awful it must be, for it is Samson which denounces the downfall of the idol, it is God who inspires the denunciation? the crisis is important, for it is that which shall decide whether God or Dagon is to triumph, it is in the strongest sense of the expression—*dignus vindice nodus*—and therefore we may boldly pronounce *Deus intersit!*

That this interpretation meets the sense of the author, is clear from the remark of Manoah, who is made to say that *he receives these words as a prophecy*. Prophetick they are, and were meant to be by the poet, who, in this use of the sacred prophecy, imitates the heathen oracles, on which several of their dramatick plots are constructed, as might be shown by obvious examples. The interview with Manoah then is conducive to the catastrophe, and the drama is not in this scene devoid of incident.

Dalila next appears, and, if whatever tends to raise our interest in the leading character of the tragedy cannot rightly be called episodical, the introduction of this person ought not to be accounted such; for who but this person is the cause and origin of all the pathos and distress of the story? The dialogue of this scene is moral, affecting, and sublime; it is also strictly characteristick.

The next scene exhibits the tremendous giant Harapha, and the contrast thereby produced is amongst the beauties of the poem, and may of itself be termed an important incident: That it leads to the castastrophe I think will not be disputed, and, if it is asked in what manner, the Chorus will supply us with an answer—

> He will directly to the lords I fear,
> And with malicious counsel stir them up
> Some way or other further to afflict thee.

Here is another prediction connected with the plot, and verified by its catastrophe; for Samson is commanded to come to the festival and entertain the revellers with some feats of strength: These commands he resists, but obeys an impulse of his mind by going afterwards, and thereby fulfills the prophetick declaration he had made to his father in the second act. What incident can show more management and address in the poet, than this of Samson's refusing the summons of the idolaters and obeying the visitation of God's Spirit?

And now I may confidently appeal to the judicious reader, whether the *Samson Agonistes* is so void of incident between the opening and conclusion as fairly to be pronounced *to want a middle*. Simple it is from first to last, simple perhaps to a degree of coldness in some of its parts; but to say that nothing passes between the first act and the last, *which hastens or delays the death of Samson,* is not correct, because the very incidents are to be found, which conduce to the catastrophe, and but for which it could not have come to pass.

The author of the Rambler professes to examine the *Samson Agonistes* according to the rule laid down by Aristotle for the disposition and perfection of a tragedy, and this rule he informs us is, that it should have *a beginning, a middle, and an end.* And is this the mighty purpose for which the authority of Aristotle is appealed to? If it be thus the author of the Rambler has read *The Poeticks,* and this be the best rule he can collect from that treatise, I am afraid he will find it too short a measure for the poet he is examining, or the critick he is quoting. Aristotle had said that *every whole hath not amplitude enough for the construction of a tragick fable; now by a whole* (adds he in the way of illustration) *I mean that, which hath beginning, middle, and end.* This and no more is what he says upon beginning, middle, and end; and this, which the author of the Rambler conceives to be a rule for tragedy, turns out to be merely an explanation of the word *whole,* which is only one term amongst many employed by the critick in his professed and complete definition of tragedy. I should add that Aristotle gives a further explanation of the terms, beginning, middle, and end, which the author of the Rambler hath turned into English, but in so doing he hath inexcusably turned them out of their original sense as well as language; as any curious critick may be convinced of, who compares them with Aristotle's words in the eighth chapter of the *Poeticks.*

Of the poetick diction of the *Samson Agonistes* I have already spoken in general; to particularize passages of striking beauty would draw me into too great a length: at the same time, not to pass over so pleasing a part of my undertaking in absolute silence, I will give the following reply of Samson to the Chorus:

> Wherever fountain or fresh current flow'd
> Against the eastern ray, translucent, pure
> With touch ethereal of Heaven's fiery rod,
> I drank, from the fair milky juice allaying
> Thirst, and refresh'd; nor envied them the grape,
> Whose heads that turbulent liquor fills with fumes.

Of the character I may say in few words, that Samson possesses all the terrifick majesty of *Prometheus chained,* the mysterious distress of *Œdipus,* and the pitiable wretchedness of *Philoctetes.* His properties, like those of the first, are something above human; his misfortunes, like those of the second, are derivable from the pleasure of Heaven, and involved in oracles; his condition, like that of the last, is the most abject which human nature can be reduced to from a state of dignity and splendour.

Of the catastrophe there remains only to remark, that it is of unparalleled majesty and terrour.

A. W. VERITY

INTRODUCTION TO *SAMSON AGONISTES*

A. W. Verity (1863-1937) was the editor and annotator of the Cambridge school editions of Milton's work in England in the latter nineteenth century, and his little volumes on the poet's work are filled with remarkably extensive introductions and helpful details. In a sense all subsequent Milton students have entered into his labors. Given here is Verity's Introduction to his edition of Samson Agonistes *(Cambridge, 1892, pp. xxiv-lxvi). Footnotes irrelevant to this excerpt have been omitted, and the remainder renumbered.*

DATE OF THE DRAMA

The date of the composition of *Samson Agonistes* can be determined only approximately. The poem was published together with *Paradise Regained* in 1671: the volume containing them had been licensed on July 2nd, 1670, and entered[1] on the register of the Stationers' Company two months later, in September. But it is

[1] Professor Masson quotes the entry: "Septemb. 10, 1670: Mr John Starkey entered for his copie, under the hands of Mr Tho. Tomkyns and Mr Warden Roper, a copie or Booke Intituled Paradise regain'd, A Poem in 4 Bookes. The Author John Milton. To which is added Samson Agonistes, a drammadic Poem, by the same Author."

uncertain when *Samson Agonistes* was actually written. Perhaps, however, the year 1667 may be accepted with some confidence.

ITS RELATION TO "PARADISE REGAINED"

The account in Ellwood's *Autobiography* of his visit to Milton at Chalfont shows that *Paradise Lost* was completed in 1665 (the year of the plague). Whether *Paradise Regained,* the natural sequel to its greater precursor, formed part of Milton's original design; or whether, as Ellwood, with pardonable self-complacence, delighted to think, it was the outcome of the famous question which he addressed to Milton when he gave back the MS. of *Paradise Lost,* it scarce can be disputed that the second epic followed close upon the first. Indeed, it is conjectured that Milton began *Paradise Regained* at Chalfont in the autumn of 1665, since he showed the MS. of it to Ellwood soon after his return to London in 1666. At that time[2] *Samson Agonistes* was probably still unwritten. The play is essentially a poet's last work, his *novissima verba* to his generation. The tone is quieter than that of *Paradise Regained:* pitched in a minor key of sad resignation. Milton has no more hope of seeing—though others will—the vindication of the cause of right. Yet the interval between the epic and the drama is not likely to have been considerable, for the closing years of Milton's life were devoted to merely mechanic work—to his *Compendium of Theology,* his *Histories* and other labours incompatible with a poet's duty. A Latin *Grammar* dates from 1669, proof eloquent that he had bidden farewell to the Muses.

Thus the issue is narrowed to the years 1667 and 1668: and of these 1667 is the more probable, since it makes *Samson Agonistes* more directly the successor of *Paradise Regained.* In the drama

[2] Stern, agreeing that *Paradise Regained* preceded *Samson,* suggests that it was purposely kept in MS. until the drama should be finished, in order that by appearing together they might each have the advantage of vivid contrast: *Paradise Regained* being "a panegyric of victorious patience, *Samson Agonistes* a glorification of revenge," *Milton und seine Zeit,* II. pp. 120, 121.

are centred the last rays of the light of epic inspiration which, late in time, had fired the heaven of the poet's genius.

THE FIRST EDITION

The first edition, as we noted, was issued in 1671. The general title-page to the volume reads thus:
"PARADISE REGAIN'D. A POEM. In IV BOOKS. To which is added SAMSON AGONISTES[3]. The Author JOHN MILTON. LONDON, Printed by J. M.[4] for *John Starkey* at the *Mitre* in *Fleet-street*, near *Temple-Bar*. MDCLXXI."

Samson Agonistes, of which the pagination is separate, has a special title-page, as follows: "SAMSON AGONISTES. A DRAMATIC POEM. The Author JOHN MILTON." And underneath stands the motto: "*Ariftot. Poet. Cap.*6. Τραγῳδία μίμησις πράξεως σπουδαίας, &. *Tragœdia est imitatio actionis seriæ,* &. *Per misericordiam et metum perficiens talium affectuum lustrationem.*"

The volume is not so well printed[5] as *Paradise Lost.* There are a number of misprints, and at line 1527 nine verses are wanting. This, however, may not have been the printer's fault. Milton probably added the passage as the poem was passing through the press. It is supplied in a page of *Omissa.*

LATER EDITIONS

The second edition, 1680, was a reprint[6] of the first, save that the absent lines were assigned to their proper place, and that the pagination of the two poems is continuous. The third edition[7], 1688, a folio, was the last in which *Paradise Regained* and *Sam-*

[3] Many of the dramatic sketches in the Trinity MS. have similar sub-titles, e.g. *Zedechiah* νεοτερίζων, *Elias* 'Ορειβάτης, *Elias Polemistes, Elisæus Hudrophantes.*

[4] i.e. Milton himself; he had had the volume printed at his own risk.

[5] Milton had changed his publisher, possibly because Simmons who issued *Paradise Lost* was slow in bringing out a second edition of it (Masson).

[6] A slight difference of reading occurs in l. 1495; . . .

[7] Some copies were bound up with Tonson's celebrated folio edition (being the fourth) of *Paradise Lost* for which Dryden's lines on the "three poets" were written.

son Agonistes were published by themselves. In the fourth, 1705, they were supplemented by the "Poems Upon Severall Occasions;" and the same description applies to the fifth. In the sixth ("adorn'd with cuts"), 1713, the volume was further enlarged by the inclusion of the *Tractate on Education;* and editions with the same contents were numerous during the last century—sufficient witness of Milton's steadfast popularity. Of *Paradise Regained* the first separate issue was that edited by Dunster in 1795: of *Samson Agonistes* there does not appear to have been any such issue till quite modern times.

To revert to the early editions, it is worthy of note that they all repeat the blunders of the first; and it was not till Bishop Newton (in 1752) revised the text that the *Errata* marked in the original volume were corrected. Since then some fresh errors have insinuated their malignant presence into the text.

THE CHIEF SOURCE OF THE PLAY

The main source on which Milton has drawn for the account of Samson's life is, we need not say, the *Book of Judges*[8], chapters xiii-xvi. Almost every detail of the scriptural narrative has been worked into the drama at some point or other: and often the language of the original is retained. So that to master the contents of these chapters aforehand is the best—indeed, the essential—introduction to the study of *Samson Agonistes.*

It were well, however, that some distinction were drawn between the story of Samson's life and the actual incidents of the drama. Strictly, only one incident in the action of *Samson Agonistes,* to wit, the catastrophe, is taken from Scripture. The dramatic mechanism whereby that catastrophe is brought about (in particular, that interview between Samson and Harapha whereof the direct sequel is the summons to the theatre of the Philistines) is of Milton's own invention. And the same holds good of all the other

[8] It is significant (says Stern) that in this drama of denunciation and personal invective M. sought his subject not in the New Testament, but in the Old, that "inexhaustible source of Puritan passion."

incidents (e.g. the meeting[9] between Dalila and Samson) which occur during the progress of the piece. The Scripture in short furnished the climax: that which led up to it the poet created for himself.

With the story of Samson's career the case is otherwise. The record of his past is conveyed to us in the form of retrospect—the method imposed on all playwrights who observe the 'unity of time:' and this record, so vivid at times that the incidents related seem to pass before us on the scene, Milton, as we have said, borrows almost in its entirety from the forecited chapters in *Judges.* He has studied them closely; how closely many passing touches indicate. The belief, for example, in Samson's supernatural power which Milton attributes to Harapha exactly represents the opinion which the Philistines were most like to have entertained.

OTHER SOURCES

Josephus; The "Travels" of Sandys

A subsidiary source from which Milton has supplemented, in a few minor details, his picture of Samson, is the fifth book of the *Antiquities* of Josephus, chapter eight. But the debt is slight. Another possible authority (which has escaped the notice of the editors) is the *Relation* of the traveller, Sandys, one of the most popular and beguiling of the writers of Milton's time. I cannot help thinking that this furnished two or three hints, notably of the description of the building at Gaza where the catastrophe occurred. Sandys apart, Milton is alone, so far as I know, in representing that building as a theatre. The Scripture speaks of a house: in other accounts we read of a temple, or a 'public hall,' as in Quarles' *Historie.* But Sandys describes the ruins at Gaza of a vast structure traditionally supposed to have been "the theatre of *Samson,* pulled doune on the head of the Philistines." And he adds, with a touch of vivid realism which would have appealed strongly to Milton's imaginative sense, that there had formerly

[9] Neither the *Book of Judges* nor Josephus speaks of their meeting after she betrayed Samson.

belonged to these ruins certain "marble pillars of an incredible bignesse," afterwards used in the construction of a mosque lower down in the valley. Were these the self-same columns with which Samson wrestled to the ruin of himself and his foes? The thought may have struck Milton and stamped the whole description on his memory. That he had read the *Relation*—who had not in the first half of the seventeenth century?—there is independent evidence; and he may well have turned to it before writing *Samson Agonistes* to refresh his recollection of the scenes mentioned in the play. No contemporary work contained a more graphic account of the Holy Land and the surrounding districts[10].

The "Historie of Samson" by Quarles

Of other poetic handlings of the subject two may be cited. A curious *Historie of Samson,* in most cumbrous verse, was written by Francis Quarles, whose *Emblems* were once not without admirers. The *Historie* is a narrative poem, divided into twenty-three *Sections*, or scenes, each *Section* having a stanza of four lines as *Argument* (cf. the introductory verses to the several cantos of the *Faerie Queene*), and a *Meditation* at the close, in which the writer 'points the moral.' Though each *Section* is nominally a narrative, yet so many speeches are introduced that the effect is mainly dramatic. The poem, which is in rhymed heroic couplets (with occasional lyrics), covers the whole of Samson's life. Quarles had been a member of Christ's College: and as the *Historie* appeared in 1632 when Milton—not impossibly—was still in residence at Cambridge, he may have read it at the time from a sense of decent piety. But there was naught to carry away, and assuredly no inducement to renew the acquaintance later on, if acquaintance there had ever been. A plagiarism-quester of the nicest scent would find it hard to show that *Samson Agonistes* owed aught to Quarles' work.

[10] Scattered throughout *Paradise Lost* are numerous pieces of description which could only have been known to him through the works of travellers, such as Hakluyt's collection of *Voyages*.

Vondel's Play

The second poem is the drama, *Samson,* by the Dutch poet, Joost van den Vondel. The question of Milton's relation to Vondel is rather complex, and requires a more detailed discussion than present space admits. In the *Appendix* at the close of this volume an endeavour is made to set forth the entire unreasonableness of the claims which have been advanced on behalf of Vondel as the inspirer of *Samson Agonistes.* Todd, it may be added, discovered a poem[11] by an Italian writer, Alessandro Roselli, and an anonymous French play[12], published in 1622, each on the subject of Samson. It is like enough that Milton had never heard of either. If he had read all the literature that has been mentioned as the 'sources' of his poems, hardly should he have found leisure to write a line of verse.

MILTON'S EARLIER SCHEMES ON THIS SUBJECT

Whatever be the precise date of *Samson Agonistes,* the drama was no new project. As early as 1641-2 Milton had contemplated treating some episode in the life of Samson. He had passed in review a number of subjects suitable, in varying degrees, to his steadfast purpose of composing some great poem—by preference a drama: and the list of these schemes has the following entry[13]:

Samson pursophorus[14] *or Hybristes, or Samson marriing or in Ramath Lechi. Jud.* 15.

Dagonalia. Jud. 16.—

[11] Printed at Florence in 1554. The title-page describes it as *La Rappresentatione di Sansone;* and 'representation' best describes a piece which is too short and altogether too slight in character to be called a play. There is no division into acts, and the whole style is lyrical. The work seems to have had some popularity, since it was reprinted in 1571, and again at Siena in 1580.

[12] There had also been an English play of *Samson,* acted in 1602, but never printed. The *Biographia Dramatica* (Baker-Reed ed., 1812), III. 239, assigns part-authorship therein to Samuel Rowley who wrote several dramas on sacred themes, e.g. *Judas* (1601), *Joshua* (1602). See Fleay's *Chronicle of the English Drama* (1891), II. 171, 308.

[13] Printed as it stands in the original.

[14] From Gk. πυρσός, a fire-brand, torch; πυρσοφόρος was used as the

OTHER INCIDENTS IN THE LIFE OF SAMSON

From this we see that four, or five[15], several scenes in the career of the great champion of Israel had occupied Milton's thoughts. These, to keep to the order in which they are enumerated in the MS., were as follows:—(i) Samson's exploit of firing the cornfields and vineyards of the Philistines (*Judges* xv. 4-6). (ii) His contemptuous treatment[16] of the Philistines after his victory over them. There may be a passing glance at this aspect of Samson's character in the present play; cf. lines 340-344, and 528-531; in each passage Samson is represented as filled with ὕβρις and disdain of his foes. Perhaps the chief incident which Milton had in his mind's eye as revealing Samson in this part of 'Hybristes' was his bearing off the gates of Gaza (*Judges* xvi. 3). (iii) "Samson marriing" clearly points to his marriage with the Philistine woman of Timnath; and (iv) "Samson in Ramath Lechi" no less clearly to the slaughter of the Philistines at Lehi (*Judges* xv. 14-17). The last entry (v) "Dagonalia" needs no comment.

---

equivalent of πυρφόρος, the latter being a title applied to several deities, e.g. to Zeus in reference to his lightning; cf. Soph., *Philoctetes,* 1198. Prometheus, too, was called πυρφόρος; and Milton knowing that πυρσοφόρος= πυρφόρος may have intended the title *Samson pursophorus* as an allusion to the drama of Προμηθεὺς πυρφόρος by Æschylus, the first, probably, of the trilogy of plays on the Promethean legend. In the Trinity MS. the word *pursophorus* is written rather indistinctly, and at first sight one would be inclined to read it as *purgophorus,* 'tower-bearing:' which would refer to Samson's carrying away the gates of Gaza, an exploit of greater dignity. The only difference is g instead of *s*: and I am not quite sure that the letter is not *g.*

[15] Whether the number of subjects be four or five depends on the interpretation we set on the word *Hybristes.* Either *Hybristes* points to the same incident as *pursophorus,* since the destruction of the corn was a special act of ὕβρις or violence; or it alludes (and this is more probable) to a separate phase of the story, viz. to Samson's habitual contempt of his enemies.

[16] Which might be inferred from the *Book of Judges.* Percival aptly refers to Josephus (*Antiq.* v. 8. 10) who says that after the battle at Lehi Samson "held the Philistines in contempt."

MILTON'S PROPOSED TREATMENT OF THE INCIDENTS

Dr. Masson's View

With regard to these five subjects—if five there be—opinions differ as to the treatment of them which Milton intended. That it was to be dramatic is, I think, past dispute: but did Milton propose to handle all five themes, and if so, after what fashion? Professor Percival suggests that he may have contemplated writing a trilogy in the Æschylean manner: the action of three dramas might have been made to comprehend the five different episodes. Professor Masson has remarked: "Milton thought . . . there might be two sacred dramas founded on the accounts of Samson's life in the Book of Judges—the one on Samson's first marriage with a Philistine woman, and his feuds with the Philistines growing out of that incident, when he was *Pursophorous* (i.e. The Firebrand-bringer), or *Hybristes* (i.e. Violent); the other on the closing scene of his life, when he took his final vengeance on the Philistines in their feast to Dagon."

The Objection to It

Against this view (and the objection applies, in some degree, to Professor Percival's theory) there is one fact which makes very strongly. It is that, at the time when these entries were written, the form of drama to which Milton leant, quite unmistakeably, was that of the Greek tragedians. The drafts[17] of his proposed tragedy on the subject of the Fall of Man, dating from this very period, leave no doubt, at least in my mind, that any drama composed by Milton about 1641-2 would have been cast in the self-same mould whence issued *Samson Agonistes*. But the five episodes whereof we are speaking were widely separated in point of time and place: and it would have been impossible to compress them into two, or even three, dramas without disregarding

[17] Four in number: two being mere lists of *dramatis personæ* from which no inference can be drawn as to Milton's idea of dealing with the subject. The other two are tolerably complete outlines of the proposed action of each play: in each the unity of place is undoubtedly, and the unity of time almost as certainly, observed.

those 'unities' of time and place which were organic elements of the structure of a Greek tragedy, and which in *Samson Agonistes* were rigidly observed. Moreover, the first of the plays of which Professor Masson has outlined the subject-matter, must have been crowded with a diversity of interest and incident wholly alien to the symmetrical structure and singleness of motive that mark the masterpieces of the classic stage. It would have partaken more of the free, romantic style of the Elizabethans: and for that style Milton had never shown any liking. I conclude therefore that the entry in the MS. simply shows that Milton had looked at the story of Samson from different points of view, and as the result of his study had decided that it presented certain incidents, each of which might yield material for a separate poem. We are not justified in assuming that he meant to combine the projects by any process of synthesis: rather, the conditions of the dramatic form which he had chosen precluded any such combination.

PECULIARITIES IN THE MS. AT CAMBRIDGE

Here it is convenient to notice certain peculiarities in the Cambridge MS. which may throw some light on the question, and certainly indicate the order in which the subjects occurred to Milton. It is clear from the script of the entries that Milton first wrote the words *Samson in Ramath Lechi. Jud.* 15. Then, in the line above, just to the right of the word *Samson,* he added *marriing or,* meaning the MS. to run *Samson marriing or in Ramath Lechi. Jud.* 15. Next, as an after-thought, he inserted, in a cramped space, to the left of the first entry and almost level with it, the words *Samson pursophorus or Hybristes, or;* so that the passage now was intended to be read, *Samson pursophorus or Hybristes, or Samson marriing or in Ramath Lechi. Jud.* 15. And underneath the original entry stands the last of the subjects, *Dagonalia. Jud.* 16. But this entry, though it occupies the fifth place as the whole passage must be printed, probably came third; for if it had not been already written, filling up the space immediately under the first entry, Milton would not have been forced to insinuate at the side the after-thought *Samson pursophorus,* etc.

The sequence therefore of themes in Milton's mind appears to have been on this wise:—(i) Samson's slaughter of the Philistines; (ii) his marriage; (iii) his revenge and death; (iv) his burning the corn; (v) his insolence towards the Philistines. And from this rather haphazard order (wherein chronology is little respected) may we not infer that Milton merely jotted down those aspects of the story which impressed him most, without investigating very closely whether their internal coherences would suffer the several episodes to be brought within the limits of two dramas, or three?

THE CLASSICAL STYLE OF THE PLAY

On one occasion when *Samson Agonistes* was mentioned in the presence of Coleridge, he remarked[18], with a just enthusiasm which did not shrink even from the most gratuitous of errors, prophecy, that it was "the finest imitation of the ancient Greek drama that ever had been, or ever would be written[19]." The classical character of the play is twofold: of the form and of the spirit: of the structure which admits analysis, and of the style which defies it. Upon the easier matter let something be commented first.

THE PLACE OF THE CHORUS IN TRAGEDY

It is often said that *Samson Agonistes* reflects the influence of Euripides rather than Sophocles: which in the main is true. But in respect of one important element in the fabric of the drama the criticism needs to be modified. That element is the Chorus—more strictly, the purpose the Chorus fulfils on the scene. The use of the Chorus at all in an English play—even a play written for the scholar's study, and for an audience as sparse as that which Mo-

[18] From Collier's *Diary;* see Coleridge's *Lectures on Shakspere,* ed. T. Ashe, p. 14.

[19] Of modern attempts to revive in English the manner of Greek tragedy, the most successful artistically is, I think, Matthew Arnold's *Merope*. He not only employs the traditional mechanism of the classical drama, but infuses into the piece, as into his *Empedocles,* much of the "antique spirit." The speech in which the Messenger reports the death of the king is strongly suggestive of the parallel scene in *Samson Agonistes*.

zart promised himself when he composed *Don Juan*—evidently seemed to Milton a notable innovation. It is the point whereon he speaks first, and most fully, in the *Preface,* when he would justify his adoption of the classical form: and perhaps nothing in *Samson Agonistes* displays more strikingly his complete mastery of the mechanism of Greek tragedy than the address—the inspiration—with which he makes the Chorus play precisely the part which had been assigned to it by the author of the *Œdipus Rex.*

Its Office in Sophocles

In Sophocles the Chorus is essentially identified with the ruling interest—the dramatic *leit-motif.* It reviews what has passed in the action: prepares the audience for what is coming: and throughout maintains a close sympathy with the characters. Indeed, it is one of the characters: howbeit, gifted with a clearer vision than theirs, because less directly affected by the fortunes or misfortunes depicted, and therefore less stirred by the passion which dims perception.

In Euripides

On the other hand, the aloofness of the Chorus from the dramatic development in the plays of Euripides is a commonplace of criticism. He assigns to the Chorus duties which make it external to the drama: and the interest of his choric interludes lies rather in themselves—in their generalisations and philosophical views—than in their bearing on the events unfolded on the stage.

In Milton

Now in *Samson Agonistes* the Chorus is so built into the structure that without it the play would fall to pieces. From the end of the prologue (where the Chorus completes the retrospect of Samson's past life, and fills us with a sense at once of his greatness and weakness, the fatal rift that ruins all) until the final ἄφοδος, the Chorus never leaves the scene at all. And so long as Samson is on the stage it serves to illustrate his character, and bring home to us what manner of man he is: partly by contrast, for the Chorus has a caution and self-restraint impossible to the protagonist: partly by sympathy—by sharing in his feelings, by taking up his words and enlarging on them, by extending the train of his thought. This is true not only of the dialogue in which the Chorus joins, but likewise of the long choric interludes. They always grow out of something which Samson, or one of the other *dramatis personæ,* has said or suggested: they always tend to make clearer to us the motive-springs of Samson's conduct, and to penetrate our minds with the atmosphere of the piece.

For example, when Samson prays for the advent of death, the releaser and comforter, the Chorus indirectly justifies his tone of despair by dwelling on the changes and chances under which the strongest may bow and grow faint. Again, when Dalila has been repulsed by Samson, the long screed of venomous invective from the Chorus against women not only carries on the idea of the foregoing scene wherein womanhood as represented by her has been held up to scorn and infamy: but it exactly reflects what we feel to be passing in the mind of Samson himself. And yet again, in the ode which closes the second great episode of the drama, the interview with Harapha, how skilfully does Milton gather up the threads of the previous interests: making the Chorus to dwell, first upon the vanity of boisterous uninspired force—an echo this of Samson's own taunt, "bulk without spirit vast:" and then on the beauty of resignation and patience—a glance at Samson's expression of his readiness to die. It were not difficult to cite other places where the utterances of the Chorus harmonise with what is, we conceive, the main purport of the play: to wit, that gradual revelation of the character of Samson which is the key to the catastrophe. And when, obeying the summons, Samson has left the stage, it falls to the Chorus scarce less than to Manoa to sustain the interest while the climax pends; and, after the blow has fallen, to exemplify the mission of tragedy in purifying and calming. Milton therefore might fairly claim to have fulfilled the prescript of Aristotle—"The Chorus must be regarded as one of the actors, and a part of the whole, and as joining in the action[20]."

[20] καὶ τὸν χορὸν δὲ ἕνα δεῖ ὑπολαμβεῖν τῶν ὑποκριτῶν καὶ μόριον εἶναι τοῦ ὅλου, καὶ συναγωνίζεσθαι, *Poetics,* 18.

DIDACTIC STYLE OF THE CHORUSES

Howbeit the choral odes of *Samson Agonistes* do recall Milton's favourite poet in one thing—their moralising sententiousness. They are full of the "just sentiments," the "maxims of wisdom[21]," whereto Euripides (with his imitator, Seneca) was most partial. With him the tendency to generalise on life and conduct was irresistible, and this speculative bent found an outlet in the choruses, to the endamagement of the coherence of his dramas: the philosopher often o'er-mastered the poet. The same reflectiveness prevails in *Samson Agonistes,* expressed in dogmatic aphorisms: only it is better disciplined; diverted into a more legitimate channel. The character of Samson epitomising, as it were, the antagonisms of human nature, its strengths and weaknesses, with their natural sequels of triumph and tragic sorrow, affords scope for a wisdom which in touching on general truths does not lose sight of the particular case that exemplifies them. And it is here—in the broad views they contain of the human tragedy, in wide-experienced justness of thought—that the choric portions of *Samson Agonistes* are strong: here, and not on their lyrical side. They show Milton as the seer rather than the singer. The force of his sentiment (διάνοια) often eclipses the beauty of its expression.

THE CHORIC ODES AS LYRIC VERSE: DIFFERENT ESTIMATES OF

Some there be who deny this, refusing to allow that *Samson Agonistes* reveals any decline from the lyric achievement of *Comus* and *Lycidas*—any loss of habit's power in the poet. There is melody, they say, here as in the earlier works: true, melody different of kind and quality, as a fugue by Bach has harmonies other than those of Mozart's sonatas: still, melody for all whose ear is sensible of delicate sound. Milton, if any other, is a 'lord of language,' a master of rhythm and cadences and balanced effects, and it is our own blame if we cannot find in the odes of *Samson Agonistes* his peculiar 'embellished speech'—τὸν ἡδυσμένον

[21] Dr Johnson, in the *Rambler,* nos. 139, 140 (July 16, and July 20, 1751).

μὲν λόγον τὸν ἔχοντα ῥυθμὸν καὶ ἁρμονίαν καὶ μέλος[22].

But to others this judgment is unpalatable. They hold that in point of style the choruses are often rugged, often crabbed, and on occasion involved to the confines of real obscurity of sense. They place "It is not virtue, wisdom" side by side with "Sabrina fair[23]:" a terrible test wherein the later poem, being tried, is found wanting. Personally I confess that my sympathies are, mainly, with this view.

No one, of course, should presume to tie Milton down to rigid principles of prosody, and scan his lines as though they were a schoolboy's copy of much-toiled iambics. A poet like Milton makes his own laws, and it is our business to find out what those laws are, ere we criticise. Again, it is scarcely fair to cavil at the odes of *Samson Agonistes* because they lack the linked sweetness of, say, *L'Allegro:* that had been ill-assorted with their didactic, ethical purpose. Further, the mere absence of rhyme is, in some degree, responsible for the impression of harshness conveyed to many readers—more especially readers from whom the classical genius of the drama is concealed. Yet, when these several points have been weighed, and due concession granted, the fact, I think, abides that the choruses seldom reach that pitch of superlative verbal beauty to which Milton has trained his audience. One sees in them—*aut vidisse putat*—the uncertain touch of a failing hand.

WHY THE LYRIC PARTS OF THE PLAY ARE, PERHAPS, INFERIOR TO THE REST OF IT

Nor were the cause far to seek. For over twenty years Milton had written scarce a stanza of lyric verse. He had been dead to poetry altogether during that dreary spell of barren controversy, and even after his return to literature had never gone outside the limits of blank verse. All his powers had been devoted to developing the last resources of that one metre: and his ear had grown accustomed to specific effects of involved and elaborate

[22] *Poetics,* 6.
[23] *Comus,* 859 *et seq.*

harmony and sheer verbal splendour such as belonged to blank verse, and to blank verse alone. Is it unreasonable therefore to think that he had lost something of his sense, aforetime so keen, of the lighter tones, the delicate graces and charms of sound, which lyric verse needs before all else; and that herein lies the reason why the blank verse of *Samson Agonistes* is superior to the choric portions?

THE DRAMATIC 'UNITIES'

Next to Milton's use of a Chorus may be mentioned his observance of those 'unities' of time, place and action which are often regarded as a malicious invention of Aristotle[24], though, in reality, they merely stand for general principles of dramatic art deduced from the study of the works of the Greek tragedians.

Unity of Time

The time of the action of *Samson Agonistes* is clearly defined[25]. It begins at sunrise, and ends at noon, thus occupying seven or eight hours. The time permitted by ancient usage was twenty-four hours, as Milton notes in the *Preface:* though the ancients allowed themselves some grace in the interpretation of the rule. The events, for instance, of the *Agamemnon* and *Trachiniæ*[26] can hardly be brought within the compass of a single day, from sunrise to sunrise. In his *Essay of Dramatic Poesy* (where the unities

[24] He discusses the unity of action at length: that of place he omits: that of time he just glances at—τῷ μήκει, ἡ μὲν (τραγῳδία) ὅτι μάλιστα πειρᾶται ὑπὸ μίαν περίοδον ἡλίου εἶναι ἢ μικρὸν ἐξαλλάττειν ("in length tragedy endeavours as far as possible to fall within one revolution of the sun, or to extend beyond it but a little"), *Poetics,* 5. One of the earliest and most interesting discussions in English of the unities is in Sidney's *Apologie for Poetrie.* As might be expected, he strongly insists on observance of "place, and time, the two necessary companions of all corporall actions:" ridiculing the haphazard method of contemporary play-wrights, wherein "at this day, the ordinary Players in Italie, wil not erre" (Arber's ed. pp. 63-64). Shakespeare had not then (*circa* 1581) shown what a drama, free from these conventions, might be made to yield.

[25] Cf. ll. II, 1596-9, 1612.

[26] Schlegel notes these exceptions to the general practice (*Dramatic Literature,* Lecture XVII).

receive full discussion) Dryden quotes a remark of Corneille, to the effect that "the choice of some signal and long-expected day, whereon the action of the play is to depend," is one of the most difficult, yet essential, tasks laid on the playwright who imitates the classical model. Milton made a very happy selection. The climax of Samson's life provided a theme which fell easily within the limits imposed, and none the less realised that completeness of action on which Aristotle lays such stress. And he has surmounted one of the difficulties which the restriction of time causes, or increases—the difficulty of explaining the antecedent circumstances out of which the complication of the play, in part, issues. Some introductory prelude is necessary: and here it is furnished by the first speech of Samson (the prologue) and the *parodos* of the Chorus. In these the historic background is illuminated. At their close we have gained an insight into the past career of Samson which has won for him our pity, and stirred in us a feeling that from misfortunes so great must come a deliverance no less signal.

Unity of Place

The unity of place is not referred to in the *Preface:* but Milton obeys it strictly—more strictly than had Æschylus in the *Eumenides* or Sophocles in the *Ajax.* The scence is laid throughout "before the Prison in Gaza." The incident which constitutes the revolution (περιπέτεια) takes place at a distance, and is reported by the familiar Messenger of Greek tragedy. The same device was used by Corneille, and Ben Jonson had employed it in *Sejanus*[27] and *Catiline* with a skill which extorted the admiration of Dryden. There are, perhaps, few pieces of more essen-

[27] Where the death of Sejanus and the portents that preceded it are narrated by Terentius, while the *Nuntius* afterwards describes what befell the children of Sejanus (Act v. Sc. 10). News of the death of Catiline is brought in the same way. Speaking of the actual presentment of death on the stage, and defending the classical manner of reporting it, Dryden says: "when we see death represented, we are convinced it is but fiction; but when we hear it related, our eyes, the strongest witnesses, are wanting; and we are all willing to favour the sleight."

tially Sophoclean narrative in English than the Messenger's speech in *Samson.*

Unity of Action: This Unity as Understood by Aristotle

Last comes the 'unity of action'—a less simple matter. Very various interpretations have been put upon this convenient but rather misleading phrase, and it may not be amiss to attempt to see what Aristotle (Milton's guide) thought on the subject: what indeed were his views in general as to the ideal construction and character of a tragedy.

The end of tragedy, Aristotle writes, is action. Action should be complete and single. By singleness or oneness of action it is meant that every tragedy should contain one ruling interest, leading up to a certain crisis or climax. There should not be diversity of interests which might conflict. A distinct underplot (such as the modern stage cannot dispense with) were intolerable. Episodes are permissible—nay, desirable: only, each episode (apart from its brevity which may be taken for granted, since herein tragedy differs from the epic) must have the closest logical connection with the predominant theme of the drama. Whatever is superfluous, inserted merely to lengthen the story, or to give the actors greater scope of display; whatever, in fact, stands a hair's breadth outside the broad course of the play, and fails to contribute to the bringing about of the climax, is defective art: "for that which illustrates nothing by its presence is no part of the whole."

And as regards the framework, let the several parts be arranged thus: first, a beginning, which prepares the way, and which does not follow anything itself, though it must lead to something: then, a middle which is that something, and is therefore linked with the beginning by causal connection: third, an end, the interval between which and the beginning is bridged by the middle. A well-constructed play is resolvable into these three divisions, so that we can say where each occurs. In the incidents the dramatist should aim at probability or necessity: one incident arising naturally out of another, and the solution of the plot issuing from the

plot itself, through the sequence of cause and effect. Above all let it be remembered that the representation of incident is the chief object of a drama: indeed, that the action lies mainly in the incidents, since they form the plot.

Such are the main directions given by Aristotle concerning the duty of a playwright in arranging and unfolding his material. In a drama framed upon these principles there would be one main motive: a sufficient variety of incident having reference to that motive: and an organic coherence between the several parts, so that to remove one, or to transpose it, would disturb the symmetry of the whole. In a great measure, of course, these are the principles upon which all great dramatists have worked. But that which appears to be peculiar to the classical stage, to Aristotle as its prophet, and to all dramas composed on its model, is this singleness of interest or motive.

The Unity of Action in Shakespeare

We should best appreciate the difference between the ancient practice and the modern, could we hear Aristotle's verdict upon *Hamlet* or *Othello*. For in Shakespeare the interest is seldom—if ever—limited to one idea, however dominant and impressive. There is a complexity of motive, a wider range of appeal. Yet the unity of the whole is not lessened. All hangs together in a golden chain of dramatic idea. The dramatist works over a much more extensive field: nevertheless he preserves an essential 'unity of action,' though not the unity advocated by the great critic. The distinction must be drawn, because the phrase 'unity of action' is used, in the vague currency of criticism, as though it were applicable in the same sense to the classical drama and the modern. This, I opine, is not so: the 'unity' of *Hamlet* does not correspond to the πρᾶξις μία τε καὶ ὅλη of the *Poetics*: the 'unity' of *Samson Agonistes* does.

THE MAIN THEME OF "SAMSON AGONISTES"

The pre-eminent interest of the play is Samson's revenge on the Philistines. That constitutes the revolution or sudden reversal of fortune, by which the relative positions of Samson and his enemies are changed: he avenged, they flung from their pride of place. All that precedes is a preparation for this catastrophe. There is no by-plot: and of the two episodes one, at least, contributes directly to the climax. Now the way to this climax leads, as it were, through the character of Samson. Until we know what type of man he is, we cannot grasp the meaning of the crisis—why it need ever have come about: to understand him is to understand it.

THE RELATION OF SAMSON'S CHARACTER TO THE ACTION OF THE PLAY

Lack of Incident

Hence Milton's duty is twofold: first, to reveal to us the character of the protagonist, partly by showing, through historical retrospect of his past life, how he has become what he is, partly by revealing his character through the action of the drama: secondly—and upon a dramatist this is the greater obligation—to create complications (i.e. circumstances or incidents) of such a nature that Samson, being what we have learned him to be, shall find himself driven to do the deed which forms the solution of those complications. It is to the first of these tasks, the revelation of the character of Samson, that Milton has mainly devoted himself: and therein is he altogether successful. It is in the second, the invention of incident, that the weakness of the play lies. The climax is adequate: the character of the hero is adequate in conception and execution: but the poverty of the plot which unites the character with the climax we are unable to dispute. A brief analysis of the drama will make the point clearer.

ANALYSIS OF THE PLAY

The First Act

Were *Samson Agonistes* divided into acts the first would end at line 325, with the announcement of the entry of Manoa. Up to this point, says Dr Johnson[28], whose design was to show that the

[28] *The Rambler,* 139.

individual parts of the play, though beautiful *per se,* lack internal unity, "there is no design laid, no discovery made, nor any disposition formed towards the subsequent event." To this it may fairly be replied, that though no incident has occurred, yet in the space of three hundred lines Milton has given us a remarkable picture of Samson. His aim has been—and this was necessary—character-revelation, chiefly by means of reminiscence. And though there has been no hint at any definite act in the future, yet the scene has prepared us for the act when it does arrive; it has afforded a glimpse, wholly essential to the plot, of the possibilities of Samson's nature, a notion of what, under the stress of circumstances, he may be ready to do.

The Second Act

The close of the second act would fall just before the entrance of Dalila. It includes the interview between Samson and Manoa, with the choral ode "Many are the sayings," down to line 710, or thereabout[29]. In this scene happens what Cumberland[30] calls an "incident of provocation:" namely Manoa's announcement to Samson of the feast which the Philistines intend to celebrate in honour of Dagon, since through him they had triumphed over Samson, and thus, indirectly, over Samson's God. In Samson's view the news is a kind of challenge to God. There must, he says, be discomfiture in store for Dagon and his worshippers: the God of Israel must manifest his might. And these words serve as a premonition of the catastrophe. We anticipate, from this point, some

[29] The exact point of division cannot be indicated. Moreover, inasmuch as the dramatist has specially avoided any such divisions, we should not, in considering the symmetry of the play, lay stress on them.

[30] Richard Cumberland, the dramatist and essayist, a kinsman of Bentley. His reply to Dr Johnson's strictures on *Samson Agonistes* is the most just and satisfactory piece of extant criticism on the literary value of the play. It is rightly based on the view that the character of Samson is the cause of the climax: and that everything which reveals, or affects, his character belongs in some degree to the 'business' or action of the piece. The essay appeared in *The Observer* (one of the many attempts to revive the style of *The Spectator*), no. 76; see Chalmers' *British Essayists,* vol. xxxix, pp. 166-173.

great deed, and interpret all that follows in the light of this anticipation. The incident therefore distinctly advances the action. Further, it is the first step in the required provocation of Samson. He is being wrought to the necessary pitch of mental agony and distress.

The Third Act: The Episode of Dalila: Its Weakness

The third act is composed of the altercation with Dalila, and the ensuing ode; it may be taken to end about line 1060. This is a true episode, and not of the class of episodical complications whereof Aristotle approved. It is lengthy: and it does not lend any material impetus to the action. No doubt Dalila, having been the fount and origin of all Samson's trouble, may fairly find a place in the plot—to see Samson in her presence is to realise more strongly than we did before the change which his character has undergone. Moreover, his scornful rejection of her offer deepens the conviction that release from all his misery, physical and mental, can only come through some deed of strength which shall make an end of all. Thus, the expectation of a catastrophe, suggested first in the interview with Manoa, is increased. Still, the final result of the scene is scarcely proportionate to the space it fills, and the method used is that of debate rather than representation of action. Dramatically this is, we think, the weakest part of *Samson Agonistes,* howbeit, in many respects, of surpassing interest: the interest, though, of autobiography, not of dramatic art.

The Fourth Act: The Episode of Harapha: Its Importance

The fourth act (ll. 1060-1440) includes the interviews with Harapha and the Officer: that with Harapha being, of course, the more significant. This has been classed as an episode: none the less, it has a vital connection with the plot[31]. Indeed, the whole

[31] It is absolutely necessary to insist upon this point, since some critics treat the whole interview as a digression which does *not* belong to the plot. Mr Stopford Brooke, for instance, writes: "Two episodes . . . interrupt the main action, the episodes of Dalila and Harapha:" and again, speaking of the later of these—"The sole importance of the scene is that it exalts

scene is the most important element of the complications of the drama. For, first, it is through the instigation[32] of Harapha, enraged at the taunts of Samson, that the summons to the feast is sent: which summons leads straight on, undeviating, to the final goal of Samson's revenge and death. Secondly, Harapha is an admirable foil to Samson. The character-contrast has almost the vividness of Shakespeare's touch. More than ever do we realise that there are unsounded depths of power in Samson, and that he must, and will, use this power to free himself from a position which makes him obnoxious to the insults of an Harapha. Thirdly, the war of words "exasperates, exulcerates" him beyond endurance: his wrath rises in a *crescendo* of passion, and when at the close of the act the summons of the Philistines is repeated he is ready in the inspiration of his anger to face the whole host of the enemy and let come what will. This fourth act seems to me one of the most dramatic parts of the play, vivid in characterisation, varied in circumstance and incident, and essential to the catastrophe.

The Fifth Act

The fifth act begins at the second entry of Manoa (l. 1441). It comprises the dialogue between him and the Chorus, just on the eve of the catastrophe; their distracted conjectures after it has fallen and before the Messenger arrives; his report of it, and their concluding reflections. Against this last act criticism cannot hint a fault or hesitate the faintest dislike. The element of terror

---

Samson in our eyes and gives occasion to a chorus (i.e. ll. 1268 *et seq.*) which has all the grandeur, the solemnity, and the simple motives of a Psalm of David" (*Milton*, pp. 164-65, *Classical Writers* series). Now the first of these episodes begins at l. 710: the second, which follows immediately, ends at l. 1300. Is it conceivable that any playwright would be so maladroit as to fill the middle of his drama with six hundred lines (more than a third of the piece) which "interrupt the action"? The one plain fact that the interview has as its sequel the command brought by the officer shows how essential the scene is: that it does *not* "interrupt the action," but does advance it.

[32] This is clearly implied by ll. 1250-1253. For some time the audience have anticipated a crisis: here the first hint is given of the quarter whence it will come.

and pervasive sense of φοβος when the "universal groan," with red ruin and deathful deeds in its echo, reaches the actors; the irony of their hope that it is well with Samson and triumphant, while the audience know that it is ill with him and that his triumph is the victory of tragic death; the narrative of the Messenger with its refrain of the old, unhappy, far-off things of the *Electra* or *Œdipus at Colonus;* the resignation of Manoa and the Chorus, showing that Tragedy is justified of her mission to purge the soul of all distress and bring it back into the haven of passionless calm: these form a perfect achievement of unfaltering art which needs no prophet.

METHODS OF CHARACTERISATION

The Analytic Method in Milton. The Use of Action in Shakespeare

But as it were idle to criticise the closing scenes, so would it be equally useless to deny the inadequacy of incident in their forerunners. The fault of the earlier scenes is that in them Milton has used a method of characterisation which belongs to the novelist's art, not to the dramatist's. There are two main ways of depicting character: by analysis and by the representation of action. The analytic method, tedious though it may prove, is permissible, within reasonable limits, to the novelist: to the dramatist it is forbidden. It is his duty to characterise his *personæ* by placing them in circumstances which will force them to act, so that the test of action may reveal their natures: and in the same way it is through action that their inborn bent should be developed or modified. Of these two instruments Milton has relied on that which pertains to the rival art of fiction. Analysis we have enough of and to spare: incident is sorely to seek. The sum of moving accident in *Samson Agonistes* is meagre. Our knowledge of the hero derives through the channel of long monologues[33]. Shakespeare, working under

[33] A curious point in *S.A.*, to which we have not seen attention called, is the comparative absence of the στιχομυθία (i.e. dialogue in alternate lines between two characters) so largely used in classical tragedy. There is nothing here to compare with the dialogue between the Lady and Comus in *Comus,* 277-290. Such στιχομυθίαι were not uncommon in the pre-Shake-

the same conditions, with the same material, and up to the same climax, would have made the character of Samson an equally forcible study, and as the means thereto would have invented a chain of incident in which the hero, under stress and necessity of action, would have shown the stuff that was in him. But Shakespeare, though not, it would seem, a keen student of the *Poetics*, knew with Aristotle that "Tragedy may exist without character—without action it cannot." Milton, too, knew this. But whereas Shakespeare could put his knowledge into practice, in Milton, unfortunately, the creative faculty was not on a level with his other powers.

TRAGIC IRONY

Perhaps we may treat the 'ironic' element in *Samson Agonistes* as part of its structure. The play is full of that irony which in the Greek theatre compensated, to some extent, for the lack of freshness in the themes treated. The classical dramatist experienced a disadvantage from which the modern playwright is exempt. In a drama of to-day there is the interest of the unknown, the feeling—'how will it end?' The subject-matter being—theoretically—of the writer's own invention is his to handle as imagination prompts: and to the audience are conceded the pleasures of conjecture. With the ordinary Greek tragedy the case stood otherwise. The audience were as familiar, from the outset, with the gist of the plot as the dramatist himself, since the chief themes of Greek tragedy were drawn from those great cycles of Hellenic history and myth which were common property[34]. Into plays based on stories so well-worn the element of novelty and surprise could not enter.

---

spearian tragedy based on Seneca; and some examples might be quoted from Shakespeare's early plays, e.g. from *Richard III*. IV. 4. 343-361. . . .

[34] Cf. Aristotle: πρῶτον μὲν οἱ ποιηταὶ τοὺς τυχόντας μύθους ἀπηρίθμουν, νῦν δὲ περὶ ὀλίγας οἰκίας αἱ κάλλισται τραγῳδίαι συντίθενται (i.e. at first poets took any plot that chanced for their subject, but now the best tragedies are composed concerning a few great families, such as those of Œdipus, or Orestes, or Thyestes), *Poetics* 13. In *Il Penseroso*, 99, 100, Milton epitomises the chief themes of classical Greek tragedy; see also the first of the Latin *Elegies*, 45, 46.

Hence as a partial remedy for this defect the tragedians, notably Sophocles[35], had recourse to that effective figure of speech termed 'irony,' by which the knowledge of the audience was turned against the *dramatis personæ.* Unconscious of their true position, and ignorant of the drift of events, the actors are made to use expressions into which the spectators, in virtue of their familiarity with the story, can read a significance that is not intended by the speakers. Very often this by-play of veiled allusiveness foreshadows the catastrophe: a character will let fall some remark exactly descriptive of the fate which himself anticipates not, though the on-lookers have been in the secret of his doom from the very beginning.

THE IRONY OF "SAMSON AGONISTES"

Samson Agonistes is illuminated with many a quivering flash of this irony. Two or three signal examples may be instanced. In line 486 Manoa says that the Philistines ought to be merciful to Samson, seeing that he "no more [can] do them harm." It is natural for Manoa to think so: Samson does seem crushed and powerless. And if the spectator did not know better, the remark would pass unnoticed: but the spectator does know better, and his knowledge throws into tragic relief the confident unconsciousness of the speaker. Again, later on Manoa bids Samson hope, since God must still require of him some service: else why this revival of his lapsed strength? "His might continues in thee not for naught" (l. 588). Here again (for the effect of irony is usually pathetic) is the same pathos of the unconscious. Manoa is dreaming of some deed whereby Samson will win rest for his soul and ease and remission of his pain. And Samson *will* win these things: but far otherwise than as his father hopes. Manoa's words are true enough and appropriate in themselves: only we who know the end add to them a something: and "the little more, how much it means!"

[35] The *locus classicus* on "The Irony of Sophocles" is Bishop Thirlwall's essay, originally printed in the *Philological Museum* (Cambridge, 1833), vol. II. pp. 483-537. At the close of the article he specially draws attention to the presence of this irony in *Samson Agonistes.*

One more example. His enemies, says Samson, would prove his best friends did they but take his life and make an end of all. Yet if they did this it would be out of no consideration for him: so let them look to it, lest in destroying him they should be self-destroyed:

> Yet so it may fall out, because their end
> Is hate, not help to me, it may with mine
> Draw their own ruin who attempt the deed.

The last line, though Samson when he speaks it has no notion of what is coming, rings ominous of the impendent crash. The words *draw* and *ruin* fall purposeless from his unconscious lips, to be caught up by the audience as a warning that the scene is not far off when the ruining structure shall, in deed, be drawn on the heads of the Philistines. In this last case the irony is purely verbal: in the others it has a wider scope; it is rather the irony of situation, springing from the speaker's ignorance, contrasted with the spectator's knowledge, of the real position in which he and the other *dramatis personæ* are placed[36]. Many other examples just as effective as those we have cited occur in the play: and it is not rash to assert that there is no other work in our literature in which this classical artifice has been turned to such effective account. Sophocles himself would have welcomed Milton to the "laureate fraternity" of poets with a friendly "*frater, Ave.*"

THE CLASSICAL SPIRIT IN "SAMSON AGONISTES"

There is an interesting reference to *Samson Agonistes* in the *Conversations* of Goethe. Speaking of Milton, Goethe said; "I have lately read his *Samson,* which has more of the antique spirit than any other production of any other modern poet. He is very great." "Antique spirit:" that after all is the gist of the matter: therein lies the uniqueness of *Samson Agonistes,* the indefinable

[36] It is particularly frequent in the speeches of Manoa, as might be expected, he being the only character in the play who from the first has hopes of Samson's being restored to a happy life: hopes which the reader knows to be groundless.

something that gives it an artistic supremacy beyond the reach of rivalry or criticism. For a man might lay to heart all the canons of the *Poetics,* and in choice of subject, in construction of plot, in delineation of his characters, deviate never a hand's breadth from the principles of the ancients, and yet fail—as French tragedians for all their pains often failed, as the early Elilzabethans habitually failed—to produce work in which should dwell the presence—the *vivida vis*—of true, living art. *Samson Agonistes* is unique because here the genius of Greek tragedy does live—really live. So oft invoked in vain, it wakes at last from the long sleep of centuries to expatiate in the warm precincts of the day. And in its train attend all these qualities of art which distinguish the classical from the romantic style.

THE ROMANTIC AND CLASSICAL STYLES

Some one has said that this drama bears the same relation to Milton's early lyric work that sculpture bears to painting. This is a very true criticism: and true, in a wider application, of the distinction between the two types of excellence between which the kingdoms and principalities of literature are divided: the classical and the romantic styles. If we took at random a page of Marlowe's *Tamburlaine* and set it beside a page, selected equally "at all aventures" (as Cotgrave has it), from the *Antigone,* the comparison of a picture to a Greek statue would best express, so far as any single comparison could, the main difference between the several aims of the two writers and the qualities which each has made the quest of his art. The one charms with a splendour of colour which delights the sense and deadens the instinct of criticism: the other with a beauty of form which translates the idea of harmony into actual embodiment of outline, and provokes a criticism that increases the gratification.

That is the gratification derived from study of *Samson Agonistes.* The more closely we scan it the more keenly conscious are we of its merits—the symmetry, the subtle union of greatness and grace, the restraint and lucidity of the art. There are none of the half-effects and—a worse thing far—the confused effects into which romanticism ofttimes lapses. In *Samson Agonistes,* as in Landor's best work (for the two poets had driven afield on the selfsame hill of Helicon), the impressions are clear, definite, precise: outcome of a sane and disciplined imagination content to wait on, never to dominate, the poet's unfaltering sense of the things that make for an art which is just and lucid and self-contained—the art of the city of the violet-crown.[37]

THE CHARACTER OF SAMSON

Among the *dramatis personæ* Samson stands out eminent. He is the central figure upon which the artist has expended his utmost skill: and in him we have bodied forth the ideal type of hero as defined by Aristotle[38]—the great man who, illustrious and prosperous once, falls from his high estate by reason of some error or fault. Fame Samson had known and good fortune, and he had lost them—lost all—through the one fatal flaw in his nature, the weakness which brought him to his present position: a position that

[37] It may be worth while to note that the attraction which *Samson Agonistes* possesses for classical scholars has borne fruit in two excellent renderings of the poem into Greek verse. The earlier of these, by an Oxford scholar, G. H. Glasse of Christ Church (who performed the same service for Mason's once-famous *Caractacus*), was published at Oxford in 1788. The British Museum has an interleaved copy full of curious and rather censorious criticisms by the Cambridge scholar, Charles Burney, brother of Madame d'Arblay. The later version by the present Lord Lyttelton was issued at Cambridge in 1867. To the same writer we owe a similar rendering of *Comus*. The Latin version of *Samson* by William Hogg (mainly into iambics) was published in his *Paraphrasis Poetica in tria Johannis Miltoni Poemata,* viz. *Paradisum Amissum, Paradisum Recuperatum, et Samsonem Agonisten* (1690). Hogg remarks in the preface to the volume that he made the translations in order that Milton might be better known to foreigners.

[38] How strongly Aristotle's conception of the ideal tragic hero had affected Milton is shown by one of the dramatic sketches in the Trinity MSS. Milton draws the outline of a play based on Abraham's proposed sacrifice of his son, and the character of Abraham which he meant to work out is that of "a noble man faln from his reputation, either through divine justice, or superstition, or coveting to doe some notable act through zeal." We may add that in this drama of *Isack redeemed* the unities of time and place were to be respected, the incident of the sacrifice reported, and a Chorus introduced.

contains all the elements of pity for him and fear for ourselves, lest we too should fare likewise.

Of the many aspects of his character those which strike us most are his sense of personal responsibility to God, and his unshaken confidence in the ultimate victory of the cause of God. When he looks back on the past it is to see how highly favoured he had been among men: adorned with special graces and gifts: destined from the womb to be the minister of Israel's Deity. On him had been imposed a special work: it should have been his privilege to execute a particular, almost personal, service to his Creator. And he had not risen to the height of this great argument. He had fallen short of the responsibility. How just therefore that he—the betrayer of such a trust—should suffer: he who of all men merited punishment. This sense of the equity of God in laying affliction on him never deserts Samson. True, there are moments when it yields to a transient mood of resentment—to that spirit of protest which animates Greek tragedy and informs parts of the book of *Job:* the spirit that rebels against the seeming injustice of the power which rules the universe, questioning its decrees and crying aloud for a fair dispensation of reward to the good and penalty for the wicked[39]. This spirit may turn to bitterness and the paralysis of cynical despair, but in Job and in Samson, after a brief sojourn in the land of despond, it comes back to the truth built on faith, and hope, and on the recognition that "whatever is, is right." The harshness of his lot—the apparent excess of his suffering over his sin—may wring from Samson an occasional cry of rebellion; but in the end calmer counsel prevails and he submits to the equity of God. Nor, though himself may complain, will he suffer others to do so: when Manoa says that God has been extreme to mark offence, Samson's reply comes unhesitating:

> Nothing of all these evils hath befallen me
> But justly; I myself have brought them on;
> Sole author I, sole cause.

[39] Cf. the essay on Milton in Professor Seeley's *Lectures and Essays,* p. 150.

It is Milton's favourite thought:

> Just are the ways of God,
> And justifiable to men.

And then when Manoa tells of the honour which the Philistines purpose paying to Dagon, an honour which involves dishonour to God, Samson's sense of physical pain gives way to a much keener distress that this disgrace to the cause of righteousness should have arisen through him. He is like a renegade who has sworn a *perfidum sacramentum* and dishonoured his standard. Howbeit, the triumph of Dagon will be short-lived. The righteousness of God will prevail as ever, and work out its own vindication: and though the contest has now passed beyond the will of Samson yet, perchance, he may be used as the instrument of that revenge, and in the struggle for the good cause find his own salvation.

Such seem to me the main aspects under which we are meant to view Samson. He is the champion of God, conscious of his weakness in the past, acquiescent in his present suffering as the direct and righteous sequel of that weakness, and confident in the future triumph of good. And perhaps no trait in his character is more beautifully conceived and worked out than this unshaken conviction that good must be the final end of ill—that right, though plunged deep in distress, must emerge the fairer for its trials. Here sounds the note of Milton's eternal optimism, the hope which springs immortal in all his great works.

Very touching, too, is the depiction of Samson's weariness of existence: his painful, purposeless *tædium vitæ*. In part the pathos springs from the impression we derive of his actual infirmity of body and sordid, servile state. He reminds us of Philoctetes on his desert island, worn with wasting labour and pain, the flame of life scarce kept alive. But far more impressive than physical distress is the tone of listless despair in some of his utterances, the sunless mood of dreary, blighting 'accidie,' born of the excess of his remorse. He rues the past too bitterly: he is like to perish in his self-contempt, and only the feeling that he may, after all, do one more deed of service to his God saves him from the annihilation of self-reproach. Herein lies his difference from the Ajax of Sophocles with whom, in other respects, he has much community. Ajax, another hero of thews and might, has fallen into folly through the blindness of self-esteem: and when the film clears from his eyes and he sees the dire fruits of his madness he, like Samson, broods over the past until the thought of the future becomes intolerable. There can be no way out of the *impasse* of difficulty save through death; and his death is really cowardice, self-chosen because he cannot face the mockery of the world. But Samson dies, not to free himself, but to vindicate the cause of God. His death is "inevitable[40]"—"by accident:" a last deed of lealty and service into which no thought of self enters.

From another point of view Samson reminds us of Prometheus[41]. Like the fire-bringing hero of Æschylus, he brought to his nation the flame of hope to kindle their hearts against the oppressor: like his prototype he has to suffer at the hands of the enemy. The Philistines regard him as the instigator of the Israelites, the author of their efforts to break the Philistine yoke; and they treat him accordingly. And worse than their cruelty is the ingratitude of those whom he had benefited. Chained to the mill, as was Prometheus to the rock, he is abandoned of all and overpowered with a sense of loneliness and desertion: an ill reward for a benefactor of his country.

DALILA

After Samson, Dalila is the most elaborate and highly-wrought portrait. If he may be understood to typify the sovereign efficacy of pain and saving grace of repentance, she is no less a study of hardened, heartless unrepentance: a contrast in this to Eve who equally embodies Milton's view that frailty is woman's name, but who is redeemed in our eyes and made worthy of sympathy by her regret for her sin. In Dalila there is no touch of remorse, no

[40] See the note on *S.A.* 1665.

[41] Samson "possesses all the terrific majesty of Prometheus chained, the mysterious distress of Œdipus, and the pitiable wretchedness of Philoctetes" (Richard Cumberland, *Observer*, 76).

strain of compunction: and this want is due to her moral callousness, to the heartlessness which seems the key to her character. Milton begins, for the sake of the foil, by investing her with all possible outward charm. Circean fairness of form and soft persuasive grace are hers, with seeming innocence; but within "all is false and hollow." Among women Dalila is what Belial had been among the fallen angels. As sign of her moral indifference we note the glib readiness with which she invokes to her defence the most solemn motives—duty to country, reverence of religion, love of her husband, though she cares for none of these things, but merely juggles with the words as if they were counters, like a clever casuist who to win a victory in debate will stoop to any sophistry.

Her cunning callousness leads her to use against Samson the argument which is at once the most effective and the most cynically shameless—his weakness. If, she argues, he had been weak, why bear so harshly on weakness in her—a weakness for which there was so much justification? Like Desdemona she had known a divided duty, drawn this way to help her country, drawn that way by loyalty to her husband: if in the distracting conflict she had erred, surely the error was pardonable, surely she could plead a cause such as Samson had not to justify *his* weakness withal. Nay, worse: it was his sin that led the way to hers: but for his folly in yielding to her she had never yielded to the Philistines. So she contends, and there is reasonableness in it all, and dialectic plausibility. Yet to clear herself at the expense of Samson and make him responsible for her fault, and then, with an affectation of generosity, to offer to merge their offences in a community of guilt—these are the unkindest of all cuts. Nor does she stick at misrepresenting his side of the case: arguing that he had revealed the secret out of mere levity and wantonness, to gratify a woman's passing whim; and leaving out of count the ceaseless importunity of sighs and reproaches wherewith she had wearied him, and through his very love of her had over-mastered his resistance. Equally false, too, is her pretence that she had never suspected to what uses the Philistines would turn their opportunity against Samson. For she had known beforehand that they sought to take Samson that they might "humble" him.

The word 'love' is often on her lying lips, but there is no love in her heart, no loveableness in her nature. Her affection is only a convenient mask, one of the many phases of her infidelity. At the end, when Samson's refusals show that concealment no longer avails, and that she may as well show herself in her true colours, she reveals the hard relentlessness of her character, unbending and keen as steel of the ice-brook's temper.

Throughout therefore Dalila personifies clever heartlessness, quick to perceive any argument, how shameless soever, that makes for her own justification, and ready to suppress what is true, to suggest what is false, to make the worse appear the better reason, to wound her husband by turning his love of herself as a weapon against his own heart; in a word, to forge with untruth and half-truth and taunt and equivocation the most specious defence that an unscrupulous wit can devise. It is a masterly character-study, consistent in conception and execution, and vivid with a number of telling dexterous strokes which show that Milton, no lover of women, put his best work and strongest feeling into the picture.

MANOA

For the introduction of Manoa Milton had no Scriptural warranty. We do not hear of Samson's father after the incident of his marriage with the "woman in Timnath of the daughters of the Philistines:" after that point (chap. xiv.) he disappears from the narrative of *Judges*. It is quite likely, however, that he was still alive at the time of Samson's death, for the reference in chapter xvi. verse 31, to "the burying-place of Manoah" may only signify the place of sepulture belonging to the family, without any implication that Manoa himself lay there. His presence in the play is so effective because it admits the element of 'irony,' whereof we have spoken. And his inability to recognise Samson's true condition, to see that death is and must be the only salvation for suffering so great and self-reproach so keen—this intensifies, by contrast, the hopelessness of Samson himself who knows that, for good or ill, his race is run.

HARAPHA

The only other character depicted in any detail is Harapha, a type of blustering cowardice beside which the courage of Samson becomes the more conspicuous. "Bulk without spirit" is the formula in which his nature were best expressed. Of the relation of the scene in which he is introduced to the general drift of the drama something has already been said. It may be added that his name, at least, was suggested by the name *Rapha* which occurs more than once in Scripture; cf. 1 *Chronicles,* viii. 37, and ix. 43, and 2 *Samuel,* xxi. 16, 18, and 20, where the text of the Authorised Version reads "the giant," while the margin substitutes the proper name *Rapha.* He was the father of Goliath and four other giant sons. From lines 1248-49 of *Samson Agonistes* it is clear that Milton identified his *dramatis persona,* Harapha, with Rapha: yet the identification is not easily reconcilable with the received chronology.

THE PERSONAL ELEMENT IN THE DRAMA

The Parallel between Milton and Samson

There are some critics for whom the personal element in *Samson Agonistes* is its great charm. That element is, at least, marked. No one can read the play without perceiving that it has something more than an artistic value. For those who are familiar with the facts of Milton's life it serves as a record of his deepest feelings at the most tragic point of his career. It is not only that there was a strong parallel in personal experience between the poet and his hero—that each was blind, that each had been unhappy in marriage, that each passed his closing years amid circumstances of isolation and disappointment, in a world which had gone against him, repelling his efforts to make it better and saner. But the parallel held good of the broad political and religious conditions of their respective times. If Samson had fought the good fight for God, yet lived to see the heathen deity, Dagon, rise in the ascendant, though but for a space: had not Milton likewise struggled for the cause of God, as he conceived it, and witnessed the overthrow of that cause, after a brief reign of power, by its old arch-enemy, episcopacy? And so in politics: it had been Samson's mission to deliver Israel from the oppression of the Philistines: it had been Milton's self-appointed office to help to deliver England from the fetters of royalty: and each had failed. True, the reasons for their several failures were different: and herein lies the great distinction between them, the point in which the parallel breaks down. For the rest, the resemblance was only too clear, and this it was that led Milton to recur to the story of Samson, and select it from the list of subjects enumerated in the MS at Trinity. Hitherto he had had no opportunity of disburthening his resentment at the outcome of the Revolution, the miserable falling away of the nation from its hard-won freedom into the old bondage. There is, indeed, a hint from time to time in *Paradise Lost* and *Paradise Regained* of what was passing in his mind; but no adequate expression of his feeling was possible within the scheme of those poems. Only in *Samson Agonistes* came the much-desired occasion. There the *sæva indignatio* of his soul found vent and made the verse.

To appreciate the intensity of that indignation, to understand at all what was the mental condition of Milton when he wrote this drama of autobiography, we must remember at once the extent of the sacrifices which he had made for his country, and the hopes which had inspired him thereto.

THE GREAT SACRIFICE MILTON MADE

Milton's Attitude towards the Revolution

Milton's natural bent was toward a life of study and self-culture as a prelude to what he conceived to be the final end and object of his existence—the composition, namely, of a great work to the glory of God, and to the honour of his country and himself. Fortune had granted the material affluence necessary to this end. Had he been so disposed—selfishly disposed—he could have prolonged his stay in Italy, perhaps remained abroad until the stress of political disturbance was overpast. And then returning he could easily have gained a livelihood by teaching, or some such occupation, and still prosecuted his studies. This life he had surrendered for one in which he ceased altogether to be a man of letters. And he had been prompted to make the surrender from a sense of civic duty, and from a conviction that the struggle on which England was embarking would lead to such glorious results. Milton, as Professor Seeley well brings out, was one of the few men who took a large view of the Revolution, a view comprehensive of all its main aspects. For some it meant a change in religion: for others a change in politics. Milton saw both sides: for him the Revolution signified complete freedom in the two vital elements of national life—political government and religion.

His Hopes of What It Would Effect

More: he looked for progress in literature and education as a result of the contest. Henceforth thought and its expression would be free. Talent would make its way to the front. High office would be open as much to genius as to birth. There would be a dissolution of the fetters of prejudice and repression, a possibility of self-advancement for merit, a real liberty in all that concerns the well-being of a people. For these views, which spring from Milton's ingrained republicanism, from his impatience of authority and restraint, we must turn to his prose pamphlets, notably to the *Areopagitica*. They give us a clear notion of the intellectual development which Milton expected that the new regimen would bring.

His Disappointment

As the hopes therefore with which Milton started were high, the disappointment which he felt when they were all falsified must have been proportionately keen. In moments of despondence it may well have seemed to him that he had thrown away nigh twenty of the best years of a man's life, sacrificing health, sight, estate—above all, poetry—and effecting nothing by the surrender.

THE UNREASONABLENESS OF THE RESTORATION

To embitter his case there was the sense that he and his party had failed through the sheer unreasonableness of the people. The national apostasy was, in his eyes, so inconceivably causeless and capricious. For Milton, be it recollected, was as thorough-paced a doctrinaire as any of the philosophers who during the earlier stages of the French revolution drew up a fresh constitution for France every morning to tear it up at night. He appealed to men's reason, ignoring the fact that the majority act—not from reason, but—from impulse and illogical emotion, seeing, it may be, the better course, and following the worse. Like Shakespeare's Brutus, Milton was an idealist, a man of logical extremes, not practical, half-way compromises. With him "it is the cause, it is the cause" that should determine action—never expediency. His intervention in politics had intensified his habit of looking at things solely from his own point of view. The happy unreason of human nature in the average lay beyond his purview, so that in his pamphlets he often beat the air, invoking principles of abstract justice quite over the head of the ordinary reader. A striking proof of this unpractical, theorising habit is his treatise on *The ready and easy way to establish a Free Commonwealth*, published in 1660. For months it had been clear to the ken of most men that a return of royalty was inevitable: yet here, with the exiles almost on the march home, and the people ready to fling open the gates and acclaim their coming, was Milton arguing against facts, laying down excellent maxims of constitutional practice about which the mass of the nation were quite indifferent, and solemnly protesting that that thing never should or could come to pass which everyone in London knew to be only a question of days. It is easy to flout at this blind pedantic belief in the efficacy of pure reason, but that belief is the key to sentiments which have left an indelible stamp upon Milton's works, *Samson Agonistes* not excepted.

THE PARALLEL BETWEEN SAMSON AND THE ENGLISH NATION

We said that the parallel between Samson and Milton ceases when we investigate the respective causes of the failure of each, Milton having been overthrown through the weakness and folly of others, Samson through his own. Hence in Samson's bitter self-reproach and remorse Milton had no share. On this side of his character Samson typified—not Milton but—the English nation, who, like him, had profaned *their* mystery of Heaven-sent freedom, selling themselves into the slavery of kings and priests and politicians[42] (worse Philistines than those of Gaza), and yielding to the fascination of the Dalila[43] of the Restoration. Moreover, this remorse of Samson would in the future—not even the far future—be the feeling of the English people, when they should reflect on their work, and reflecting should see how evil it was, how they had sinned in restoring all the ills that the Revolution had swept away.

MILTON'S PROPHECY OF A SECOND REVOLUTION

That the day of repentance would come Milton, of course, never doubted. No man ever held opinions with more unwavering confidence in their absolute correctness. So here, as in all his other controversies, the right (he thought) lay with him, the wrong with his enemies. Their triumph was the supremacy of evil over good: how then could it endure? how could the victory be to

[42] Of course, this is only meant to represent Milton's view; see *S.A.* 1653-4. . . .

[43] *Samson Agonistes* is not the only work in which Milton has used the character of Dalila allegorically. In the *Reason of Church Government* (1641), bk. II, he makes Dalila typify the ensnaring power of Episcopacy, which had increased its authority by cajoling and flattering the King, *P.W.* II. 506.

any but the just? Milton knew only one answer to these questions: nor did he hesitate to foreshadow the time when the baseless fabric of the Restoration Court would be overturned, and the reign of right be renewed, the greater order of things begun.

THE REMOTENESS OF "SAMSON AGONISTES" FROM THE RESTORATION STAGE

In the *Preface* to *Samson Agonistes* Milton insists with rather unnecessary emphasis that the work was not intended for the stage. The most relentless of Puritan denouncers of the theatre could scarce have found an occasion of stumbling in a work so remote from the conventional type of acted drama. *Samson Agonistes* is an isolated masterpiece, no more akin to the contemporary drama of the reign of Charles II. than to the drama of the present day: and it appears to us altogether a labour of supererogation to take account of what was then being produced by Dryden and Shadwell (most unjustly traduced by his great rival), and the inglorious throng of Restoration playwrights—too 'easy' Etheredge, and the Killigrews, and Wilson (whose masterly comedy *The Cheats* even Milton might have admired), and Lord Orrery, and other faded immortals of whom memory lingers in the pages of Downes' *Roscius Anglicanus.* Not one of their works presents the slightest point of contact with *Samson,* which stands by itself, linked with no period in the history of the English drama, but deriving all its artistic worth from its observance of the principles of the ancients.

BISHOP ATTERBURY'S SCHEME TO ACT IT

It is interesting, however, to note that, in spite of Milton's clearly expressed wish, the play did, on two occasions in the last century, come within measurable distance of representation. In his *Life* of Milton prefixed to the edition[44] of *Paradise Lost* which he issued in 1749, Bishop Newton, speaking of *Samson Agonistes,*

[44] vol. I. p. xliv, whence it was copied by the editors of the *Biographia Dramatica;* see the *Biographia* (ed. of 1812), vol. I. p. 519.

says: "Bishop Atterbury had an intention of getting Mr Pope to divide it into acts and scenes, and of having it acted by the King's Scholars at Westminster[45], but his commitment to the Tower put an end to that design." What authority Newton had for this statement I have been unable to discover. His information may have been derived through some friend of Pope or Atterbury—some member, perchance, of the literary coterie whose *obiter dicta* are chronicled in the *Anecdotes* of 'Polymetis' Spence. There is no definite allusion to the project in the correspondence of Atterbury with Pope, though the following passage in one of the Bishop's letters may well refer to it. "I wish," he writes, "you (i.e. Pope) would review, and polish that piece (*Samson*). If upon a new perusal of it, which I desire you to make, you think as I do, that it is written in the very spirit of the ancients, it deserves your care, and is capable of being improved, with little trouble, into a perfect model and standard of tragic poetry[46]." The date of this letter is June 15, 1722: it tallies therefore with Newton's explanation that the scheme fell through because of Atterbury's committal to the Tower, which took place in August of that year.

A LATER ATTEMPT TO REPRESENT IT

Never Acted

The tradition as to the second attempt to adapt *Samson* to the stage rests on the authority of the *Biographia Dramatica.*[47] The play, we read, was prepared for representation at Dublin (then a very important centre of theatrical activity) in 1741-2; and Baker, the first editor of the *Biographia,* mentions that he had himself seen the acting version of the piece which had been got ready, and even the play-bills of the performance which at the

[45] i.e. Westminster School: the English tragedy was to take the place of the ordinary Latin Comedy acted in the great dormitory at Christmas.

[46] See the *Works* of Pope (in the Elwin-Courthope edition), vol. IX. p. 49. The editor of the *Correspondence,* Mr Courthope, does not give any note on the passage; but I think it must refer to this scheme.

[47] vol. III. p. 240 (ed. of 1812).

last moment was frustrated through some dispute among the actors. Twice therefore did *Samson Agonistes* escape the fate which its author deprecated, and Geneste[48] was doubtless correct in including it in his list of "Plays unacted." May it always be conceded such immunity.

HANDEL'S ORATORIO

Handel and Milton

To the public of the last century *Samson Agonistes* was, probably, best known through Handel's oratorio[49], written in the autumn of 1741, and first rendered at Covent Garden Theatre in the Lent of 1743, immediately after that visit to Dublin during which the *Messiah* was produced. The original title-page of the libretto, printed by Tonson, describes the oratorio as "alter'd from the SAMSON AGONISTES of *Milton:*" but some portions were taken from his early poems: e.g. the air "Thus when the sun," which comes from the *Nativity Ode,* and the famous "Let the bright Seraphim," from the ode *At a Solemn Musick*—a poem which musicians now associate with a later setting, under the title *Blessed pair of Sirens.* For the rest, the text of the drama receives very free treatment at the hands of the librettist, whose rhymed commonplace would have been more distateful to Milton than even Dryden's paraphrase of *Paradise Lost* in the *State of Innocence.* Not, indeed, that *Samson* fared worse than did *Comus* when it was arranged for Dr Arne; or *Lycidas*[50] when it was tortured into a musical medley expressive of a nation's lament over the death of the Duke of York; or *L'Allegro* and *Il Penseroso* when at Han-

[48] vol. x. p. 142.

[49] The MS. of the Musical Score is in the Library of Buckingham Palace. It shows that the Oratorio was composed in September and October, 1741, save the three concluding numbers which bear the date October 12, 1742.

[50] The elegy was arranged as a musical cantata and performed at Covent Garden Theatre on November 4, 1767, the night after the funeral of the Duke (*Geneste,* v. 186). The music was by William Jackson, organist of Exeter Cathedral, a well-known composer of the last century. One of his operas, *The Lord of the Manor,* held the stage for many years.

del's bidding they were made to take unto themselves an ignoble partner in *Il Moderato.* Handel, who really did much to increase the general acceptance of Milton's poetry[51], though perfectly indifferent himself what liberties his librettists took with the text, never could quite decide whether he preferred *Samson* to the *Messiah,* and during the 18th century the former seems to have been very popular[52]—perhaps more popular than it is now[53].

THE BLANK VERSE OF "SAMSON AGONISTES"

In the blank verse of *Samson Agonistes,* as distinguished from that of *Paradise Lost,* one peculiarity is noticeable—the prevalence, namely, of lines with an extra syllable at the close, such as the following:

> Why thou should'st wed Philistian women rath*er*.

Here the italicised syllable is superfluous. The percentage of verses in which this metrical license occurs is very small in Milton's epics, but not inconsiderable in his dramas. According to Professor Masson the percentages read as follows: in *Comus* 9; in *Paradise Lost* 1 (about); in *Paradise Regained* 3-4; in *Samson* 6.

[51] Joseph Warton in his *Essay on the Genius and Writings of Pope* attributed the popularity of *L'Allegro* and *Il Penseroso* to the fact that they had been "set to admirable music by Mr Handel" (see the Pitt Press ed. of those poems, p. xxxvi); and Bishop Newton was of opinion—very justly—that the genius of the great musician was exactly suited to illustrate that of the great poet (*Introduction to Paradise Lost,* ed. 1749, I. xliv).

[52] Thus the reprints of the libretto were numerous: the Catalogue of the British Museum mentions seven editions issued before 1765.

[53] Apart from Handel's oratorio there have been several musical works based on the story of Samson: e.g. an oratorio by the celebrated Italian Church-composer, Giovanni Paolo Colonna, of Bologna, whose *Samson* was written only a few years after Milton's drama—viz. in 1677; a French opera by the Court-composer Rameau, for which Voltaire prepared the text-book (1732); a German opera, *Samson,* by Raff, never acted; and the *Samson et Dalila* of the living French musician Saint-Saëns. The libretto of this opera (produced at Weimar in 1877) is interesting because it deals with the last day in Samson's life, and in it, as in *Samson Agonistes,* Dalila is one of the chief *dramatis personæ.* In the last scene (laid in the temple of Dagon) she attempts to kill Samson by offering him a poisoned chalice. This she does at the bidding of the priest of Dagon; cf. *Samson Agonistes,* 857-861.

The extra syllable is far more suitable to dramatic than to epic verse, since it knits a passage together with a rapidity of movement akin to the naturalness of ordinary conversation. Epic narration requires a statelier, slower effect[54].

THE USE OF RHYME

Milton's occasional use of rhyme in the play is not easy to explain. In some instances the rhyme is probably accidental: in others[55] it may be intended, as Professor Percival suggests, to express contempt.

In the choruses it serves to emphasise their lyrical character, and Milton may mean it to compensate, in some degree, for their lack of division[56] into strophe, antistrophe and epode.

[54] Mr Bridges, who has done so much to elucidate the principles of Milton's prosody, shows in his recently published pamphlet on the verse of *P.R.* and *S.A.* that these poems contain several elisions and metrical licenses which Milton did not allow himself in *P.L.*; in fact, that their verse is of a somewhat freer type than that of *P.L.* But it would not be profitable to discuss the point without considering the whole question of elided syllables in Milton.

[55] Cf. ll. 1010 *et seq.*

[56] See Milton's *Preface* to *S.A.*

R. C. JEBB

SAMSON AGONISTES AND THE HELLENIC DRAMA

In 1908, the tercentenary of his birth, the British Academy produced several papers in honor of John Milton. The following paper on "Samson Agonistes *and the Hellenic Drama*" *was prepared by the British classicist R. C. Jebb (1841-1905) and read on December 10, 1908. The essay is reprinted from* Proceedings of the British Academy, *III (1908), 1-8.*

I

Samson Agonistes may fairly be called classical both in language and in structure. The language has throughout elevation and temperate dignity, resembling that of *Paradise Lost,* but colder, and with fewer bursts of great eloquence. The structure fails only in one point, the metre of the choruses. The lyrical beauty of the choral odes in a Greek tragedy depended much on their division into corresponding parts, the strophe, the antistrophe, and the epode. It is the balance and symmetry of these strophic movements to which the regular grace of the choruses is chiefly due. Milton here has freed himself from the restraint of strophe and antistrophe, and the measures of his Chorus are entirely arbitrary. This very irregularity has, it is true, a certain grandeur, but is not the grandeur proper to a tragedy on the Greek model; it is rather the sublimity of some of the bursts of eloquence in the Hebrew prophets.[1]

Another criticism, upon the structure of the drama, is offered by Johnson—that the action of the drama makes no continuous progress from the beginning to the end. The opening is fine; the catastrophe is just; but there is no dramatic progress. This criticism appears to me far too strongly expressed. The *Samson Agonistes* falls into five Acts:—

1. Act i, 1-325: Samson and the Chorus.
2. Act ii, 326-731: Samson and Manoah.
3. Act iii, 732-1060: Samson and Dalila.
4. Act iv, 1061-1299: Samson and Harapha.
5. Act v, 1300-1758: Samson and the Philistines.

Is it true that, as Dr. Johnson declares, after the point at which Manoah informs Samson of the feast to Dagon (vv. 433-47), no incident which advances the plot occurs until the catastrophe?

The catastrophe, let it be observed, consists in Samson deliberately pulling down the temple of Dagon on his own head and those of the spectators. Samson's will is the agent of the catastrophe. Everything, therefore, which helps to determine Samson's will and to define his purpose leads to the catastrophe.

Now (*a*) the last part of Act ii, vv. 606-731, cannot from this point of view be thought, as Johnson thinks it, idle. In that passage Samson expresses his resolution to die—a resolution fixed in him by the tidings just brought by Manoah of the honour to Dagon and the consequent dishonour to God, resulting from Samson's own weakness. He tells his father that he must not propose to seek his release. Thus the issue is so far narrowed; we see that one way of escape is closed; Samson will not allow himself to be ransomed.

But perhaps Dalila in her remorse will intercede for him, and he will be extricated in that way? The third Act brings Dalila on the scene, and at once she proffers her good offices (vv. 743-7).

[1] See, for instance, the last choral song, vv. 1660-1707.

It is now clear that Samson will accept no kind of mediation, and that he will die in captivity, either worn out by sorrow or in some great agony, which his treatment of the Philistines may hasten or delay. At this moment the giant Harapha enters, and to his insults Samson replies with defiance. As he leaves the scene the Chorus say:

> He will directly to the lords, I fear,
> And with malicious counsel stir them up
> Some way or other yet further to afflict thee.

Thus all is at last ready. Samson, crushed by despair and shame for himself and Israel, has rejected the proposal of Manoah to treat for his release; has made the intercession of Dalila impossible; finally, by bitter defiance of Harapha, has prepared for himself some crowning ignominy at the hands of his captors.

Surely, then, it cannot be said, as Dr. Johnson says, that the action of the drama makes no progress between the opening and the close. The action is, indeed, a still action, because the force which is to produce the catastrophe is the inward force of Samson's own despair, not an external necessity pressing upon him. Precisely the same is the case in the *Prometheus Vinctus* of Aeschylus, a drama consisting, like *Samson Agonistes,* of a series of interviews.

II

A more interesting inquiry than any regarding the form of the *Samson Agonistes* is that regarding its spirit. Granting it to be in diction and in structure representative of that Greek drama which was its model, how far, we ask, is it animated by the spirit, by the dominant idea, of its original? This point appears to have been too little considered by the critics of Milton's great poem; and it is to this point especially that I wish to direct attention.

Mr. Matthew Arnold, in his essay entitled 'Culture and Anarchy', has made the terms Hebraism and Hellenism familiar as designating two opposed, or at least widely divergent, moral habits. Hebraism, as used by him, means the tendency to energetic action under the pressure and control of strict conscience. Hellenism denotes the desire to appreciate justly in the light of a free consciousness. The Hebrew acts strongly with an earnest faith. The Hellene thinks, and then acts in temperate obedience to his thought. The characteristic of Hebraism is direct intensity. The characteristic of Hellenism is flexible intelligence. The Hebrew has force, the Hellene has light.

I am not proposing now to broach the question whether the terms Hebraism and Hellenism accurately or completely express a fundamental antithesis between two permanent types of human activity. But these terms, in a narrower and stricter acceptation, form the contrast which immediately concerns us here.

Milton's mind was, in the literal and proper sense, Hebraic. Among those things which Hebrews have always believed and felt most strongly, and by believing and feeling which they have been characterized, are these:—(1) that God is the personal head, the immediate King, the very leader in battle, of His servants; (2) that the Hebrew people are, in a special sense, His *chosen* servants; a peculiar people, chosen by Him from other peoples; (3) that, as the interpreters of His will to His chosen servants, He from time to time selects men whom He directly and specially inspires, and who become what we denote by the Greek word προφῆται—i.e. *speakers forth, utterers* of His will.

Now, Milton habitually thought of the English people as holding the same place under the New Covenant which the Hebrews had held under the Old Covenant. He regarded them as a peculiar nation, selected by God to proclaim to the modern world the purest form of Faith, as the Hebrews had been chosen to declare to the old world the highest form of Law.[2]

[2] *Areopagitica*: 'God is decreeing to begin some new and great period in His Church . . . what does He then but reveal Himself to His servants, and, as His manner is, first to His Englishmen?'

Doct. and Disc. of Divorce: 'It would not be the first or second time since our Ancient Druides . . . that England hath had this honour vouchsafed from heaven to give out Reformation to the world.' Cf. the *Tenure of Kings and Magistrates.*

He compares the English Commonwealth to the Hebrew Theocracy. In adopting that form of government, he says the people chosen by God under the New Covenant have resolved to have for their one Supreme Ruler no other than God Himself. Men endued with great gifts are now, as of old, His prophets. From his early youth Milton's genius had that which is seldom separate from genius—a certain still consciousness of itself; and from his early youth this consciousness was solemn—joined to a sense that these powers were destined to be employed in the ministry of a government whose Head was God Himself; that he was, in his place and time, to be an interpreter to England of the best things imparted to him—that he was to be a prophet.

When a man with this bent of thought selected as the subject for a poem an episode of Hebrew history, the treatment of the subject was sure to be genuinely Hebraic. It would be needless to point out how, or how thoroughly, the spirit of the *Samson Agonistes* is the spirit of Hebraism. Samson is the champion of the Israelites against the Philistines. Jehovah is the God of the Israelites; Dagon is the protecting deity of the Philistines. Samson, through disloyalty to himself, has been permitted to fall into the hand of the idolaters; and Israel shares in his humiliation. Yet, even in this abasement, Samson is confident that the Lord of Hosts will finally assert His own majesty against the idol. This confidence is justified: the honour of the true God and of His chosen people are vindicated by the catastrophe which punishes the weakness, as it closes the penance, of His individual minister. This is the issue of the drama—Jehovah has prevailed over Dagon; Israel is avenged on Philistia.

Is this tragedy Hellenic in its spirit? If the names were changed—if the supernatural and the mortal agents were different—would it be possible to conceive this subject thus treated by Aeschylus, by Sophocles, or by Euripides?

The first characteristic of Hellenic tragedy in the hands of its greatest masters was an ideal grandeur of agony depending on a real grandeur of contrast. The contrast was between man and fate. The subject of Greek tragedy in all its forms, in all the fables over which it ranged, was the conflict between free will and destiny, between an absolute inward liberty and an inexorable external necessity. The gods themselves are subordinate to fate, either as administrators or as rebels; and the question so often asked, what is the source of imaginative pleasure in tragedy? is thus answered by Hellenic tragedy: it is the sense, on the one hand, of the heroic in man; on the other hand, of a superhuman controlling power.

It would not be difficult to select from the dramatic poetry of Greece passages which would interpret this statement. But there is one which, though limited in its scope, is, perhaps, better suited to the purpose than any other single passage. In his tragedy *Eumenides* Aeschylus has put into the mouth of the Furies themselves the theory of that government which, as the executants of the Fates' darkest decrees, they exercise over the whole human race. The Furies are not the Fates; but they are their most potent and most certain ministers; and the sublime Chorus in which they describe the sway committed to them is no imperfect expression of the deepest religious feeling of the ancient Greeks.[3]

Hellenism contrasts man with fate. Hebraism contrasts God and His servants with idols and their servants. The difference will be best illustrated if the Hebrew personification of strength is compared with the Hellenic personification of strength; if Samson and his destiny are compared with Herakles and his destiny. It may be proper to inquire at the commencement—how far is the parallel just? What are the points of analogy between the history of Samson and the legend of Herakles? For convenience, I will speak of Herakles, a Hellenic idea, as if he was no less actual than Samson, a Hebrew fact.

They may be described as analogies of epoch; of mission; of temperament; of sufferings; of death.

Of epoch. Each was a strong man in a rude age—an age of widely-spread physical violence and fierce passions; an age of spasmodic efforts.

[3] *Eumenides,* vv. 306-80.

Of mission. Each was a deliverer. Samson was the champion, immediately, of his own tribe, the tribe of Dan, against the Philistines—who were straitening them in their already narrow borders between the mountains and the sea—and thereby of all Israel; Herakles, as he is himself made to say, 'ridding the earth of plagues, vexed his soul on the sea and in all forests.'

Of temperament. In his lectures on the Jewish Church Dean Stanley has well brought out the 'rough humour' which is a leading characteristic of Samson. 'As a peal of hearty laughter breaks in upon the despondency of individual sorrow, so the joviality of Samson becomes a pledge of the revival of the greatness of his nation.' Precisely this quality is prominent in the Greek Herakles; and no one will forget the interpretation of this trait in Browning's *Balaustion.*

Of sufferings. Each becomes a thrall; and the most bitter thraldom of each is due to misplaced affection. Herakles is the slave of Omphale and the victim of Deianeira, as Samson was plotted against by his first wife, and successfully betrayed by Dalila.

Of death. Each passed away in agony—Herakles on Oeta; Samson in the temple at Gaza.

Such are some of the principal points of analogy between Herakles and Samson; and the analogy appears sufficient to justify a general comparison of poems which concern the two heroes.

The central idea of Samson's history, and, in harmony with that history, the central idea of Milton's poem, is the idea of a national champion, first victorious, then abased, then finally triumphant in a national cause. The feeling uppermost in Samson's mind is this —that the strength entrusted to him for the honour of God and of Israel has, through his own weakness, been betrayed and crushed; and that the great cause which he was commissioned to uphold has thereby been dishonoured. When Samson has perished in the temple of Dagon it is Manoah's comfort that this stain has been effaced (vv. 448-71, 1669-1720).

The central idea of the story of Herakles is that of a champion of the whole human race, persecuted throughout his mortal life by a cruel destiny. In his supreme agony—when the robe anointed by the unsuspecting Deianeira with the poisoned blood of the Centaur Nessus is burning into his flesh, as he writhes in his torment by the altar at Cenaeum, whence he is borne to his fiery death on Mount Oeta—his foremost thought is this, that the strength which had been used for all mankind has been overcome by an unworthy adversary through the working of destiny. Samson in his death triumphs over the Philistines; Herakles in his last agony is the victim of fate.[4]

[4] *Trach.*, vv. 1046-63:

Ah me, whose hands and shoulders have been tried
In many a burning trial! Not the hate
Of Hera, not Eurystheus, ever laid
Aught on me like to this, her gift, the gift
Of Oeneus' daughter, falsely beautiful,
This garment of the Furies on my back,
This clinging woven snare in which I die.

* * * *

Again that scorching dart of deadly pain
Shoots through my sides—the evil-eating pest
Gives me no space from torment. Oh, receive me,
Ruler of darkness—strike me, flash of Zeus!
O king, send down thy thunders! O father, hurl
Thy thunderbolt upon me! Again, again
It gnaws me, it has blazed into new fire!
Ah hands, ah shoulders, breast, ah trusty arms,
Yes ye, ye in this plight, are they who quelled
The habitant of Nemea; the shepherds' scourge,
The lion, before whose face no man might come,
And Lerna's hydra and the Centaur host
Separate from men, fierce, lawless, great in strength,
And the Erymanthian beast, and the hound of hell
Three-headed, an appalling enemy,
Born of Echidna, and the serpent-guard
Of golden apples in Earth's utmost clime,
And of trials ten thousand other I had taste,
And no man took a trophy from my hand.
So now—joint loosed from joint—flesh rent to shreds—
I perish by this blind pest! I—I, the son

Vaunted of royal mother—I proclaimed
The son of Zeus, whose throne is in the stars!

These are the last lines of the *Samson Agonistes:*—

> All is best, though we oft doubt
> What the unsearchable dispose
> Of Highest Wisdom brings about,
> And ever best found in the close.
> Oft He seems to hide His face,
> But unexpectedly returns,
> And to His faithful champion hath in place
> Bore witness gloriously; when Gaza mourns,
> And all that band them to resist
> His uncontrollable intent;
> His servants He, with new acquist
> Of true experience, from this great event
> With peace and consolation hath dismiss'd,
> And calm of mind, all passion spent.

and these the last lines of the *Trachiniae:*—

> Who shall look into the future?
> But these things are anguish for us
> And shame for the Gods;
>
> * * * *
>
> And these things are Zeus' alone.

The task of Samson descended to Samuel; and it may well be that, as Manoah forebodes, the grave of Samson among his native hills, between Zorah and Eshtaol, was long visited by the men of his tribe and people with the remembrance only of a triumph—of a victory which his successors had perpetuated, the continuous victory of Jehovah over Dagon. But it was with another feeling that the Greeks of a later age saw the mountain, consecrated by tradition, which looked on the Malian Gulf—the mountain which had witnessed the fiery apotheosis of Herakles:—

> Where the great warrior, wrapt in heav'nly flame,
> High above Oeta's steep,
> Was taken, a god, unto Gods.

This was no link in a chain of unbroken victories, no incidental assertion of a good power ever triumphant over evil; it was, for them, a lonely instance of superhuman strength towering above the rugged, low range of human history, and confronting, though not vanquishing, except by the death which led to immortality, the awful malignity of fate.

The *Samson Agonistes* is a great poem; it is also a noble drama, though its rank as a poem is far higher than its rank as a drama. But neither as poem nor as drama is it Hellenic. Its sorrow is the sorrow of Jeremiah; its joy is that which inspires the songs of Miriam and of Deborah.[5]

[5] 'Hear, O ye kings; give ear, O ye princes; I, even I, will sing praise to the Lord God of Israel. Lord, when thou wentest out of Seir, when thou marchedst out of the field of Edom, the earth trembled, and the heavens dropped, the clouds also dropped water. The mountains melted from before the Lord, even that Sinai from before the Lord God of Israel.'

JAMES HOLLY HANFORD

SAMSON AGONISTES AND MILTON IN OLD AGE

Often called the dean of American Milton scholars, James Holly Hanford (1882-) has prepared numerous studies on the life and work of the poet. The article which follows appeared in Studies in Shakespeare, Milton and Donne by Members of the English Department of the University of Michigan [University of Michigan Publications in Language and Literature, 1] *(New York, 1925), pp. 165-189.*

Paradise Lost, the "monumentum aere perennius" which Milton had planned in youth but whose execution he perilously delayed till beyond his fiftieth year, stood complete and glorious by the summer of 1665. Before its publication in 1667 its author had probably finished the second masterpiece of his maturity, *Paradise Regained.* The composition of *Samson Agonistes* presumably fell within the immediately succeeding years. The two poems appeared together in 1671. Were these later works really afterthoughts, as Thomas Ellwood's well-known anecdote regarding the first of them suggests? Despite the gentle Quaker's unquestionable candor I cannot think so. At his comment, "Thou hast said much here of Paradise lost, but what hast thou to say of Paradise found?", the poet sat in silence and seemed to meditate. We are under no compulsion to believe that he was struck dumb by the novelty of the idea! There is, to be sure, the later very explicit statement, quoted by Ellwood as made when Milton showed him in London the manuscript of *Paradise Regained:* "This is owing to you, for you put it in my head at Chalfont which before I had not thought of," but is it not quite possible that Ellwood is here innocently twisting some merely polite or even ironical remark of Milton's into conformity with his own self-flattering opinion that he was the "fons et origo" of an epic poem?

However this may be, there is a kind of inevitability in these last two works which makes it difficult to accept the idea that a chance suggestion in any very important way determined either of them. In form and general character, at least, we may regard them as predestinate. The evidence goes back to a passage in the *Reason of Church Government,* written in 1641, where Milton takes the reader into his confidence regarding his literary ambitions. He is in doubt, he tells us, whether to adopt the form of an extended epic like the *Aeneid,* or of the brief epic which he says is illustrated by the Book of Job, or of drama, "in which Sophocles and Euripides reign." Since life and energy endured he did all three, taking thereby a triple bond of fame. *Paradise Lost* is the new *Aeneid,* exhibiting all the recognized technique of the full and perfect epic; *Paradise Regained* is something more unusual, a heroic poem composed entirely of dialogue, save for a narrative introduction and conclusion and a few links. Its formal precedent is obviously the Book of Job, regarded not as a drama but, more strictly, as a modification of the epic type. *Samson Agonistes,* finally, is Hellenic tragedy restored.

With his plan of life endeavor thus beyond expectation fulfilled, it seems unlikely that Milton would ever have considered a further addition to his poetical works. The lengthy list of dramatic subjects in the Cambridge manuscript (which includes a "Samson Agonistes" under the title "Dagonalia" and a kind of "Paradise Regained" under that of "Christus Patiens") together with the corresponding one of epic themes which Professor Gilbert supposes him to have drawn up at the same time[1]—these lists were not in any sense a program. Milton was not given, like the dreamer Coleridge, to projecting vaguely a host of works which he could never write. The manuscript materials are notes taken in the process of canvassing the whole range of available materials before making a final choice. Had Milton enjoyed twenty more years of life and had there been twenty Ellwoods to urge him on, we should never have had at his hands the suggested epic on the deeds of Alfred, or the drama of "Sodom Burning" or the new Macbeth. To write any one of them would have been to mar the antique symmetry of his achievement.

It is not, however, from the standpoint of outward form alone that Milton had reason to regard his contemplated work as done. The three poems are complementary in theme and in ethical idea. Taken together they constitute a complete and unified embodiment of Milton's Christian humanism, the full working out of the didactic purpose which he had accepted as a responsibility implied in his abandonment of the office of preacher for the more congenial onc of poet. Let us, as an approach to the present object of giving sharper definition to the significance of *Samson Agonistes* as a work of the poet's last years, consider first the relation of the two companion epics. This relation is clearly not the mechanical one which their contrasting titles might at first suggest, and which, had *Paradise Regained* been named but never written, we should naturally have inferred from Milton's initial statement of his theme:

> Of man's first disobedience and the fruit
> Of that forbidden tree whose mortal taste
> Brought death into the world and all our woe,
> With loss of Eden till one greater man
> Restore us, and regain the blissful seat.

These lines appear to promise a scheme of salvation, according to the ideas of traditional Christianity, and for such a scheme we do

[1] *The Cambridge Manuscript and Milton's Plans for Epic, Studies in Philology,* 16 (1919). 172-176.

not have to await a second work. It is already amply given in the first. But the truth is that Milton pays little more than lip honor to the theological system which his work bears in its superscription. His deeper interest is to be sought elsewhere. At the close of *Paradise Lost* the Archangel Michael, after revealing to Adam at somewhat wearisome length the history of redemption, instructs him in quiet but thrilling words how he may regain what he has lost and build for himself "a paradise within thee happier far."[2] The program is that of all humanity, for Adam is the representative of man. Mere repentance and the sacrifice of Christ are but the form of salvation. The thing itself involves the coöperating will as manifested in the successful meeting of future trial. It is the work of no vicarious and of no single act, but of patient moral discipline in a world of evil, according to a pattern from above. The actual exhibition of the process is not included in *Paradise Lost*. The unique situation of Adam made it impossible for him to serve as an illustration of the struggles and triumphs which raise man from his degraded state. His story is of a fall. It remained for Milton to embody in another work its counterpart, to set forth in detail the successful encounter of humanity with the manifold forms of evil which present themselves in the complexities of a developed civilization. In this view *Paradise Regained* becomes a necessary sequel of *Paradise Lost*. Its theme, in its ethical as distinct from its theological aspect, is, indeed, already foreshadowed in the earlier poem, where the Christian virtues of faith, hope, love, humility, patience are indicated by the angel for Adam's attainment.[3] Their exemplification is in Christ, who becomes for Milton the second Adam, protagonist of a humanity confronted with choices which the first Adam in the freshness of the world could not have known. This is the key to the development of the temptation scenes in *Paradise Regained*.[4] The first and third

[2] Book XII, lines 574 ff.

[3] *Loc. cit.*

[4] This view of the theme of *Paradise Regained* and the corresponding interpretation of the conflict in *Samson Agonistes* are set forth in a different connection in my article *The Temptation Motive in Milton*, *Studies in Philology*, XV (1918). 176-194.

temptations are special, having to do with the peculiar character and mission of Christ. The second—the kingdoms of the world and the glory of them—is universal, implying all human moral issues. Milton accordingly elaborates it into a "survey of vice with all its baits and seeming pleasures," for which Christ's calm answers afford the antidote of reason. The critical objection that the temptations, given the nature of Christ, are not tempting, is beside the point. They are such temptations as experience shows to be the characteristic ones of men at large—luxury, wealth, power, fame, the pride of knowledge. By his indifference to these allurements and by his Socratic exposition of their emptiness Christ instructs all men how they may despise them. It is no mere piece of biblical commentary that Milton is composing, nor is it an attempt at portraiture of the historic Christ (though this motive from time to time appears). It is rather a pictorial map of the moral universe, a representation of the happier inner Paradise of life according to right reason, an image of redemption in the only sense in which Milton in his maturer years could even pretend to understand redemption.

The theme was one which commanded the full resources of a life of meditative study, not in the dubious realms of demonology and Christian myth, but in the sun-clear walks of moral and religious wisdom, in history and political philosophy, in the biography of good men and great, in the exalted teachings of poet and seer, most of all in the gospels taken in their plain historical and moral sense, and such a theme gave Milton the opportunity to be altogether his humanistic self. In *Paradise Lost* he had been committed to a more or less inflexible story and to a traditional system of ideas which his best endeavor could not wholly rationalize or adopt to his own more individual thought, with the result that though his imagination was stimulated to unexampled activity, the work is but an imperfect and distorted image of his philosophical point of view. In *Paradise Regained* he was largely free. It is no wonder that he resented the suggestion that the second work was inferior to the first. Though lacking in color and vivid outward incident, it had even its points of superiority. Its drama was of an inward intensity like that of the Book of Job. Its truth was unmixed with the accessory element of fiction. To Milton, in the severity of his age, this was argument of excellence. He knew, moreover, that the poem was more harmonious than *Paradise Lost,* simpler if less sensuous, and woven more close in "matter, form, and style."

It is now possible to consider the less obvious position of *Samson Agonistes* in Milton's poetic scheme. Formally and theologically the poem has no relation at all to its predecessors. For Milton does not, in his interpretation of the Old Testament material, adopt the point of view of the medieval religious drama, which built everything it treated into a single structure, regarding the events and characters of Hebrew history as episodes in an action which proceeded logically from the creation of the angels to the day of judgment. The story of Samson has for him an independent human value, neither implying nor prefiguring the life of Christ. For this very reason it adapts itself more naturally to his purposes, and affords the means of completing his representation of the state of man. The function of Christ we have already seen. He is, besides being the redeemer, the second Adam and the model man. But unlike Adam, Christ is without sin. Hence while he is the pattern and guide of human life, his victory is not, as ours must be, a recovery of something lost. The full account of man in his relation to the forces of good and evil demands another picture—the representation of frail humanity, burdened with the memory of former sin, but now repentant, restored to strength, and wrestling successfully with further trial. To what extent can *Samson Agonistes* be shown to fit this ideal prescription? The question raises some points of interpretation which appear to have been neglected by the numerous critics who, since Samuel Johnson, have discussed the merits of the work as drama.

When Milton, in 1641, first considered the life of the great but erring Hebrew champion as possible literary material and set down five subjects from it in the Cambridge manuscript, he was doubtless prompted chiefly by the coincidence of the story with characteristic themes of ancient drama. Samson was blind through his own guilt like Oedipus. In all other respects he was a Hebraic Herakles—the performer of incredible labors, enthralled by woman, sealing his baffled strength by a final destructive act. Such circumstances meant much in Milton's pre-disposition to a literary theme. More influential, however, in his final decision in favor of the subject was his perception of the parallel between Samson's sin and that of Adam. The point had already impressed itself upon him when he wrote of Adam's fall in the Ninth Book of *Paradise Lost*,

> So rose the Danite strong,
> Herculean Samson from the harlot lap
> Of Philistean Dalilah, and waked
> Shorn of his strength, they desolate and bare
> Of all their virtue.[5]

In the tragedy itself he is concerned with the fallen Samson's recovery of God's lost favor. The process involves his punishment and repentance, and the facing of new trials with a firmness won of experience and faith. It involves also a reward in the consciousness of God's having again accepted him as a worthy instrument of his purposes.

The trial itself is, I believe, the real center of the inward action, providing the play with such vital dramatic conflict as it exhibits. The Chorus and Manoa continually suggest distrust and compromise. They imply, in their attempted consolation, that Samson has been deceived in his belief that he once enjoyed God's special favor and was his chosen vessel. His marriages were not, as he had supposed, of a divine suggestion. God's dealings in sending the angel of his birth and apparently electing him as the champion of Israel, only to desert and leave him impotent, are unintelligible, if not unjust, for all has been turned to the glory of the Philistines. Against this Samson opposes, on the whole, the attitude of faith. He resists the suggestion that God was not really

[5] Lines 1059-1062.

with him in the past. He reiterates the cry that nothing of all his evils has befallen him but justly. He meets the challenge of Manoa's

> Yet Israel still serves with all his tribes,

with the rejoinder that it is they themselves who through their own weakness have neglected God's proposed deliverance. For himself he knows that he has forfeited all hope, but he remains unshaken in the belief that God will not

> Connive, or linger, thus provoked,
> But will arise, and his great name assert.

Throughout the dialogue there are marked similarities to the Book of Job. Manoa and the Chorus have a function analogous to that of the friends who sharpen Job's agony by their mistaken comfort. Samson's resistance of the attempt to shake the convictions of his innermost experience has its counterpart in Job's passionate denial of the imputation of unrighteousness. There is, of course, a formal contrast between the two, in that Samson, unlike Job, is afflicted by a sense of sin, but both are loyal to truth and both maintain their positions against the apparent facts. Both, finally, are rewarded for their consistency by a manifestation of God's approval. With Job it is the voice out of a whirlwind, with Samson the renewal of "rousing motions" of innermost impulse, which have stirred and guided him to great deeds before his fall.

Of these motives there is in the Scriptural account of Samson not the slightest hint. The hero of the Hebrew chronicle is a naïve and semi-humorous märchen figure, whose sluggish intellect is far removed from any capability of spiritual conflict. Milton preserves the traits of his impulsiveness of temper and his original simplicity of spirit, but endows him, after his disillusionment, with extraordinary force of mind and with penetrating insight. The infusion into this mighty champion of old, of the complex emotions of the maturest and most profound creation of Hebrew thought, is the last masterful stroke of Milton's genius. For it, he had, to my knowledge, no precedent in literary tradition.

But if Milton is indebted to Job for the most essential elements in his conception of Samson's character, it is to his own constructive imagination, working within the artistic forms provided by occidental drama, that he owes the development of his theme. In the Book of Job there is little outward action and no clear progression. In *Samson* there are both. The framework of the plot is that of a Greek play. It is simple even to meagerness. Samson is consoled by the Chorus, worried by Dalilah, insulted by Harapha, summoned before the Philistines by an officer. Old Manoa is busy meanwhile with misguided plans for his release, the moment of his success ironically coinciding with that of Samson's death. A messenger relates the catastrophe. The Chorus sings of Samson's fate and triumph.

Within this formal action the spiritual movement is richer than one at first observes. At the opening Samson is a spectacle of tragic misery and debasement. Out of his intense depression there rises higher and higher the note of active pain. At first his utterance concerns chiefly his physical and outward state:

> O loss of sight, of thee I most complain!
> Blind among enemies! O worse than chains,
> Dungeon or beggery, or decrepit age!

The first chorus, unheard by the protagonist, echoes and interprets his lament, with emphasis on the contrast between what once he was, is now. In the ensuing dialogue Samson's attention is diverted from his present wretchedness to its causes and significance. The memory of his fault is more bitter than the punishment wherewith it has been visited.

> Ye see, O friends,
> How many evils have enclosed me round;
> Yet that which once was the worst now least afflicts me,
> Blindness, for had I sight, confused with shame,
> How could I once look up, or heave the head,
> Who, like a foolish pilot, have shipwracked
> My vessel trusted to me from above.

The sight of Manoa wakes "another inward grief," and his

words are as a goad to Samson's bitter remembrance. His proposal to treat with the Philistine lords serves only to reveal his son's indifference to his outward fate. The scene culminates in a spiritual outburst, expressive no longer of the hero's physical misery and obvious disgrace,

> Ensnared, assaulted, overcome, led bound,
> Thy foes' derision, captive, poor, and blind,

but of the inner agony of soul which springs from full contemplation of his sins, "and sense of Heaven's desertion." The opening words of the passage clearly indicate the forward movement:

> Oh, that torment should not be confined
> To the body's wounds and sores,
> With maladies innumerable
> In heart, head, breast, and reins,
> But must secret passage find
> To the inmost mind,
> There exercise all his fierce accidents,
> And on her purest spirits prey,
> As on entrails, joints, and limbs,
> With answerable pains, but more intense,
> Though void of corporal sense![6]

The conclusion is one of unrelieved despair and marks the darkest moment of Samson's suffering, corresponding precisely to Adam's remorseful misery as he meditates upon his sin:

> Hopeless are all my evils, all remediless.
> This one prayer yet remains, might I be heard,
> No long petition–speedy death,
> The close of all my miseries and the balm.

Henceforth we have recovery. By confronting his own guilt without evasion, and by resisting the temptation to doubt God's ways are just, or to fear for the ultimate triumph of his cause, Samson has won the right to be put to proof a second time. His firmness is subjected first to the insidious approaches of Dalilah,

[6] Lines 606-616.

whose visit, however doubtfully motivated in itself, is essential to the idea of the drama. Her plea is specious, but Samson remains unmoved, the significance of his victory being pointed out in the choric comment,

> Yet beauty, though injurious, hath strange power,
> After offence returning, to regain
> Love once possessed, nor can be easily
> Repulsed, without much inward passion felt
> And secret sting of amorous remorse.

He next confronts physical force in the person of Harapha, who collapses, like all brute menace, before the champion's indifference to fear, and the Chorus, participating for the moment in Samson's strength, sings the great ode,

> O how comely it is, and how reviving,
> When God into the hands of their deliverer
> Puts invincible might,
> To quell the mighty of the earth, the oppressor,
> The brute and boistrous force of violent men.[7]

They are, of course, like Samson himself, still blind to what is to come, and they go on to sing of patience as the final crown of saints.

The coming of the officer creates a problem. Samson's refusal, at first, to do his bidding illustrates his uncompromising allegiance to the God of his fathers and his contempt of personal safety. The Chorus suggests the easier way of yielding, pointing out the fact that he has already served the Philistines (with the old implication that he cannot regard himself as a being set apart). Their reasoning is met with a clear distinction between compromise in things indifferent and the surrender of a point of conscience. Then, as if in answer to this final proof of Samson's single devotedness to God's service, comes again the inner prompting, "disposing to something extraordinary my thoughts." He obeys it unhesitatingly and goes forth under divine guidance as of old. He

[7] Lines 1267 ff.

has, in a sense, regained his own lost Paradise, and in his story Milton, by vindicating the power of a free but erring will to maintain itself in obedience and be restored to grace, has again asserted eternal Providence and justified the ways of God to man.

The fact that Samson is an Old Testament figure and achieves his triumph before the time of the Redeemer shows the true place of Christ in Milton's system. The blood of his sacrifice is plainly no necessary instrument of salvation; even his example may be dispensed with by those who enjoy a direct and special relation with the Divine. Yet the Hebrews did have Christ in prophecy, and for the men of later time he is the way. By his present example the path is open, not for chosen heroes alone, but for all, to

love with fear the only God, to walk
As in his presence, ever to observe
His providence, and on him sole depend,
Merciful over all his works, with good
Still overcoming evil, and by small
Accomplishing great things—by things deemed weak
Subverting worldly-strong, and worldly-wise
By simply meek;[8]

Such is Milton's final teaching and the ethical goal of his poetic art. The desire expressed in the introduction to Book IX of *Paradise Lost* to sing "the better fortitude of patience and heroic martyrdom," is fulfilled by the portrayal of a divine pattern in *Paradise Regained. Samson Agonistes* is its nearest possible fulfillment in the life of mortal man. To embody it more completely by representing the humbler trials and victories of daily life would have been incompatible with the tradition of Milton's literary allegiance—incompatible, too, with the memory of the heroic struggle in which he himself had been engaged.

Of this experience and this struggle I have as yet said nothing. How deeply it enters into the bone and sinew of *Samson Agonistes* no one can doubt. That Milton felt the parallel between his own situation and that of Samson and that he in some way iden-

[8] *P. L.*, XII. 562-569.

tified himself with his hero is obvious and has been emphasized by the biographers. I have myself elsewhere pointed out that in making Samson wrestle with despair Milton was championing his own faith assaulted by inward murmuring and challenged by the apparent failure of his cause.[9] It remains to enquire as to the extent and nature of this personal identification and to analyze more exactly the psychological reactions, conscious and unconscious, which are implied in the composition of the play.

Let us recognize at once that *Samson Agonistes* is a work of art and not a disguised autobiography. To a reader unacquainted with Milton's life the poem would seem as monumentally independent as *Prometheus Bound.* It deserves to be so judged and would, perhaps, stand higher as a masterpiece of art if it had been less often used as an illustration of Milton's personal life and temper. It should not, however, suffer from interpretation in the light of the poet's characteristic moods and thoughts, if we clearly recognize the conditions of their operation in his creative work. His most intimate emotions are invariably sublimated by the imagination and so far depersonalized. The process enables him to project himself with sympathy into characters and situations which have only a partial analogy with his own. So it is with his representations of Comus, or of Satan and Adam in *Paradise Lost.* In other cases, as in those of Dalilah, Eve, or Mammon he is capable, within a limited range, of being as objective as any artist of essentially romantic temper.

In the representation of Samson, Milton has undoubtedly put more of himself than in other of his imaginative creations. The sense of power and dignity, the "plain heroic magnitude of mind," the will toward championship are Milton. So too is the noble self-pity, expressed in the consciousness of deprivation in the loss of sight ("The sun to me is dark, and silent as the moon"), and the feeling of physical helplessness ("In power of others, never in my own"). But all this is heightened and idealized for purposes of art. The tragic gloom and flat despair of Samson, the

[9] *Studies in Philology,* XV. 176-194.

wretchedness of pain, the distaste of life, are the embodiments of an aesthetic mood which owes quite as much to literature as to personal experience. As a matter of fact the impression left by such direct biographical records as we have of Milton in old age is quite the reverse of this, suggesting the persistence in him to the end of a temper unspoiled by tribulation. The "cheerful godliness" of Wordsworth's sonnet appears to be an entirely appropriate description of the poet's habitual outward mood in the last years of his life.

With regard to his blindness it is worth noting that the most poignant allusions to it were written longest after the event itself. At the actual moment of the catastrophe Milton was silent. His poetical occupation in the immediately succeeding years was the translation of Psalms, a literary and religious discipline. In 1654 he gives expression in prose, not to his sense of irrecoverable loss, but to the consciousness of spiritual compensation in "an anterior illumination more precious and more pure."[10] In 1655, on the third anniversary of his loss of sight, he allows himself to consider how his "light is spent ere half his days," and to give voice to the pathos of his condition, only, however, as a preparation for the expression of acquiescence and of the consolations which come from the sense of having sacrificed himself in a noble cause. The utterances in *Paradise Lost* are touched with a deeper pathos, but it is first in *Samson,* where they are no longer directly personal, that they become a tragic cry:

> Dark, dark, dark, amid the blaze of noon,
> Irrecoverably dark, total eclipse,
> Without all hope of day.

A similar account might be given of the poet's antifeminism. It is entirely absent from the sonnets which belong to the days of his estrangement from Mary Powell. Indeed the two poems written at that time, *To a Virtuous Young Lady* and *To the Lady Margaret Ley,* are sincere though sober tributes to female virtue. The general indictment of the sex begins with Adam's words to Eve in

[10] *Defensio Secunda, Prose Works* (Bohn), I. 239.

Book X of *Paradise Lost* and reaches a strain of unrelieved bitterness in *Samson Agonistes.*

Such are the facts, as we read them in the chronological consideration of Milton's works. One cannot fail to be struck by the analogy which exists between the processes of the poet's expression of certain phases of his inmost experience in this last epoch of his literary life and the youthful development which we have studied in the preceding essay. The position of *Samson Agonistes* in its relation to the complex of emotions and ideas which centered in the poet's blindness is singularly like that of *Comus* with reference to the conflict of sensuous and ideal impulses in his adolescence. Each represents the culmination of a train of introspective thoughts which may easily be conceived to have been disturbing to Milton's mental equilibrium. In each work he appears to achieve for the first time a full expression of these emotions, and in achieving it to obtain a spiritual mastery of them. The result is one which is always, perhaps, in some degree present in the intenser activity of the creative imagination, and it has received general recognition from the critics and philosophers of literature. The most luminous statement is the following by Croce in his *Aesthetic.*[11] "By elaborating his impressions man frees himself from them. By objectifying them, he removes them from him and makes himself their superior. The liberating and purifying function of art is another aspect and another formula of its character as activity. Activity is the deliverer, just because it drives away passivity. This also explains why it is usual to attribute to artists both the maximum of sensibility and the maximum of insensibility or Olympian serenity. The two characters are compatible, for they do not refer to the same object. The sensibility or passion relates to the rich material which the artist absorbs into his psychic organism, the insensibility or serenity to the form with which he subdues and dominates the tumult of sensations and passions."

It is scarcely possible to determine the degree to which Milton,

[11] Chapter 2. Douglas Ainsley's translation, 1922.

in recreating and transforming emotions which in their rawer form made inroads upon his carefully cherished serenity, experienced a similar deliverance. Some light may be gained, however, by a consideration of certain neglected aspects of the play itself, the indications, namely, which the poet has given of what he himself thought of its function as a work of art. These indications refer mainly, to be sure, to what he looked for in its effect upon the reader or spectator, but they are not without application to the artist as well and it seems to me quite clear that Milton must have been guided in his interpretation of the power of tragedy to effect spiritual benefits upon others by what he had himself experienced in creating it.

The question centers in his understanding of the formula for tragedy and its purgative effect as given in the famous Aristotelian definition. The importance of this formula in Milton's thought and the degree to which he must have been conscious of it in constructing his drama are suggested by the fact that he quotes it in Latin on his title page and devotes the first part of his prose preface to its elaboration. His opening statement is as follows: "Tragedy as it was anciently composed hath been ever held the gravest, moralest, and most profitable of all other poems; therefore said by Aristotle to be of power by raising pity and fear, or terror, to purge the mind of those and such like passions, that is to temper and reduce them to just measure with a kind of delight, stirred up by seeing those passions well imitated."

In considering the application of this principle to *Samson Agonistes* we must observe, first of all, that, by representing a clearly marked triumph of the human will over its own weakness, and by the substitution of Providence for blind fate as the power which overrules the action, the play provides material for a different understanding of catharsis from that contemplated by Aristotle, an understanding which falls in with the first part of Milton's description—that tragedy is the gravest, moralest, and most profitable of poetic forms—rather than with the last—that it transforms painful emotions into pleasurable. On a superficial view we might, indeed, be tempted to regard the purgation, as Milton actually worked it out, as a purely ethical and religious process, the result of a consciously didactic purpose by which our faith is strengthened and our sympathy with Samson's pain swallowed up in our exultation in his triumph. It is the function of Manoa's last speech and of the final chorus to emphasize this motive:

> Come, come, no time for lamentation now,
> Nor much more cause; Samson hath quit himself
> Like Samson, and heroicly hath finished
> A life Heroic. . . .
> With God not parted from him as was feared,
> But favouring and assisting to the end.
>
> . . . .
>
> All is best, though we oft doubt,
> What the unsearchable dispose
> Of highest wisdom brings about
> And ever best found in the close.

To some critics[12] these quotations have seemed an adequate formula for the poem as a whole, and a mark of the failure of *Samson Agonistes* to embody the genuinely tragic motive of the unsuccessful struggle of man with fate. Such a judgment is obvious and in part correct. It fails, however, to take account of the actuality of the tragic impression which the drama must leave upon every reader who comes to it unhampered by definitions and comparisons. The pain of the earlier scenes is something which cannot be so easily displaced. Sealed as it is with the hero's death, it outlives all consolation, as the tragic suffering of Hamlet outlives the accomplishment of his purpose, the choric benediction of Horatio, and the restoration of a wholesome commonwealth by Fortinbras. The pronouncement "All is best" is of scarcely more avail than the identical formulae which bring Greek plays to their conclusion and from which this one is derived. The consolation which is offered of "what can quiet us in a death so noble" is not enough. Samson should have gone on from

[12] See Paull F. Baum, *Samson Agonistes Again*, *Publications of the Modern Language Association*, XXXVI (1921). 365 ff.

one glad triumph to another and emerged unscathed. Outward circumstances, the treacheries of others, and his own conspiring fault have brought him low, and have constrained him to wear, however gloriously, the crown of martyrdom. Here surely is tragedy enough. Though Providence is proclaimed, its ways are dark and its face, at times, is hardly to be distinguished from the countenance of Fate herself. The secret is that there remains an irreducible element in the midst of Milton's faith—a sense as keen as Shakespeare's of the reality of suffering which neither the assurance of God's special favors to himself nor his resolute insistence on the final triumph of his righteousness can blot out. The antique strain in Milton's experience and thought stands side by side with the Christian, and the two alternate or combine in their domination of his artistic moods. It is in vain that he repudiates stoicism as a futile refuge and a false philosophy; he is betrayed by the vehemence of his declarations against it, and he instinctively adopts its weapons.

These considerations prepare us to examine the operation in *Samson Agonistes* of catharsis in its strict Aristotelian sense. Milton's effort to demonstrate in his drama the truth of Aristotle's pronouncement is part and parcel of a thoroughgoing conscious classicism, which extends far beyond such matters as the ordering of the incidents and the employment of ancient devices like the messenger. It is shown in a more philosophic and intrinsic way in the subtle turns which the poet gives to the intepretation of his theme in order to bring it more nearly into conformity with the spirit of ancient tragedy. Professor Baum[13] counts it a major defect of *Samson Agonistes* that the hero's tragic fault is undignified and sub-heroic. But observe the means which Milton takes to dignify it. He associates it with the most dignified of all tragic faults—rebellious pride. Intoxicated by success Samson forgets to refer his victories to their source, and so becomes, in Milton's interpretation, an instance of classical hybris. Like Shakespeare's Mark Anthony he "struts to his destruction."

[13] *Loc. cit.*

Fearless of danger, like a petty God,
I walked about, admired of all, and dreaded
On hostile ground, none daring my assault.
Then swollen with pride, into the snare I fell
Of fair fallacious looks, venerial trains.[14]

This is somewhat forced, one must confess, and Milton appears to be aware of it. Witness the shading he is compelled to give to the idea in the following:

But I
God's counsel have not kept, his holy secret
Presumptiously have published, impiously,
Weakly at least and shamefully—a sin
That Gentiles in their parables condemn
To their Abyss and horrid pains confined.[15]

The cloak of Prometheus and Tantalus evidently refuses to fit the less majestic Hebrew Titan. The conception of hybris and Ate applies more perfectly to the Philistines and is accordingly invoked in the triumphant semi-chorus beginning in line 1669:

While their hearts were jocund and sublime,
Drunk with idolatry, drunk with wine
And fat regorged of bulls and goats,
Chaunting their idol, and preferring
Before our Living Dread, who dwells
In Silo, his bright sanctuary,
Among them he a spirit of phrenzy sent,
Who hurt their minds,
And urged them on with mad desire
To call in haste for their destroyer.
They, only set on sport and play,
Unweetingly importuned
Their own destruction to come speedy upon them.
So fond are mortal men,
Fallen into wrath divine,
As their own ruin on themselves to invite,

[14] Lines 529-533.
[15] Lines 496-501.

Insensate left, or to sense reprobate,
And with blindness internal struck.

Both passages, however, are illustrative of the degree to which Milton had grasped the central motive of Greek tragedy and the pains he was at to bring his own material under the ethical, religious, and artistic formulae afforded by it.

A more vital result of his assimilation of the point of view of his ancient models is to be found in the great chorus which follows Samson's deeper expression of despair, in lines 608-650. If anything in Milton or indeed in all modern literature deserves to be called a reproduction of antiquity it is this passage. It is as perfectly representative as Milton could have wished of "Aeschylus, Sophocles, Euripides, the three tragic poets unequalled yet by any, and the best rule to all who endeavor to write Tragedy," and it comes little short of their noblest choral odes in the grandeur and intensity of its tragic feeling. In the majestic rhythms of the opening the Chorus sings of the vanity of consolation in the ears of the afflicted and expostulates with Providence in its uneven course with men. Thoroughly Greek and as thoroughly Miltonic is the centering of attention on the woes, not of the common rout of men who grow up and perish like the summer fly, but on those of heroic mould, "with gifts and graces eminently adorned." The ensuing lines embody the idea of the excess of evil which rains down on the head of the tragic hero according to Aristotle's description in the *Poetics:*

Nor only dost degrade them, or remit
To life obscured, which were a fair dismission,
But throw'st them lower than thou didst exalt them high—
Unseemly falls in human eye,
Too grievous for the trespass or omission;
Oft leav'st them to the hostile sword
Of heathen and profane, their carcasses
To dogs and fowls a prey, or else captived,
Or to the unjust tribunals, under change of times,
And condemnation of the ungrateful multitude.
If these they escape, perhaps in poverty

> With sickness and disease thou bow'st them down,
> Painful diseases and deformed,
> In crude old age;
> Though not disordinate, yet causeless suffering
> The punishment of dissolute days. In fine,
> Just or unjust alike seem miserable,
> For oft alike both come to evil end.

The personal note here is too distinct to be mistaken. "Unjust tribunals under change of times," "their carcasses to dogs and fowls a prey" are certainly echoes of the Restoration, with its brutal trials of men like Henry Vane, and the indignities to which the bodies of Cromwell and Ireton were subjected. The parallel and not less wretched fate of poverty and disease is Milton's own. He goes so far as almost to specify the rheumatic ills from which we know him to have suffered—"painful diseases and deformed"—with the bitter reflection that these afflictions, justly the fruit of dissipation, may come also to those who, like himself, have lived in temperance. Nowhere else in his works, not even in the laments of Adam, does Milton permit himself to indulge in so unrelieved an expression of pagan sentiment. He does so under the shield of dramatic objectivity, yet none of his words spring from deeper sources in his consciousness. Here momentarily he faces the world with no other arms than those of pure humanity, giving utterance to a view of life directly opposed to that to which he had subdued his thinking as a whole.

It is in such a mood as this and in such an utterance that Milton must, if ever, have felt, in his own emotional experience, the reality of the Aristotelian catharsis, and the need of it. The question of the means whereby affliction may be soothed is one which had always interested him, and his works contain numerous suggestive utterances on the subject. It is prominent in the discussion of the case of Samson. Thus, contemplating, at this point, his hero's misery, he makes the Chorus tell how useless for the sufferer in his pangs are those wise consolations of philosophy, "writ with studied argument, lenient of grief and anxious thought." It is only, they affirm, by "secret refreshings from above" that the afflicted wretch can be restored. But such refreshings are obviously not always to be commanded. To prepare for their benign influence the mind must first be emptied of its pent-up bitterness, and for such a process tragedy, in the Aristotelian conception, supplies the means. So, one would suppose, might Milton have thought and felt. And if such was his experience it is not surprising that he should have dwelt with such insistence on the rationale of the process in his prose preface.

His initial statement I have already quoted. Pity, fear, and like passions, it implies, are, in their raw state, dangerous and painful. Objectively represented, they are tempered and reduced to just measure by a kind of delight. "Nor is Nature," adds Milton, "wanting in her own effects to make good his assertion; for so, in Physic, things of melancholic hue and quality are used against melancholy, sour against sour, salt to remove salt humours." This passage has often been cited with approval by classical scholars as expressing the soundest modern interpretation of the dark oracle of Aristotle's pronouncement, and there has been discussion of Milton's priority in employing the medical analogy. No one, I think, has called attention to his application of this conception to the analysis of Samson's spiritual ills in an outstanding passage in the play itself. The hero has just expressed his indifference to the efforts proposed in his behalf and his expectation of an early death. Manoa replies:

> Believe not these suggestions, which proceed
> From anguish of the mind, and humours black
> That mingle with thy fancy.[16]

There follows the great lyric outburst of Samson's spiritual woe, which must now be given at greater length.

> O that torment should not be confined
> To the body's wounds and sores,
> With maladies innumerable
> In heart, head, breast, and reins;

[16] Lines 599-601.

But must secret passage find
To the inmost mind,
There exercise all his fierce accidents,
And on her purest spirits prey,
As on entrails, joints, and limbs,
With answerable pains, but more intense,
Though void of corporal sense!
My griefs not only pain me
As a lingering disease,
But, finding no redress, ferment and rage;
Nor less than wounds immedicable,
Rankle, and fester, and gangrene,
To black mortification.
Thoughts, my tormentors, armed with deadly stings,
Mangle my apprehensive tenderest parts,
Exasperate, exulcerate, and raise
Dire inflammation, which no cooling herb
Or medicinal liquor can assuage,
Nor breath of vernal air from snowy Alp.
Sleep hath forsook and given me o'er
To death's benumbing opium as my only cure;
Thence faintings, swoonings of despair,
And sense of Heaven's desertion.

The idea which Milton here develops with somewhat shocking explicitness is obviously the same as that which underlies his conception of catharsis—the idea, namely, that the passions operate in precisely the manner of bodily poisons, which, when they find no outlet, rage destructively within. Samson is given over to pity and fear, and there is no apparent prospect of relief, no cooling herb or medicinal liquor to purify the "black mortification" of his thoughts. It is quite clear, then, that Milton intends to suggest a kind of Aristotelian diagnosis of Samson's tragic state, parallel to the more obvious religious interpretation which I have previously expounded. But if he partly identified himself with his hero, then such a diagnosis would serve also to that extent to describe his own. As, however, he draws a sharp distinction on the religious side between Samson's spiritual darkness and his own illumination by an inner light, so here he must have been conscious of a difference in the manner of their deliverance from the morbid introspection to which they are equally subject. The intensity of Samson's pain lasts only so long as he remains inactive. His lyric elaboration of his inward woe is immediately followed by the unexpected visits of his foes. His attention is thus distracted from his suffering to a series of situations which confront him and he finally loses himself in glorious though disastrous action.

For Milton, in the impotence of his situation after the Restoration, there can be no such deliverance. He is enrolled perforce among those "whom patience finally must crown." But he has in his possession a recourse without which the way of patience is at times too hard. The purgation which the untutored champion of Israel must find in deeds is available to the man of culture through the activity of the mind and spirit. It offers itself to Milton in a dual form, corresponding to his twofold inheritance from the Reformation and the Renaissance. As the play draws to an end the two motives are subtly balanced and as nearly reconciled as, perhaps, it is within the power of human skill to reconcile them. The champion's final deed and the triumph of God's uncontrollable intent promote in us a sense of exultation and confirm our faith, but the greatness of his suffering and the pathos of his death produce a different effect, making possible the serene dismission of the close:

> His servants he, with new acquist
> Of true experience from this great event,
> With peace and consolation hath dismissed
> And calm of mind, all passion spent.

It is characteristic of the critical self-consciousness which Milton carries with him even in his moments of highest creative inspiration and suggestive also of the vital uses to which he turned aesthetic as well as religious doctrine that the last word of all should be an almost explicit reference to the tragic formula which he had derived from the authority of "the master of those who know."

UNA ELLIS-FERMOR

SAMSON AGONISTES AND RELIGIOUS DRAMA

Scholar of Renaissance interests, Una Ellis-Fermor (1894-1958) has written the following two selections on Milton's drama. Both are here reprinted from The Frontiers of Drama *(London, Methuen & Co., Ltd., 1948); the following selection is from pages 17-33. Footnotes irrelevant to this excerpt have been omitted, and the remainder renumbered.*

Milton, in his prefatory note to *Samson Agonistes,* made it clear that he regarded his play as a tragedy; but some modern readers do not find it precisely the kind of play that they have been accustomed to call tragedy, either ancient or modern. It ends with the death of Samson, and has a clear technical claim to inclusion in the category. But few of us, if thinking in terms of experience and not of names, are content to call Samson's triumphant death a tragic catastrophe. How could we, indeed, when 'nothing is here for tears'? We are accustomed to associate with tragedy a balance between conflicting moods, between the sense of pain, grief, or terror on the one hand and, on the other, something that triumphs and illuminates. But in Milton's play we find instead a progression towards triumph and illumination which gradually subdues the sense of pain, grief, and loss and at the end transcends and utterly destroys it. Here is clearly something other than the balance of tragedy. Milton oversets the balance in the direction of positive interpretation; by justifying the ways of God to man he leaves no room for tragic ecstasy and substitutes an ecstasy of another kind. He has written, that is, a play that belongs to the rare category of religious drama, a kind which, by the nature of some of its basic assumptions, cannot be tragic.

This distinction between tragedy and religious drama is not a quibble; it goes to the root of the nature of each kind. If it be nearly impossible, as we have already suggested, to subdue the matter of religious experience to the form of drama, it is a frank contradiction in terms to equate religious with tragic experience. The tragic mood is balanced between the religious and the non-religious interpretations of catastrophe and pain, and the form, content, and mood of the play which we call a tragedy depend upon a kind of equilibrium maintained by these opposite readings of life, to neither of which the dramatist can wholly commit himself.

What, then, are the characteristics of content and form which distinguish religious drama and entitle it to a category of its own? Of what kinds of plays, besides *Samson Agonistes,* do we think when we speak of religious drama, and how has the reconciliation between this apparently irreconcilable content and form been brought about? The first part of this question can perhaps be answered by separating out those plays which have just claim to inclusion from those that, for one reason or another, have none; the second part by considering the play of *Samson Agonistes* itself.

By religious drama I would be understood to mean that kind of drama which takes religious experience for its main theme. It is not, as we have said, a common type; indeed, it is its comparative rarity at all times, and the extreme rareness of great drama of this kind, which first leads us to suspect an inherent incompatibility between drama and the matter of religious experience.[1] The

[1] There is an appearance of paradox here when we remember that, in the few cases in which we can trace the origins of any stream of drama, we find it to have risen in religious ritual. But the paradox vanishes when we

greater part of the material which seems at first glance to claim consideration has no valid claim, and we may well begin by cutting away what is irrelevant.

We may discard first all plays in which religious experience, though touched on or approached, is not the main subject of the action. A play in which a man of apparently saintly life and experience played an incidental part, without his sainthood affecting the lives or actions of the other characters, would not be religious drama, though it might throw some interesting light on the dramatist's convictions or sympathy with such persons. There is every reason to suppose, for instance, that the Abbot with whom Edward II takes refuge is such a man, but we do not for that reason call Marlowe's *Edward II* religious drama. Nor do we in the infrequent cases in which such figures appear in Shakespeare's plays. In none of these has the playwright made that figure the centre, nor its experience the main subject of the play. Whether or not he could have done it is beside the point; to have done it he would have had to write a different play, with a different centre and a different theme. At the opposite extreme of the same category is the play of *King Lear,* which contains a series of profound, interrelated studies of conversion. But the religious experience of Lear or of Gloucester is not the main or ostensible subject of the play; it remains among the underlying implications.

This suggestion is quickly despatched, but others require more examination.

There are many plays in which religious practices and habits are assumed as part of the background, and that to such an extent as to affect the action itself. Yet even here we shall, I think, find at least three kinds which we should not, upon reflection, include.

There are, first, those in which characters approach the experience, touch upon it or make play with the idea. Shakespeare's Richard II does this in moments of despondency or self-display; but we are hardly tempted to confuse his sentimental religiosity

---

notice that the greater part of the drama so derived either rapidly becomes secular, or, if secularisation is delayed, occupies itself with the accompaniments, not the essence of the experience.

with any form of conversion or complete religious experience. In fact, genuine experience is the one thing we are sure he lacks. This case is unlike our first; we are not here concerned with the presence of genuine religion in a subordinate character, but with something like it but *not* it in the chief character. The Peer Gynt of the fourth act, again, plays in a somewhat different way, with the edges of the experience. But we do not confuse his utilitarian and belated attempts at propitiation with religious experience; if the play had stopped there we should not class any part of it as religious drama.

There are, in the second place, certain plays about religious people in which discrimination begins to be more difficult. Here we are asked to accept religious inspiration as the source of the characters' actions and the controlling factor in their behaviour; the subject of the play is the course of action resulting from this inspiration or experience. Are we or are we not to include Mr. Shaw's *Saint Joan* in the group we are trying to compose? I think the answer, for all plays of this kind, will depend upon whether the religious experience is itself the main subject of the play or only the accepted starting point of the action; whether the play is concerned with the process or with the exterior effects. In *Saint Joan* we are clearly concerned with the effects, though, inevitably, as we watch the character in action, we perceive that the process is continuing its work. But we see also that the experience itself is not the theme; the theme is the outward career of the character that it has formed. Even clearer is the case of certain late nineteenth- and early twentieth-century plays in which religion was rediscovered as a dramatic theme. Henry Arthur Jones, in *Saints and Sinners* and *Michael and his Lost Angel,* shows us some of the effects of the experience; but, least of all in the second, a grandiose attempt to dramatize the conflict between the 'world' and the 'spirit', do we meet any positive revelation of the experience itself. T. C. Murray, in *Maurice Harte,* has come nearer to it, with his profound understanding of the mental conflict of the young peasant who finds himself committed to the priesthood without vocation. But even he has chosen to reveal the conflict in terms of its effects, and not to make it the actual theme, though, unlike Henry Arthur Jones, he never leaves us in doubt that the experience is real.

There is, in the third place, the deliberate propaganda play, designed to teach the dogma or the ethics of a particular religious system. If we were to include this, we should find our category swelled to enormous bulk, for the whole body of Bible History Plays, Miracle Plays, and Moralities written in Western Europe between the tenth and the sixteenth centuries would immediately enter it. But most of this is 'religious' only in the most formal sense of the term; it is occupied either with stories taken from the history of the Jews, in which the religious convictions of the characters are an accompaniment rather than the main theme, or with episodes in the life of Christ or of the saints, of which practically the same holds good, or with allegories on the conduct of life that represent the ethical counterparts of the dogmas embodied in both the other kinds. Only very rarely, in an individual play such as the Brome *Abraham and Isaac,* in a single, incidental speech or an isolated conversion scene, do we come upon a direct presentation of religious experience in action.

Finally, before we leave this question of what is *not* religious drama, we must mention certain plays, some of them among the greatest, in which a profound psychological experience is revealed (akin to conversion), without it being certain that the author conceived it as religious.

Ibsen's *The Master Builder, Rosmersholm,* and others of his latest group are all plays of conversion, and the conversion is, unlike those in *Lear,* a central part of the mental action of which the play consists. But though some kind of psychological conversion is, in each case, the dominant theme of the play, there is no suggestion that this, like the conversions in *Lear,* has any metaphysical implication. The characters arrive at a greater or less degree of understanding of their own experience; they rid themselves of their illusions, they see what has happened to them and its significance. But they do not (unless in the latest of his plays, which I do not profess as yet to understand) arrive at more than a resolution of their perplexities, a fuller understanding of their relation to the society about them and the underlying moral laws. Their experience does not, apparently, bring them into relation with a spiritual universe from which these moral laws derive. And some perception of the reality of this spiritual universe I should hold to be indispensable in religious experience of any strict mystical kind. If Solness in *The Master Builder* had had the same order of experience as Lear and Gloucester, the play would have been religious drama of a clear kind; if the spiritual experiences of the characters in the play of *Lear* had been made the central theme of the play, as is the psychological development of John Gabriel Borkman, then Lear would, on precisely the same terms, have entered our category.

But there are, I think, a few plays which, as I have suggested, effect a union of the content of religious experience and the form of drama; plays that do not, upon inspection, prove to have evaded the issue by drawing upon some other, related, field.[2] I do not propose to attempt a comprehensive list, but I would include, as instances to lead us to the positive issue with which we are concerned, the *Oresteia* of Aeschylus, the Brome *Abraham and Isaac*, the Dutch *Elckerlijc* and its English translation *Everyman*, Marlowe's *Faustus*, Milton's *Samson Agonistes*, Ibsen's *Brand*, and (two out of several representative moderns) W. B. Yeats' *Hour Glass* and T. S. Eliot's *Family Reunion*. It is obvious that these are not of equal magnitude and power, though I think all are at least fine pieces of dramatic art. But they all have in common one thing, the thing for which we are looking, the dramatic presentation of religious experience in one or other of its essential phases.[3]

[2] Since we are concerned here with the art of drama and not with the literature of religion, I have not considered that interesting body of plays in the early and the contemporary religious drama of India, in which fidelity to content is maintained partly at the expense of dramatic form or of what the European tradition considers dramatic form.

[3] Generally, though not always, the phase chosen is conversion, a crisis which most readily satisfies the demands of the dramatic mood. But the

They do not all offer in equal degree the characteristic concentration and immediacy of drama, but, though the structural modifications of some of them are original and even startling, none of them sacrifices the essentials of dramatic mood and form. At the same time, whatever the aspect chosen, the world of experience to which they testify is the world we find in the writings of St. Augustine, Dante, Vaughan, Penn, Bunyan and Blake, in the book of Job and in the Apocalypse. Here, then, if anywhere, we have the paradox of a reconciliation between the experience whose consummation is the resolution of conflict and a form whose power derives from tension and balance.

Can we now draw a few conclusions as to the way in which the reconciliation of matter and form has been made? We notice that all these plays have in common first the choice of religious experience as their main theme, and second the direction the action takes. A dramatic presentation of religious experience is, we find, generally a presentation of the progress into that experience. It may, as in the case of Marlowe's *Faustus,* move in a negative direction towards damnation (the religious experience being, if one may venture the paradox, negative), or it may, as in all the other cases, move, at whatever pace the theme demands, towards beati-

---

plays of conversion are themselves of different kinds. In some the phases of conversion (or, it may be, of re-conversion) are evenly distributed throughout the play (as in *Everyman* and *Samson Agonistes*); in some, the preliminaries are treated at great length and lead us gradually to the crisis (this is especially so in the *Oresteia,* where the 'conversion' is less that of an individual than of a society); in one (the preposterous case of Brand) it is postponed until the last half-line of a 5,000-line play—though its promise has been kept steadily in mind throughout. In one kindred play, Shelley's *Prometheus,* the process is consummated well before the end and the subsequent phase of beatitude occupies the whole of the fourth act, thus attempting to subdue to dramatic form content associated rather with the music of Beethoven or the poetry of Dante. One or two plays choose a phase which, even if not the dramatically obvious one of conversion, is still near the centre of religious experience. Thus the testing of Abraham's faith *(Abraham and Isaac)* is nearer to the crisis of martyrdom than to that of conversion. The play is exquisite in its kind, that of the single-episode or one-act play, but it is hard to imagine this subject supporting the greater magnitude of a play on the grand scale.

tude. In either case, in so far as it is dramatic, the progress will be through conflict to the victory of one of the contending forces, the religious or the anti-religious, and it must necessarily dwell more upon the emergence than upon the experience, whether of beatitude or damnation, or there will be no conflict strong enough to give dramatic intensity.[4] Since, in practice, religious drama (with the exception of Marlowe's *Faustus*) is almost invariably positive, the only type of conflict that this subject can offer for the use of drama is that of a heroic contest rising to exultation and passing on, in a few rare cases, into beatitude. This is the only point at which this content and this form can be reconciled, and it is at this point that, in all genuine religious drama, the reconciliation has been made. Are we now on the way to understand why the drama of religious experience is rare at all times and why the great plays of this kind can be counted almost upon the fingers of one hand?

We may perhaps draw one more distinction. In some of the plays we have chosen, the contest, though belonging essentially to the domain of the mind, is mirrored in event; a part at least of the character's inner experience is revealed to us in action and not only or mainly by his words. This is true of the *Oresteia* (though Aeschylus could elsewhere use another method), of *Abraham and Isaac,* of *Faustus,* and of *Brand;* all these plays belong to that main division of drama to which event is essential. (*Everyman,* which is an allegorical play, is not strictly of this kind, and the relevant part of *Peer Gynt* [Act V] is perhaps as purely symbolic

[4] Only one kind, the victory of the anti-religious forces, could produce tragedy even in the earlier phase of the experience. In fact, Marlowe's *Faustus,* the only example of strict religious drama of this kind that is known to me, almost passes out of the category of tragedy in the negative direction. Marlowe's complete rejection of reconciliation with a beneficent world-order oversets the tragic balance. . . . This, of course, does not exclude it from the category of religious drama. But since progression into beatitude cannot, in the nature of things, give us tragedy (even though it may present the technical appearance of a catastrophe in death), we are left in the position of finding no actual example of strict religious drama which is also a balanced tragedy.

as *Everyman.*) A notable exception is *Samson Agonistes,* in which the contest takes place entirely in the 'theatre of the soul'. It is a precursor of much modern psychological drama (some of which is also religious in the strict sense) where the inward conflict is revealed directly in the speeches, and the function of event is to occasion or stimulate that progress of the mind which constitutes the real action of the play. It is not necessary to remind either modern readers or good Aristotelians that 'action' may be a psychological contest with no effect upon the outer world except, possibly, at the end of the play, when the two worlds of thought and event fall together in what is technically the catastrophe; Samson's thought is translated into the act which destroys the Philistines, just as the self-discovery of Rosmer and Rebecca finally transfers itself to the plane of event and cuts off their lives.[5]

But it may be well to remind ourselves that Dr. Johnson thought differently of *Samson Agonistes* and condemned it as having no 'middle' in Aristotle's sense of the term and so, properly speaking, no action. He goes through the play[6] looking for a 'well-connected plan' and finding, to a miracle, the exact opposite of what the modern reader finds: 'At the conclusion of the first act' (by which he means the end of the 'solemn vindication of divine justice' in the first choric ode) 'there is no design laid, no discovery made, nor any disposition formed towards the subsequent event.' It 'wants', that is to say, 'a middle, since nothing passes be-

[5] Although the number of plays in which the action consists in this kind of mental or spiritual contest has grown far greater in the last sixty or seventy years than in the centuries preceding the work of Ibsen, it should be borne in mind that *Samson Agonistes* is, in this respect, as much a descendant of the *Prometheus Vinctus* as a forerunner of *Rosmersholm.* (See for a more detailed comment Chapter II, Section IV, of that fine contribution to the æsthetics of drama, H. D. F. Kitto's recent *Greek Tragedy.*) Certain medieval moralities, again, carry the process to the logical (and undramatic) extreme, which recurs, with the necessary modifications, in a few modern experiments, such as Evreinoff's *Theatre of the Soul.*

[6] Rambler, 139-140. The observations made in these two essays are supported, but not extended, in the brief references in the *Life of Milton.*

tween the first act and the last that either hastens or delays the death of Samson'. And 'this is the tragedy which ignorance has admired and bigotry applauded'.

'Ignorance' and 'bigotry', in the persons of Jebb, Ker, Bailey and others, to the present day, have continued in various ways—some slightly more subtle than Dr. Johnson's, and revealing a somewhat sounder understanding of the æsthetics of drama—to admire and to applaud. But his view serves well to remind us that the ground on which drama and religion can meet is narrow, so narrow that a genuine union of the two can be misjudged, even in *Samson Agonistes* and even by Dr. Johnson. The question in dispute between him and the modern critics is whether or not religious (or psychological) experience can constitute the 'action' of a play. We believe that it can, and so, we may remind ourselves, did Aristotle. But, even as Aristotle's generalizations were unable to take *Hamlet* into consideration, so, it is but just to remember, were Dr. Johnson's unable to take in *Rosmersholm*.

May we, then, once again consider *Samson Agonistes,* and now as a play whose 'action' consists not only in a mental progress (akin on one side to the *Prometheus* of Aeschylus and on the other to *John Gabriel Borkman*), but in a progress of a particular kind, drawn from material that is normally, by the nature of its emotion, compatible with drama only within narrow limits yet here shaped into dramatic form. We shall, that is to say, trace moods, phases, and states of mind instead of actions (of which, as Dr. Johnson pointed out, there are none until the end). If the play is what we have supposed it to be, these moods will be causally related as events are related in a finely built drama of action, and there will be a psychological beginning, middle, and end as plain to trace as in the plot of *Macbeth.* And all this will be achieved within the narrow limits left to drama when it embodies religious experience and to religious experience when it takes on dramatic form.

The mood of the opening speeches appears to be the motionless inertia of despair. There is no hope; not even continuity of thought. Samson's mind is, like his body, 'carelessly diffus'd'. Were it not for the 'restless thoughts that rush upon [him] thronging', there would not even be the promise of action. In effect the inertia is not absolute or the despair complete, for there are periods of sustained bitterness, rebellious impulses that show a fitful power. There is also an intermittent effort to trace detachedly the causes of the disaster; a survival of the habit of disciplined thought. But when the chorus enters there are still, as it were, but the unassembled elements of a mind; inertia and despair, if not absolute, prevail. This, and what immediately follows, may fairly be said to constitute a beginning.

The first choric speech, unheard by Samson, has an important dramatic function, both arousing the sympathies of the audience and enriching their knowledge (or memories) of the past and its contrast with the present. But these, though necessary, are subsidiary functions, part of the exposition of the play, and the action proper only begins with their address to Samson (l. 178). The chorus (like most visitations of friends from the time of Job downwards) soon falls into the question, Why did you do it? and calls up the superb, frank egoism of Samson, which had already appeared at intervals, in a passage of self-justification (l. 241 *seq.*). This leads immediately to the lines (298 *seq.*) in which the chorus, ceasing to be interlocutors, take on another function and reveal, in a debate on the justice of God, the thought that is in Samson's mind. The doubt that had lain unexpressed since the beginning is admitted and, if not resolved, at least rebutted, and a main cause of division in the mind is weakened. It is from this point, I think, that that unification of the mind which is a necessary preliminary to any action begins.

Milton wastes no time, but immediately brings in Manoa. Manoa enters lamenting, and we know that for the purposes of the action he could not have done a better thing. For the lament rouses Samson to defend the decrees of Heaven and to lay the blame steadily upon himself. The timing of this is exquisite. The lamentations would have been useless before the slight tonic effects of the choric dialogue had worked upon Samson's mind, and perhaps no other impact would have served the same purpose as they do, following immediately upon that dialogue. The quality and kind of stimuli that Milton applies to Samson's mind are like a highly skilled course of psychotherapy: each comes at its due moment, before which it would have been overpowering and after which inadequate. We are in the hands of a man who knows this experience intimately and of an artist who can assemble the raw material of life into form. Event, even minor event, such as Manoa's visit, serves simply to stimulate that mental progress which is the action. The sole function of event is thus, until the climax of the play, to produce thought or emotion, not, as in the drama of action, to reveal them. Samson's mind moves forward a necessary stage on its journey because Manoa—or Harapha or Dalila—visits him; by the way he receives each successively he reveals the stage to which the last has brought him. Only at the end does his mind show itself in action and event cease to function solely as the cause and become simultaneously the result of thought.

The inspired blunders of Manoa serve the same purpose throughout. The news of the feast of Dagon, which a little earlier in the play would have led to despair, falls upon a mind now capable of being roused by the challenge 'So Dagon shall be magnified', to draw a distinction between his fortunes and those of the God of his worship. Despairing for and still condemning himself, he perceives, in a sudden leap of the mind forward, the power of God to accomplish His own purposes ('God doth not need either man's work or his own gifts'). A preliminary climax, a foretaste of exultation is reached.

> This only hope relieves me, that the strife
> With me hath end; all the contest is now
> 'Twixt God and Dagon; Dagon hath presum'd
> Me overthrown, to enter lists with God,
> His Deity comparing and preferring
> Before the God of *Abraham*. (460–5.)

As Manoa (whose mind, like that of Dr. Johnson's, interprets Samson's story in terms of events and not of inner experience) suggests alternative means of escape from his bondage, Samson's vision grows proportionately clearer and he distinguishes more sharply the life of the mind from the subsidiary life of the body. From this point onward Milton makes it plain that the death of the body will never be more than an incident in Samson's life, the significant episodes disengaging themselves more and more clearly.

> All otherwise to me my thoughts portend,
> That these darks orbs no more shall treat with light,
> Nor th' other light of life continue long
> But yield to double darkness now at hand:

The impulse then exhausts itself and the action seems as if it will go no further. Indeed, without fresh stimulus from event, it might end on the note 'God of our Fathers, what is man', the challenge that shows Milton's bitter knowledge of the dark night of the spirit that he seems here for the first time to understand.[7] But just as, when the movement of a normal drama of action appears to flag, an episode, arising naturally from the circumstances of the plot, may turn the whole accumulated force into a fresh channel, so here, the entry of Dalila rallies the momentarily flagging force of the play and sends it triumphantly to its conclusion. For Dalila brings a different and fiercer conflict, sterner than the disputes (themselves of steadily increasing force) with the chorus and with Manoa. She provokes Samson to wrath and self-determination. She concentrates his imagination not upon the heroic part of his miscarried glory, but on the matter-of-fact, the practical, the petty, everyday things that have deflected the currents of the mind. He grows more alert, he puts out more strength; this victory costs more than the earlier ones. And as she engages him closer and closer we notice how severely logical is the argument (even Dr. Johnson gave Milton due credit for this), how nobly clear and sustained the survey over their past as they uncover

[7] One of the most surprising qualities of *Samson Agonistes* is this, that Milton, who could write *Paradise Lost* without any indication of mystical experience, in this play suddenly associates himself with those who have made strong, original contributions to the records of the experience and the analysis of its phases.

layer by layer the conduct and motives that brought it about.[8] Even in the exultation of Dalila's last speech this quality remains. Then, its work done, the work of disciplining and welding together the faculties of Samson, the episode ends and leaves him lifted above even that degree of self-despair which had remained, roused by anger and disciplined by logic into a mood resolute and ready for inspiration.

The dialogue with Harapha makes clear how far the last episode has advanced the action. Samson's speech reveals the active presence of certain moral qualities; courage, self-respect, self-control, faith, and the intellectual virtue of disciplined and ordered thought. The restoration of these we have traced step by step through the earlier episodes. The conflict with Harapha, which is the direct result of the state of mind into which he has been brought, now transfers a part of the action to the plane of event; what had been purely psychological action begins to express itself simultaneously in thought and in deeds. But it has still some steps further to go. From the exit of Harapha the mind of Samson enters upon a phase in which it is resolute, clear, and steady. The process of rehabilitation is complete and energy of spirit and power of continuous thought return. From now onward Samson's speech, and that of the chorus which echoes him, is illuminated with prophetic flashes of exultation. It still needs the first visit of the Philistian officer to assemble them and give them direction. The heroic contest is completed; exultation takes possession, and from this moment the play sweeps up easily to the triumphant climax:

> Be of good courage, I begin to feel
> Some rowzing motions in me which dispose
> To something extraordinary my thoughts. . . .
> If there be ought of presage in my mind,
> This day will be remarkable in my life. . . .

It is to be noticed that the accident of physical death (which, if

[8] This is a delightful anticipation of the method used with supreme art by Ibsen in *Rosmersholm* and extended in details (though not in essentials) by Pirandello in our own day.

we read the action of the play in terms of its events, is the catastrophe) is clearly separated now in Samson's mind from significant experience. It is hardly important, one way or the other:

> Happen what may, of me expect to hear
> Nothing dishonourable, impure, unworthy
> Our God, our Law, my Nation or myself,
> The last of me or no, I cannot warrant.

From this point onward the outward events bear the impress of this exultation achieved through contest, and, despite the ironic relief of Manoa's speeches before the death of Samson, the play passes on undisturbed to the mood of beatitude which is the natural conclusion of religious drama:

> All is best, though we oft doubt
> What th' unsearchable dispose
> Of highest wisdom brings about,
> And ever best found in the close.

There is, then (*pace* Dr. Johnson, of whom we may now take leave), a profound and dramatic psychological contest in this play, and, if it be not 'action', it is difficult to apply that term to much of the major drama of the Greeks and of the moderns. The earlier episodes of the play do not merely illustrate or reveal but cause that progress of the mind which is the real theme, and the final episodes mutually cause and are caused by it.[9] The severest dramatic economy is revealed in the ordering of both, and the play is as strict and unified a work of art as any we could examine.

If this be a just conclusion, we shall find this unity revealed in every aspect of the play which we can study. Since a great work of art is an organism and not an amplification of a schematic de-

[9] If this does not constitute 'a beginning, a middle and an end', it is difficult to say what a middle is. It is perhaps when we misuse the term 'tragedy' that we are liable to misplace the emphases (especially upon the death of Samson), and find ourselves complaining with Dr. Johnson that the middle part of the play does not further the end and so is no Aristotelian 'middle'.

sign, we shall find the main theme revealed and interpreted not only by the ordering of the episodes and their variations of tension and pace; the relations of the characters, the accompanying commentary, the prosody and the imagery will also show continuity, a progression reflecting that of the main movement. For it is a distinctive mark of a great work of art that each of these would itself—isolated, if that were possible, from all the others—offer a rendering of the main theme and of the essential mood of the play. Since we are concerned here with a play in which one of the most notable limitations of drama is transcended, it is perhaps worth while to remind ourselves to what extent it has that organic nature which is characteristic of a great work of art. Can we perhaps indicate something of this by looking in a little more detail at one of these other aspects?

To many readers, the prosody of *Samson Agonistes,* the musical technique which carries so easily the bold, almost arrogant, variations, a technique as supreme as Shakespeare's later prosody, is more satisfying than that of any other phase of Milton's work. This alone would suggest that the play was a fully harmonized work of art, and this suggestion is confirmed when we see that the prosodic form of the play is itself a living organism. The play is a sustained, continuous musical composition, the parts resiliently related each to each and to the whole, and can no more be understood prosodically than logically if it is only considered line by line; the one aspect offers a texture as seamless as the other.

The progressive modulations of the verbal music are, that is, an aspect of the psychological progression that forms the main theme,[10] passing from the rhythms of flat, inert despair, through those of restless conflict and turmoil to the clear, hard movement of argument, or, again, through the swinging, marked rhythms of exultation into the level verse of serenity, plain and relatively unvaried.

[10] I shall not attempt here to analyse the details of the effect; the relation in individual lines of verbal music and meaning has been examined by Bridges. I am only attempting to indicate the outlines of the musical composition referred to above.

This can be demonstrated in some detail, though even a sketch of the musical form of the play does but scant justice to that form, which reveals itself as a series of exquisitely related curves in sculptural design. As in all great poetic drama, the prosodic form of *Samson Agonistes* can constitute an experience complete in itself, a reinterpretation of the main theme in terms of verbal music. The dramatic function of the imagery is akin to that of the prosody. For it also follows, reflects, and reinterprets in another medium the experience which is the theme of the play. This consonance, this close relating of all the aspects of its technique with the main design, is a sure sign—if we needed signs to convince us—that the play is a living organism, no sterile and artificial product, but a major work of art.

The form of *Samson Agonistes,* then, whether we consider the relation of episodes and the general shaping of the play or the progression revealed in the similarly related prosody and imagery, is peculiar to its kind. The theme of religious experience when, as is rare, it takes dramatic form, appears to follow certain broad lines of action, and these themselves determine the form in general and in detail. Milton's play is no miscarried tragedy, but a major work of this rare, but distinctive kind, among the finest of that kind in our experience. The doubt whether it is a living work of art, the doubts as to its formal soundness, falter when we realize the firm lines with which the theme is developed; the steady psychological progression from despair through heroic conflict upwards to exultation and the final assumption into beatitude; the unerring reflection of this in the relation of the episodes each to each and to the main theme, in the steady development in tempo and tension, and in the simultaneous and equivalent progression in imagery and prosody. It is not the formal weakness, but the formal wholeness of the play that astounds us. Seldom was an artistic experience more unfalteringly sustained and more clearly communicated. The hesitations of certain critics are perhaps due in part to their attempts to judge it as tragedy, but probably more to the attempt to judge it by criteria of form and construction based on our experience of the more familiar kinds of drama.

For, as has been indicated in this essay, this specific content determines for itself a special form, and often dispenses with event and outward action to substitute a progression of inward crises or phases of mood causally related and leading to their own resolution. If this resolution is simultaneously imaged on the plane of action, by death or some other apparent outward catastrophe, it is possible to regard the play as an intended but miscarried tragedy, and to point out that the earlier phases do not lead naturally to the catastrophe. What is overlooked in this view is that the apparent catastrophe is as purely subsidiary to the real action as is (for example) commentary in the final phases of the drama of event. The earlier phases do not lead consistently towards it because it is not, in itself, the significant climax of the action. What they do lead to (and this often with consummate skill in architectural grace and solidity) is the resolution of the spiritual conflict which the apparent catastrophe serves only to image in terms of event.

UNA ELLIS-FERMOR

A NOTE ON THE DRAMATIC FUNCTION OF THE PROSODY OF *SAMSON AGONISTES*

This selection is by the author of the preceding selection and is from The Frontiers of Drama, *pp. 148-152.*

The prevailing movement of the opening passage, up to about the sixty-fifth line,[1] is slow, lifeless, and inert. The lines drag, like the thought. Sometimes they are deliberately unmusical and formless; they seem again and again about to drift into silence. When a feeble impulse revives the rhythmical movement and carries it forward again, it gives us no confidence that the impulse will last or the movement continue. This is the natural musical opening for the play; in these first phases Samson's mind, like his body, lies 'at random, carelessly diffus'd'.

> There am I wont to sit, when any chance
> Relieves me from my task of servile Toyl,
> Daily in the common Prison else enjoyn'd me,
> Where I a Prisoner chained, scarce freely draw

[1] Line-divisions in the prosodic sequence are, except in a few cases where the end of a speech marks the end of a movement, a somewhat arbitrary way of indicating transitions. If I use them here I would prefer them to be regarded as approximations rather than precise divisions. The references in all cases are to the Oxford edition.

The air imprison'd also, close and damp,
Unwholsom draught: but here I feel amends,
The breath of Heaven fresh-blowing, pure and sweet,
With day-spring born; here leave me to respire. (4–11)

Passages of more vigour, in thought as in movement, break in here from time to time, but the inertia re-asserts its weight throughout the opening phases and even at intervals up to the entry of Dalila.

The next group of movements, from about l. 68 to about l. 187, has more range and flexibility. As Samson's mind tosses between dejection and sharp protest, the verbal music flashes from one extreme to the other of tempo and cadence, alternating between heavy, dragging verse and lines of the utmost irregularity, harsh in the pitch and relation of their sounds. The emotions are echoed with fidelity, even to the note of unassuageable grief in the iterated 'ai' sounds of the long passage on blindness (ll. 68-109). There is more vigour, in sound as in feeling, than in the opening lines, but it is still undisciplined, restless, unsustained:

The vilest here excel me,
They creep, yet see, I dark in light expos'd
To daily fraud, contempt, abuse and wrong,
Within doors, or without, still as a fool,
In power of others, never in my own;
Scarce half I seem to live, dead more than half.
O dark, dark, dark, amid the blaze of noon,
Irrecoverably dark, total Eclipse
Without all hope of day! (74–82)[2]

These characteristics are continued into the speeches of the chorus, but with modifications. The movement is less often sharp and restless, more often irresolute, wavering, uncertain. The verse, that is to say, is less stridently irregular, less full of contrasts in tempo and sound, but it more often lacks

[2] Cf. ll. 100-109 in the same speech, where the cadences of despondency recur with increased effect, after the vigorous protest and grief that have gone before.

definition, drifting into broken fragments and cadences that are almost prose. It follows closely the emotions of the speakers, whose minds reveal by sympathy something of what is passing through Samson's. The choric verse at this point has a significant and organic relation to the verse of his speeches.[3]

In the passages that follow (ll. 187-448) there appear to be three related movements. First the short passages of dramatic verse which break in intermittently, as gusts of energy sweep over Samson's mind, disconnected still, but still gathering force. These passages have something of the immediacy of emotional speech in the hands of an experienced playwright; they unite with the cadences and tempo of dramatic verse those of familiar speech:

And for a word, a tear,
Fool, have divulged the secret gift of God
To a deceitful Woman: tell me Friends,
Am I not sung and proverb'd for a Fool
In every street, do they not say, how well
Are come upon him his deserts? Yet why? (200–5.)

Second are the passages, steadily increasing in number, in which a steadier, firmer moulding of the verse begins to show, as the defensive mood of the debate and argument develops:

That fault I take not on me, but transfer
On *Israel's* Governours, and Heads of Tribes,
Who seeing those great acts which God had done
Singly by me against their Conquerors
Acknowledged not, or not at all consider'd
Deliverance offer'd. (241–6)[4]

Throughout this speech of Samson's there is a tendency (as here) for the lines to form into brief verse paragraphs, a rhythmic

[3] Cf. with the speech just examined, the movement of ll. 115-75, especially the transition from 115-27 to the middle of the speech and the similar transition, after l. 150, to the last part.

[4] Cf. also ll. 373 *seq*.

movement strictly in harmony with the growing cohesion of Samson's thought and passion.

In sharp contrast is the designed confusion, the wavering, weak rhythm of some of Manoa's speech (especially ll. 340-72). Perhaps the most important prosodic function of this passage is to emphasize the growing formal restraint and shapeliness of Samson's lines, especially of the speech (373-419) which immediately follows. Throughout this part the metres are all tending to greater smoothness and steadiness; even Manoa and the chorus are gradually affected by it.

In lines 448-709, which appear to constitute another prosodic group, we find for the first time (448-71) a complete verse paragraph, a musical passage which moves continuously from beginning to end and is composed of a sequence of related passages; a continuous passage of thought is now for the first time co-terminous with a speech. As the thought rises to a climax of conviction its mood is reflected in the prosodic movement; in the gradual quickening of pace and increase of emphasis and tension, in the momentary restlessness of lines 458-59 and in the sudden exhilaration as the movement becomes one of exultation (ll. 460-65). There is no need to analyse the strong, emphatic cadences of these lines, but we may note how far they are from the rhythms and sound-relations of the opening lines of the play. There is relaxation at the end of the passage, as the music and the emotion sink down again to quiescence.

The resignation that follows, though seeming at first glance a reversion to the dejection of the earlier part, is as clearly distinguished from it prosodically as it is psychologically. This is a slow and even movement—lacking variation, it is true, and strong emphases, but musical and not formless:

> All otherwise to me my thoughts portend,
> That these dark orbs no more shall treat with light,
> Nor th' other light of life continue long,
> But yield to double darkness nigh at hand:
> So much I feel my genial spirits droop,

My hopes all flat, nature within me seems
In all her functions weary of herself. (590–96.)

This is followed by a series of passages (606-709) in which Samson's doubts beset him again, and the prosody, following the inner turmoil, returns to a restless movement, fiercer than the corresponding earlier passages,[5] just as the steadier movements now are firmer. Coherence and definition of thought or emotion are followed closely by the corresponding prosodic distinction.

In the next passage (the arrival of Dalila and the rising dispute between her and Samson), the prosody, like the thought, shows a steady increase of firmness and form. The verse becomes tough and resilient; it hardens as the moods and tempers harden.

Such pardon therefore as I give my folly,
Take to thy wicked deed: which when thou seest
Impartial, self-severe, inexorable,
Thou wilt renounce thy seeking, and much rather
Confess it feigned, weakness is thy excuse,
And I believe it, weakness to resist
Philistian gold. (825–31)[6]

This steady metallic rhythm is the fitting accompaniment to the hard mood of dispute and debate,[7] and gives stability to the pro-

[5] See particularly ll. 617-27.

[6] Compare also the whole passage, 748-959.

[7] There is no room here for a detailed analysis of the technique, but we may perhaps notice three things which contribute to this effect. The contrast between light and strong stresses in the individual feet is reduced, both strong and light approximating, in many cases, to half accents, a stress midway between both; by this means the spring of the lines is subdued; the method is precisely the opposite of that by which Marlowe, for example, emphasizes the throb of the individual line in the main passages of *Tamburlaine*. In the second place, the lines are relatively regular, with little substitution or inversion (accentual anaepaest, spondee, pyrrhic, or trochee) and the comparatively level feet are allowed to succeed each other with little variation from the prosodic base. In the third place, the tempo does not vary greatly from line to line (rapidly spoken lines of multisyllabic words are not followed by and contrasted with the slow paces of lagging monosyllables), so that there is little elasticity in the line groups. Thus each prosodic unit from the smallest (the individual foot) through the single

sodic foundation from now onward. When the exultant movement already noticed in an earlier phase returns,[8] it grows out of this tougher verse and becomes itself firmer and more even, passing into a grave, majestic movement which increasingly reflects the growing assurance and clarity of Samson's spirit:

> Be of good courage, I begin to feel
> Some rousing motions in me which dispose
> To something extraordinary my thoughts.
> I with this messenger will go along,
> Nothing to do, be sure, that may dishonour
> Our Law, or stain my vow of *Nazarite*.
> If there be aught of presage in the mind,
> This day will be remarkable in my life
> By some great act, or of my days the last. (1381–89.)[9]

After an interval on a lower level, reflecting the false relief of Manoa and the chorus, there is a passage of rising excitement gathered together by the messenger's speech. This part (1426-end) shows a gradual lowering of tension from the sublimity of Samson's final mood towards the conversational tempo of verse in the drama of everyday life; from this it is guided again through the messenger's speech into the final movement, in which extreme simplicity, of blank verse and choric ode alike, mirrors the serenity of the end of the play. The rhythm is now strongly marked and regular, but the variations are reduced again and we reach a prosody which in its compactness and stability is in complete contrast with the opening phases of the play.[10]

---

line to the larger unit of the line-group plays its part in producing this complex sound effect that so accurately reflects the state of mind of the speaker.

[8] See ll. 1076-1426 and compare the earlier passage, ll. 460-65.

[9] Cf. also 1423-26.

[10] See especially 1711-14, 1745-48.

WILLIAM RILEY PARKER

THE DATE OF *SAMSON AGONISTES*

In the following two selections the subject of the date of composition of Samson Agonistes *has been pursued by American Milton scholars William Riley Parker, Indiana University, and Ernest Sirluck, Dean of the School of Graduate Studies, University of Toronto. The first article is reprinted from* Philological Quarterly, *XXVIII (1949), 145-166. In Volume II of his biography of Milton, Professor Parker has augmented his argument on the date of composition.*

When was *Samson Agonistes* written? *Paradise Regain'd. A Poem. In IV Books. To which is added Samson Agonistes* was published in 1671. The book was licensed July 2, 1670, registered September 10, 1670, and advertised for sale in the Term Catalogue for Michaelmas 1670.[1] Neither in the preface to *Samson* nor

[1] The circumstance that the book was licensed in July and registered in September led Masson (*Life,* VI, 651) to infer that, though dated 1671, it "may have appeared late in 1670." For some unexplained reason Wood (and, after him, Toland) gave 1670 as the date. *Paradise Regained* and the *History of Britain* were both advertised in the Michaelmas Term Catalogue, 1670; and, as a comparison of type and ornaments in the two books will show, both were printed by the same "J.M.," whom Helen Darbishire identified as John Macock (*The MS of Paradise Lost Book I,* p. 72). This printer dated the *History* 1670; indeed, it must have been out before November 3, 1670, when its publisher, James Allestry, died. The delay in the appearance of *Paradise Regained* was probably due to the time taken for

elsewhere in print did Milton say anything about the date of composition of his dramatic poem. The early biographers, John Aubrey and Anthony à Wood, although they attempted catalogues of Milton's published works, did not mention the *Samson* at all. The Anonymous Biographer merely lumped it with seven other works "finished after the Restoration"—an unhelpful comment. Toland mentioned it but said nothing about the time of its composition.

When Bishop Newton stated, in 1749, "This I conceive to be the last of his poetical pieces," he expressed an uncritical assumption which has generally prevailed down to the present day. *Samson Agonistes* was printed last; *ergo* it was written last. No one, of course, would dream of applying such dubious logic to Milton's *Grammar* or *History of Britain,* but it has been convenient to leave unchallenged the assumption about the late composition of the *Samson,* especially, one may suspect, because so many critical and biographical inferences have been based upon this assumption. The more that such inferences have gained currency, the more unassailable the initial assumption has seemed. Thus, in modern studies of Milton it has often been taken for granted that the tragedy contains transparent expressions of the poet's feeling about the Restoration and about his marriage to Mary Powell. Even those writers who have objected to reading a dramatic work as a spiritual autobiography have not been disposed to doubt that *Samson Agonistes* was written after 1660.

The matter is important, because, if the venerable assumption of late composition is wrong, or even open to serious doubt, then a good many widely accepted generalizations about Milton's art and thought are invalidated. Whatever we are going to believe about the date, we had better have some good reasons for it.

I propose to show, first, that the traditional date is open to very serious doubt; second, that the usual autobiographical inferences

---

blind Milton to superintend the proofreading of the *History* (308 pages) and the two poems (220 pages).

are highly questionable; and third, that there are some reasons for dating the inception of *Samson Agonistes* as early as 1646-1648.

1. THE TRADITIONAL DATE DOUBTFUL

The *Samson* is traditionally dated after the composition of *Paradise Regained.* Masson gave the great weight of his authority to the years between 1666 and 1670, and many writers have, for no discernible reason, singled out the year 1667. Only a few critics, notably Hayley and Dunster, have argued that the drama was composed immediately after the Restoration. To the best of my knowledge, no one has presented in print an argument for composition prior to the Restoration, although Harris Fletcher, in his fine edition of the *Poetical Works* (1941), sceptically observed that the *Samson* might have been largely composed in its "general outlines at almost any time after 1640, and slowly brought to completion between 1650 and 1670"; and more recently, in his provocative remarks *On the Composition of "Paradise Lost"* (1947), Allan Gilbert indicated his belief that the *Samson* was begun in the early 1640's. What, then, are the reasons against assigning the drama to 1667-1669, the dates usually accepted?

Insufficient attention has been paid to Edward Phillips' words about the date of the *Samson.* As a student in Milton's household during the years 1640-1646 and as one of the amanuenses for *Paradise Lost,* Milton's nephew was in a better position than any of the other early biographers to know when the tragedy was written, and one might expect him to be helpful. In his *Life of Milton* (1694) he declares that he paid his uncle "frequent visits to the last." Of *Paradise Lost* he says, "I had the perusal of it from the very beginning." Of *Paradise Regained* he is confident that it was "begun and finished and printed after the other [*Paradise Lost*] was published, and that in a wonderful short space considering the sublimeness of it." From 1667 until 1670 seemed to Phillips "a wonderful short space" for the composition of the 2,070 lines of *Paradise Regained.* How much greater the wonder would be if, in the same space, Milton also composed the 1,758 lines of *Samson Agonistes!*

What does Phillips say about the date of the *Samson?* Although he seems to have read the drama immediately upon its publication, perhaps in manuscript before publication,[2] he nevertheless says, frankly, that he does not know when it was written. This is a most significant confession. Consider his exact words:

> It cannot certainly be concluded when he wrote his excellent Tragedy entitled *Samson Agonistes,* but sure enough it is that it came forth [i.e., was published] after his publication of *Paradise Lost,* together with his other poem called *Paradise Regained* . . .

"Cannot certainly be concluded" certainly means what it says, and it carries a rebuke to the easy assumptions of modern editors. However (and this point is important), his remarks about the composition of the tragedy, taken with his remarks about *Paradise Regained* and the "wonderful short space" of its composition, make it quite clear that he, for one, does not believe the *Samson* to have been written after *Paradise Lost.* And this fact gives us one serious reason for doubting the traditional date.

A second reason is the presence of rime in *Samson Agonistes.* In 1668, to late issues of the first edition of *Paradise Lost,* Milton added a well known little paragraph on "The Verse." This was ostensibly a defence of the unrimed pentameters of his epic, in which he boasted of his "example set, the first in English, of ancient liberty recovered to heroic poem from the troublesome and

[2] The third edition of Phillips' *New World of Words,* published in 1670-71 and advertised in the Michaelmas Term Catalogue of 1670 along with the *Samson,* contains some indirect commentary on Milton's drama. For example, the account of Samson in the 1670 dictionary is much enlarged and there appears for the first time an account of Harapha. See my note on "Milton's Harapha" in the *Times Literary Supplement,* Jan. 2, 1937, p. 12. One may also notice that in the 17th edition of John Buchler's *Thesaurus* (1669) there appears for the first time an essay on the verse of the Greek tragedians—an essay written by Edward Phillips.

modern bondage of riming." But it was more than a defence of *Paradise Lost:* it was an emphatic, a needlessly severe statement of a new artistic credo. Almost all of Milton's minor poems had rimed, but in 1668 he was convinced that rime is

> no necessary adjunct or true ornament of poem or good verse, in longer works especially, but the invention of a barbarous age, to set off wretched matter and lame metre; graced indeed since by the use of some famous modern poets, carried away by custom, but much to their own vexation, hindrance, and constraint to express many things otherwise, and for the most part worse, than else they would have expressed them.

Milton need only have confined himself to the place of rime in heroic poetry, but he chose, instead, to generalize. With *Paradise Lost* in print, and *Paradise Regained* presumably being composed, he called rime a "jingling sound," "a fault," "to all judicious ears trivial and of no true musical delight." Some of the best Italian and Spanish poets had rejected it even in shorter works, we are told.

All of these remarks might be taken to apply only to non-dramatic poetry. But, no doubt aware of the current debate between Dryden and Sir Robert Howard, Milton went out of his way to mention drama too, asserting that "long since our best English tragedies" had rejected rime.

What about rime in *Samson Agonistes*? There is not much; some 154 lines—about one-eleventh of the poem—contain rime. But how to account for the presence of these 154 lines? Commentators have explained them in several ways, although, as A. W. Verity confessed, "Milton's occasional use of rhyme in the play is not easy to explain." He is certainly right if the play was written in 1667-1669. A. J. Wyatt declared: "It needs no great perspicacity to discover that Milton's use of rhyme is so far in accord with his previous renunciation of it, that he intends in the rhymed passages to produce a curious effect of contempt or aversion." This is ingenious and sounds plausible; but a sympathetic application of Wyatt's theory accounts for not half of the riming passages; and

Wyatt himself, in a list of "the chief passages," omits the superb final chorus, the intricate rime pattern of which is reminiscent of a sonnet.

Perhaps some of the rimes, particularly those few in dialogue, were accidental;[3] but there are eleven separate passages in which four or more consecutive lines rime, and these can hardly be accidental.[4] Milton knew he was riming; and when he composed the magnificent *kommos* upon which the drama ends, giving the choral odes thirty-seven riming lines out of sixty-two, he could not have felt about riming as he did while composing the paragraph on "The Verse" for *Paradise Lost.* I do not assume that Milton had become fanatical on the subject of rime, for, after all, he published *Samson Agonistes* three years after his pronouncement, and in 1673 he published a second edition of his minor poems. Moreover, he was quite able to change his mind. My point is, simply, that we are justified in suspecting the years *immediately preceding or immediately following* Milton's public rejection of rime as a period for the composition of *Samson Agonistes.*[5] In other words, the traditional date is, on a second count, open to serious doubt.

2. THE AUTOBIOGRAPHICAL FALLACY

Apart from the assumption that late publication implies late composition, the only arguments for the traditional date of *Samson Agonistes* have consisted of critical and biographical inferences from the drama itself. These we may now consider briefly. We shall have to separate and classify them because, unfortu-

[3] E.g., lines 922, 926, 928, 931, 994, 996. There are even rimes in *Paradise Lost,* but they are so inconspicuous and infrequent that a scholarly article was published to call attention to them—John Diekhoff, "Rhyme in *Paradise Lost,*" *PMLA,* XLIX (1934), 539-543.

[4] S.A. 170-175, 286-289, 303-306, 672-675, 688-691, 1010-24, 1030-33, 1051-60, 1660-65, 1697-1707, 1745-58. Consider also the following couplet rimes: 134-135, 160-161, 297-298, 555-556, 610-611, 615-616, 658-659, 668-669, 973-974, 1041-42, 1117-18, 1519-20, 1667-68, 1687-88, 1691-92.

[5] This argument for an early date on the basis of rime and the opinion of Phillips was elaborated in a paper on "The Date of *Samson Agonistes*" which I read on March 18, 1937, before the Johns Hopkins Philological Association.

nately, they have never been dignified by thorough and orderly statement.

Since the late eighteenth century, the *Samson* has been widely interpreted as thinly disguised autobiography. Let us recognize at once that, right or wrong, most of this interpretation has no real bearing on the traditional date of the tragedy. If Samson's feeling about blindness is Milton's feeling also, if Dalila is something of Mary Powell, if Harapha is something of Salmasius, the *Samson* might still have been written before the Restoration. The only biographical inferences that concern us here are those that supposedly reflect Milton's feeling after 1660. In all my reading of commentary on the play I have met with no inferences that point definitely to the period 1667-1669, and with very few that are supposedly post-Restoration. These few—such as Samson's reactions to captivity, to sickness and disease, and the choral reference to slain heroes and "unjust tribunals under change of times"—can all be related, if we *must* relate them to Milton's experience, to events in an earlier period.

A detailed, point by point refutation of the autobiographical fallacy as it applies to *Samson Agonistes* can easily be made,[6] but I do not think it really necessary. Let us observe, instead, a few pertinent facts. The personal element in the drama, so apparent to modern critics, was evidently not so apparent to the early biographers and critics. Why? And what evidence is there that Milton himself would condone using drama as a vehicle for disguised autobiography? There is strong evidence that he would not. In his *Apology* (1642) he insisted that "the author is ever distinguished from the person he introduces." In his *Defensio Prima* (1651), although he conceded that "poets generally put something like their own opinions into the mouths of their best characters," he reiterated:

[6] See, for example, the M.A. thesis by Alma Frances Sams, "*Samson Agonistes:* its date and fallacies in the autobiographical interpretation," written at Duke University in 1942 under the supervision of Professor Allan H. Gilbert.

> One must not regard the poet's words as his own, but consider what person in the play speaks and what that person says; for different persons are introduced, sometimes good, sometimes bad, sometimes wise men, sometimes fools; and such words are put into their mouths as is most fitting to each character, not such as the poet would speak if he were speaking in his own person. [Columbia ed., VII, 306; also p. 326.]

This is a perfectly clear and sensible attitude. But let us, for the sake of argument, assume that Milton either did not mean what he plainly said or was incapable of applying the precept in his own practice. What then?

If there was one attack which Milton probably resented above all others, it was the widespread idea, published and talked by royalist sympathizers, that his blindness had been God's punishment upon him for misdeeds. If such a disturbing thought ever crossed Milton's own mind (and it may have!), he would certainly not have put it on paper to comfort his enemies; on the contrary, in his second and third *Defences* (1654-1655) he is at great pains to prove that it simply cannot be true. Yet Samson's blindness, as Milton repeatedly makes clear, was God's punishment for disobedience and loss of virtue. When one reflects on this, *the marvel is that the drama was ever printed, even as late as 1671.* The last thing in the world that the poet wished was for readers to identify Samson with John Milton. Samson was not only blind; he had shown great weakness, he was possessed of more strength than wisdom, he had been uxorious, he had brought dishonour to God. Modern proponents of the autobiographical interpretation ignore, of course, these central aspects of Samson's character. Fletcher is quite right in saying that "the autobiographical parallels in *Samson Agonistes,* regardless of how striking they seem, are much more accidental than real. Not a one of them can be completely trusted."

There are those who believe that Milton's tragedy is, at least in part, a political allegory of England before and after the Restoration. I have met this view in print, although I have yet to meet a thorough demonstration of it. Personally I do not think that *Samson Agonistes* is any kind of allegory at all, and I offer my conviction for whatever it is worth. I cannot prove the point. However, if someone will show how the drama allegorizes England before and after the Restoration, I will cheerfully undertake to show that it allegorizes England before and after 1649 instead; then we can cancel each other out and concentrate on more demonstrable matters.

Still another kind of criticism, which I may call "the swan-song theory," would seem to argue for late composition of the *Samson.* This is the view, often expressed in the last century, that Milton's tragedy reveals (as Henry Hallam put it) "the ebb of a mighty tide." J. C. Collins found it the work of an artist "whose enthusiasm and imaginative energy were beginning to flag." Verity thought that "the play is essentially a poet's last work, his *novissima verba* to his generation . . . pitched in a minor key of sad resignation." The case was best expressed by H. M. Percival, who shrewdly observed that much in the style and tone of the *Samson* must be attributed to the author's effort to reproduce in English the severity of Greek tragedy, but who insisted that "one strong circumstance . . . indicates, as far as internal evidence can, that *Samson Agonistes* was a later utterance of Milton's spirit than *Paradise Regained.*" This one circumstance he described as "the transition from that tone of confidence in the future vindication of the Puritan cause, so clearly marked in [*Paradise Regained*] . . . to the extinction of hope and the weariness of life most touchingly depicted" in the drama. There are, however, at least two good ways of answering such an argument. One may stand on his rights as a subjective critic and disagree, perhaps quoting Tillyard, who also thinks the *Samson* was written late but who finds in the play evidence of confidence regained. Or, on the other hand, one may agree with Percival about the tone, and then ask for any evidence that such a tone expresses Milton's mood in the last years of his life but not in 1646-1648. As a matter of simple fact, all such inferences tell us little or nothing about the date of the drama, for they have a way of cancelling each other out. If *Samson Agonistes* reveals a pitiable flagging of poetic energy, it was not necessarily written late. If it is vital and confident, it was not necessarily written early.

There are other kinds of internal evidence which seem to me a good deal less debatable and more helpful. I have in mind, not parallels of character, not individual lines or passages which may express Milton's views, but a few dramatic and intellectual emphases which were certainly of Milton's making and which may tell us something about the date of composition. I venture my observations, however, while still on the subject of the autobiographical fallacy, for my own views are possibly open to objections similar to those I have advanced against the opinions of others. Let my excuses be that it is a game at which anyone can play blindfold, and that the scales of subjective criticism need balancing.

One of the dominant ideas of Milton's drama seems to me the conception that God chooses a few men—individuals, not nations—for the fulfilment of His mysterious purposes. Samson was "designed for great exploits." He was not one

> Whom long descent of birth
> Or the sphere of fortune raises

but one "whom God hath of His special favor raised" to be a champion and deliverer. He was "select"; he was "chosen" to worthiest deeds "and the work from heaven imposed." He was not "of men the common rout" but one of those

> solemnly elected
> With gifts and graces eminently adorned
> To some great work, Thy glory,
> And people's safety . . .

This idea is repeated again and again as the drama unfolds. It is more than a necessary detail taken from the Old Testament story;

it is emphasized to a degree that makes it seem a passion, a deep personal conviction of the author.

If this should be granted, we might have, I think, a useful clue to the date. Milton had this belief early and probably held it long, but there was one period in his life when political and religious crisis brought it to the foreground of his thinking and gave it almost prophetic force and flavor. This was not in 1641-1645, for although he felt some need then to state the belief, in justification of his own lay preaching, his faith was still in Parliament and in the English people themselves, who (he fondly believed) were about to rise and achieve quickly a new reformation. It was after his disillusion, and conspicuously in the period 1648-1654, that his belief in chosen ones amounted to an emotional necessity. Perhaps the first evidence is the 1648 sonnet to Fairfax, but the sonnets of 1652 and the tracts of 1649-1654 are eloquent with the idea. Cromwell was elected to power, not by the will of the majority, but "by the special direction of God." Milton wanted to believe that the great Protector was "almost instructed by immediate inspiration," just as Samson acted "from intimate impulse," from "divine impulsion." The justification of success is, of course, a dangerous doctrine, and Milton found it increasingly difficult to hold as the Restoration grew imminent; and after the Restoration he could not, in logic, believe it. One by one England's apparently "chosen" leaders failed to accomplish God's work. To the last Milton may have thought of himself as "solemnly elected" to some great task, but the emphasis upon this idea, *as an idea,* gradually disappears from his writing. Neither *Paradise Lost* nor *Paradise Regained* contains such an emphasis; but the *Samson* contains it, reiterates it, insists upon it, and dramatically gives it illustration. Is there anything in Milton's life after the Restoration which can explain a revival of this conviction?

In his *Milton & Wordsworth: Poets and Prophets* (1937), Sir Herbert Grierson makes a point which has some bearing on our problem. Up to the beginning of the Revolution, Grierson reminds us, Milton was an artist unburdened with any prophetic messages, although "if ever a poet wished to be a prophetic poet it was Milton." In his *Ad Patrem* he has spoken yearningly of the bard as a prophet, and with the "two-handed engine" of *Lycidas* he had ventured upon prophecy himself; nevertheless, his early verse is almost entirely conscious experiment, reflecting many new states of mind but never the mind of God's chosen Spokesman. It was only when Milton entered the pamphlet warfare and became "rapt in a vision of a regenerate England" that his writing became more prophetic than practical. Grierson is at great pains to show that in his early tracts, especially the anti-Episcopal tracts and *Areopagitica,* Milton writes in the authentic spirit of prophecy. He is at equal pains to show that both *Paradise Lost* and *Paradise Regained* are essentially didactic, not prophetic. Yet, "with *Samson Agonistes* there is an abrupt and decisive change of tone. In no poem since *Lycidas* have the poet and the critic of life been so at one."

Grierson does not directly call *Samson Agonistes* prophetic, nor does he attempt to cope with the biographical problem presented by the assumption of late composition; but his penetrating analysis of Milton as poet and prophet has, it seems to me, some light to throw on the problem of date. A prophetic poet Grierson describes as

> a poet putting into the language and pattern of poetry his deepest intuitions as these have been evoked by a great political and religious experience. . . . Of intuitive, prophetic poetry the characteristic is this . . . that style and thought are inseparable, that these poets and orators write most imaginatively when their thought is at once profound and passionate.[7]

These remarks apply to the *Samson* with unexpected pertinence. Milton's treatment of the story seems to me, not political allegory, but dramatic prophecy. The element of didacticism, so strong in *Paradise Lost* and *Paradise Regained,* is subordinated in

[7] My quotations from Grierson's book may be found on pp. 25, vii, 136, 83, and 95 respectively.

the tragedy to an emotional and intuitive faith in God's mysterious use of his chosen ones in the punishment of wickedness. All is best, but the dark dispose of highest wisdom is forever "unsearchable." Just are the ways of God, but God is not tied "to His own prescript": He made "our laws to bind us, not Himself." "Down reason, then; at least vain reasonings down!" Samson acts "from intimate impulse"; he goes to death and triumph when he feels

> Some rousing motions in me which dispose
> To something extraordinary my thoughts.

In nothing else that Milton wrote, either in prose or in verse, did he sound so much like an Old Testament prophet. There is bitterness in the poem, and pain, and disillusion—but there is also the promise that God "unexpectedly returns" and bears witness gloriously to His own.

It is easy enough to say—indeed, it has often been said—that such were Milton's thoughts after the Restoration. But where is any evidence apart from the tragedy itself? We cannot have our critical cake and eat it too. Evidence there is, and enough, for moods of prophecy in an earlier period; but in the works known to have been written after 1655 we are confronted with moods of a strikingly different sort. Why could Milton write like a prophet in the ecclesiastical controversy of 1641-1642 and not in the religious tracts of 1659? Why is there no tone of prophecy in the great epics? The answer, I submit, is quite simple, and only the assumption of a late date for the *Samson* has obscured it. After writing his *Defensio Secunda,* Milton was driven by disappointment to feel national policies of far less importance than the fate of the human soul. To the last he fought for human liberty as he envisaged it, but he lost his vision of a regenerate England and concerned himself instead with a rational justification of the ways of God to men. There is nothing known about Milton's experiences after 1660 which encourages us to believe that the mood of prophecy was somehow recaptured and given final utterance in *Samson Agonistes.*

3. REASONS FOR AN EARLY DATE

If the statement of Edward Phillips and the presence of rime in the drama combine to cast serious doubt upon the traditional date; if, moreover, the usual autobiographical interpretations of the *Samson* are ambiguous, contradictory, and highly questionable; it would seem to follow that *Samson Agonistes* was probably written earlier than has long been supposed. Here the argument might rest. There is some evidence, however, which gives positive support to an early date, and this we must consider finally.

Most stylistic tests seem to me largely inconclusive. Milton was extremely conscious of "decorum," and a deliberate imitation of Greek tragedy could not, in his thinking, call for a style found suitable for epic. Let me illustrate. In *Comus,* his first ambitious experiment with blank verse, there are a large number of lines ending with an extrametrical syllable ("feminine ending"): the proportion is about one in nine. In the two epic poems this kind of verse is comparatively rare, but in *Samson Agonistes* it is conspicuous, the proportion being about one in six. Nevertheless, this fact does not seem to me a valid argument for dating the *Samson* between *Comus* and the epics, because the similarity is better explained on the grounds that *Comus* and the *Samson* are dramatic pieces.

Not so easily accounted for are the audacious metrical experiments in the choruses and monologues of *Samson Agonistes.* The strange rhythms and irregular lines have been often remarked, but never satisfactorily explained. When he published the drama, the poet added a note of self-conscious comment:

> And though ancient tragedy use no prologue, yet using sometimes, in case of self defence or explanation, that which Martial calls an Epistle, in behalf of this tragedy coming forth after the ancient manner, much different from what among us passes for best, thus much beforehand may be epistled: . . . The measure of verse used in the chorus is of

> all sorts, called by the Greeks *monostrophic,* or rather *apolelymenon,* without regard had to strophe, antistrophe, or epode . . . or, being divided into stanzas or pauses, they may be called *allaeostropha.*

At only one other time in his life did Milton compose a poem with such metrical freedom and feel called upon to explain the irregularity. About his Latin *Ode to John Rouse,* written early in 1647, he commented:

> . . . the strophes and antistrophes do not perfectly correspond either in the number of verses or in divisions which are strictly parallel . . . a poem of this kind should perhaps more properly be called *monostrophic.* The metres are in part regularly patterned and in part *apolelymenon* [i.e., free from the restraint of correlation].

The Latin lines of *Ad Rousium* are, in fact, quite as irregular, and have been almost as often damned by perplexed critics, as the English lines of *Samson Agonistes.* The parallel is striking. Both poems appear to be experiments in the free rhythms of the Greek chorus. Milton's poetical development offers many examples of experiments in technique being closely allied in point of time, and the transition from Latin to English (with Greek as the model) would have bothered him not at all. We have, therefore, a reason for *suspecting* that *Samson* was in process of composition as early as 1647.

But is there any evidence that Milton was interested in writing a drama so early as 1647? As a matter of fact, the *only evidence* of Milton's interest in dramatic composition dates from the period 1641-1645. Both the statement of literary ambitions in *The Reason of Church Government* (1642) and the titles and sketches for plays in the Trinity Manuscript indicate clearly that Milton was contemplating the writing of a tragedy in 1641. Aubrey tells us on the authority of Edward Phillips that some verses for a drama on the theme of *Paradise Lost* were actually written "about fifteen or sixteen years before ever his poem was thought of"—in other words (if we accept Aubrey's additional statement that the epic was begun as such about two years before the Restoration), in the period 1642-1643. Milton "was diverted from it by other business," presumably the six pamphlets of 1643-1645. But when this "other business" was completed and the poet enjoyed almost four years of freedom from pamphleteering (1645-1648), he almost certainly returned to his idea of writing a tragedy. One of the four muses depicted on the 1645 portrait of Milton is Melpomene, singularly inappropriate as a patroness of the *Minor Poems.* But in 1642 Milton had promised his readers a literary achievement within "some few years," and he had evidently decided then that a drama could be brought to completion with less difficulty than a longer poem. Is there the slightest reason to suppose that he changed his mind in 1645? *Paradise Lost* was eventually dropped as a dramatic subject, we know; but it does not follow that the idea of writing a drama was also dropped.

Some further clues to the date of the *Samson* may perhaps be glimpsed in the none too distinct career of Edward Phillips, who, we remember, did not know when the tragedy was composed and, quite obviously, did not think it was written after *Paradise Lost.* One gathers, therefore, that it was chiefly done during some period when Phillips' "frequent visits" to his uncle were interrupted for a considerable time. Unfortunately, to determine this we need to know a good deal more than we now know about Milton's nephew.[8] But let us glance at the problem. Edward was born in August of 1630, and by his own statement he "was put to board" as a student with his uncle "not long after" Milton took a house in Aldersgate Street. This was almost certainly in 1640, when Edward was about ten. And almost certainly both residence and tuition ceased about 1646[9]—making it at least possible that

[8] Sidney Lee's life in the *D.N.B.* is spotted with inaccuracies. Wood wasted little time on Phillips in the *Athenae Oxonienses.* William Godwin resurrected the two Phillipses in 1815 on Milton's account; but although he took the trouble to look up their various performances, literary and not so literary, he wrote with a biased and careless pen. Masson, busy with more important matters, leaned heavily on Godwin for his comments about Phillips. And since Masson, silence, except for occasional comments and queries.

[9] Since the point is crucial to our problem, the evidence had better be

Samson Agonistes was begun in the year 1647, when Phillips might have known nothing about it.

In 1650-1651 Phillips was for a short time at Oxford, but from 1649 Milton was busy with his *Tenure of Kings, Iconoclastes, Defensio Prima,* and a good deal of routine writing for the Council of State. In 1652 Phillips was back in London and on February 13 acted as Milton's amanuensis for a letter to Hermann Mylius; Milton was then ill and practically blind. It is conceivable that work was done on the *Samson* during 1653, unknown to Phillips; but in 1654-1655 Milton was occupied with the dictation of the *Defensio Secunda* and *Defensio Pro Se.* In 1655-1656 he was certainly, among other things, writing sonnets, and again he might have worked on his tragedy. Phillips, however, makes the following report on Milton's literary activities after 1655:

> Being now quiet from state-adversaries and public contests, he had leisure again for his own studies and private designs, which were his foresaid *History of Britain,* and a new *Thesaurus Linguae Latinae* . . . a work he had been long since collecting from his own reading and still went on with at times, even very near to his dying day . . . But the height of his noble fancy and invention began now to be seriously and

summarized. Phillips, in discussing the education given him by his uncle, enumerated the many authors who "were run over within no greater compass of time, then from Ten to Fifteen or Sixteen Years of Age." Since we know that he was about ten when he went to live with his uncle, it seems reasonable to infer that his tuition ended when he was about sixteen (i.e., in 1646). Moreover, since it was in 1646 that Milton's household was suddenly crowded by the arrival of his wife's family and by the birth of a daughter, the probability increases of an end to Phillips' studies at this time. In his *Life of Milton,* Phillips has little to say about the years 1647-1648: he knows merely that the poet's father died, that the Powells "soon after went away," and that Milton moved to a smaller house where "he lived a private and quiet life." There is one odd bit of further evidence: when Milton recorded in his Bible the birth of his first daughter (July 29, 1946), he noted also that "Edward Phillips was 15 year old August 1645" and "John Phillips is a year younger about Octob."—notes whose very vagueness suggests that the Phillips boys were not on hand in July of 1646 to supply more exact data.

> mainly employed in a subject worthy of such a muse, viz. a heroic poem entitled *Paradise Lost* . . .

Phillips, let us remember, claimed to have had "the perusal of it from the very beginning" and added, moreover, that for some years he "went from time to time to visit him." He told Aubrey that the epic was finished about three years after the Restoration, and in his 1694 *Life* he stated further that it was finished in Milton's house in Bunhill, to which the poet moved "not long after" his third marriage, in February of 1663. If this is true, Milton could have worked again on the *Samson* in 1664-1665, while Phillips was living at Sayes Court, near Deptford, as a tutor to John Evelyn's son.

CONCLUSIONS

When, exactly, was the play written? Unless additional external evidence comes to light, I do not think it possible to give a final answer to this question. My own guess, after more than a decade of studying the problem, is that *Samson Agonistes* was begun in 1646 or 1647, near the time of the *Ode to Rouse*, and that composition was discontinued in April of 1648, when Milton turned to the translating of psalms. My further guesses are that the drama was taken up again for its possible *katharsis* in 1652 or 1653, that Milton had some thought of including it in a revised edition of his *Poems* in 1653,[10] that the projected edition was abandoned (per-

[10] The Trinity Manuscript contains unmistakable evidence of amanuenses preparing Milton's poems for publication—making fair copies, supplying titles, ordering the sonnets, etc. The following facts indicate that this was done in 1653 (and not twenty years later): (1) The amanuensis who made fair copies of Sonnets XI-XIV also added the title, on Milton's copy of the sonnet to Lawes: "To Mr Hen: Laws on the publishing of his Aires"—and the first volume of Lawes' *Ayres and Dialogues* was published in 1653. (2) This same amanuensis made corrections in four lines of a copy of "On the new forcers of Conscience" which happens to be in the hand of the amanuensis who also copied the sonnet to Vane, at the top of this same page—and the sonnet to Vane was, of course, composed in 1652. (3) This same amanuensis also wrote Milton's letter to Bradshaw, dated February 21, 1653 (see the facsimile facing p. 124 in Sotheby's *Ramblings*).

Humphrey Moseley was still advertising Milton's 1645 *Poems* for sale

haps when the death of Salmasius plunged Milton into the composition of his *Defensio Secunda,* perhaps when Milton realized that many readers would gleefully identify blind Samson with a certain blind regicide), and that composition of the tragedy was again discontinued in August of 1653, when Milton turned again to translating psalms. Whatever the exact facts, both the style and the characterization of *Samson Agonistes* in its present form persuade me that its composition was several times interrupted.

The reader may wonder at my inclination to link conjectured interruptions with experiments in translation. It seems to me that Milton's mood in April of 1648 was obviously unable to sustain original composition, and that it is clearly reflected in his translations of nine psalms into English riming verse. The consolation and relief which Milton found in this exercise are easily guessed, for his choices are an eloquent suggestion of a troubled soul. The first, Psalm 80, is the lament of a desolated country, tired of strife and tears, praying God to return His divine favor. Israel, of course, becomes England in the translator's mind, although in a few lines he can hardly avoid thinking of his personal unhappiness:

> A strife thou mak'st us, and a prey,
> To every neighbour foe;
> Among themselves they laugh, they play,
> And flouts at us they throw.

The spirit of *Samson Agonistes* is everywhere in these psalms. Psalm 81 explains why God is not now delivering His people as in days past: it is their own stubbornness of heart which is at fault. Psalm 82 is a vision of divine judgment against the high spiritual powers whose rule "in darkness" is responsible for the wickedness of the world: these rulers, who fail to "regard the weak and fa-

---

in 1654; see sig. ²A5ᵛ of Thomas Washbourne's *Divine Poems* (registered April 8, published on or before June 28, 1654). My reason for thinking that Milton may have intended to include *Samson Agonistes* in a new edition of his *Poems* is that there were too few additional shorter poems to justify republication of a book still "in print."

therless," may be sons of God but they shall die like men. Psalm 83 is also a song of judgment, a prayer that God will punish the enemies of His people; and Psalm 85 is an anthem of trouble and divine deliverance. Psalm 86 is a kind of liturgy, highly personal in feeling, and it may have brought Milton a special *katharsis.* He ended this series of translations with Psalm 88. Like the first of the series it is an elegy, a lyric lament of tribulation; but unlike the first, and like *Samson Agonistes,* it is an expression of deep personal woe. The psalmist fears a lifelong severance from human intercourse as the result of some incurable affliction. Beyond doubt Milton was attracted to this poem by his own dread of approaching blindness, for it was not even necessary to modify the wording of the original to make it apply to himself:

> Thou in the lowest pit profound
> Hast set me all forlorn,
> Where thickest darkness hovers round,
> In horrid deeps to mourn. . . .
> Thou dost my friends from me estrange,
> And mak'st me odious,
> Me to them odious, for they change,
> And I here pent up thus.
> Through sorrow and affliction great
> Mine eye grows dim and dead;
> Lord, all the day I thee entreat,
> My hands to thee I spread. . . .
> In darkness can thy mighty hand
> Or wondrous acts be known,
> Thy justice in the gloomy land
> Of dark oblivion? . . .
> Lover and friend thou has removed
> And severed from me far.
> They fly me now whom I have loved,
> And as in darkness are.

In April of 1648, when Milton translated these psalms, his left eye had grown "dim and dead," and his health was wretched, probably as a result of the medicines he was frantically taking to preserve his remaining sight. It was some comfort, for a man in such personal misery, to realize that another poet had walked through the same shadows. It was some confort, for a man who saw in his country's troubles the rebuke of an angry God, to reflect that it had happened before. Milton's translations were exercises in morale as well as in linguistics; they compensated for unaccountable stoppages in direct personal expression.[11]

Unlike the translations of 1648, which were all in the common service metre, Milton's psalm translations in August of 1653 contain a great variety of rime and metrical patterns, and strangely anarchic rhythms which may remind one somewhat of *Samson Agonistes.* Psalm 6 could have attracted the blind poet to this particular sequence:

> Pity me, Lord, for I am much deject,
> Am very weak and faint; heal and amend me,
> For all my bones, that even with anguish ache,
> Are troubled, yea my soul is troubled sore.
> And thou, O Lord, how long? Turn, Lord, restore
> My soul . . . . mine eye
> Through grief consumes, is waxen old and dark
> In the midst of all mine enemies that mark.

But in most of the others are the cry of human trouble and the sense of God's protection. Thinking of how his character had been defamed in the abusive *Clamor,* Milton might have found relief in translating Psalm 7. He knew, too, that his enemies were pointing to his blindness as God's punishment upon the regicide, and Psalm 3 was reassuring:

> Lord, how many are my foes,
> How many are those
> That in arms against me rise;
> Many are they
> That of my life distrustfully thus say,

[11] The suggestion sometimes made, that Milton hoped to produce a new hymnal, ignores both the nature of the psalms chosen and the state of the poet's mind in 1648 (also reflected in parts of his *History of Britain*), to say nothing of the fact of a hymnal not produced.

"No help for him in God there lies."
But thou, Lord, are my shield, my glory . . .
. . . Of many millions
The populous rout
I fear not, though encamping round about
They pitch against me their pavillions. . . .

With his translation of Psalm 8 he stopped:

When I behold thy heavens, thy fingers' art,
The moon and stars which thou so bright hast set
In the pure firmament, then saith my heart,
O what is man that Thou rememberest yet?

The poet, destined never more to behold God's handiwork, turned to other tasks.

Whether or not there is any connection between these translations and the composition of *Samson Agonistes,* it is a simple matter to reconcile a conjectured early date with other facts of Milton's thought and art. This let me attempt finally.

In brief, here is what happens in *Samson Agonistes:* At the outset the hero is almost unconscious of his returning strength; his spirit is not yet reconciled to God. But from his conversation with the Chorus he learns to put the divine will before his own. Manoa's visit depresses him momentarily, but Dalila shows him that he is at last master of himself. The quarrel with the giant Harapha, by completing the reconciliation with God and bringing the urge to act, prepares him for the catastrophe. All is best, but only because Samson had "quit himself like Samson" *before* he pulled down destruction upon the Philistines. The psychological development is the thing that makes the play. And this psychological development, the regeneration of the fallen leader, is Milton's invention; it is not even hinted at in the Old Testament story. It provides, therefore, a potential clue to Milton's choice of Samson as a subject for tragedy.

About 1640, when he made an orderly search through the Old Testament for suitable dramatic themes, Milton had jotted down several topics dealing with Samson; but these notes give no hint of special interest or of interpretation; we cannot even say with certainty how many possible plays they indicate. When he came to write *The Reason of Church Government,* however, he realized that the Samson story had allegorical potentialities. Discussing the "mischief that prelaty does in the State," he compared King Charles to Samson, the laws of England to Samson's strength-giving hair, and the Episcopal bishops to Dalila. Late in 1641 he was still hopeful that the King, like Samson, would "nourish again his puissant hair, the golden beams of Law and Right, and, they sternly shook, thunder with ruin upon the heads of those his evil counsellors." But the political allegory breaks down at its conclusion, for Milton did not then wish the death of Charles; he explained, rather lamely, that royal punishment of the prelates would be "not without greater affliction to himself." There is no psychological development implied in this use of the Samson story, for the hero acts automatically, "knowing his prelatical razor to have bereft him of his wonted might." Still, the allegory proves that Milton had Samson on his mind. Three years later, in the *Areopagitica,* he described England as "a noble and puissant nation rousing herself like a strong man after sleep, and shaking her invincible locks." In *Colasterion* (1645) he declared that he had no fear "who can shake" the two pillars of the temple of his divorce doctrine. In *Iconoclastes* (1649) Samson was still a useful analogy, and in the *Defensio Prima* (1651) "that renowned champion" who "made war singlehanded against his rulers" became a symbol of lawful regicide: "Since he had first duly prayed to God to be his help, it follows that he counted it no wickedness, but a duty, to kill his masters, his country's tyrants, even though the greater part of his countrymen refused not slavery." A new interest had now entered: Samson is the lonely champion, who fought his country's enemies while "his countrymen blamed him."

It is not difficult to see how Milton came more and more to look upon Samson as a moving symbol of man's weakness and strength. In 1646-1648, when he realized that blindness threatened him, when the clergy were still damning his views on marriage and divorce, when he felt lonely and miserable and frustrated in his life's work, he may have wondered how Samson managed to rise above his troubles and fulfil, at last, his great purpose. The moment at which the poet first considered the mental process that led to Samson's regeneration was the moment at which the drama was conceived; for then, and only then, did the Old Testament story cease to be a possible plot, listed with a hundred others in a notebook, and become instead a compelling theme for tragedy. We cannot say, of course, just when the moment of creative insight came; but we can believe that Milton felt little personal interest in Samson's attitudes until he, too, was a rejected champion facing the grim fact of blindness. This could hardly have happened much before 1647.

But what of Samson's great speeches on blindness, those passages in the tragedy which cry with acute awareness of horror? In simple truth we cannot tell when these passages were written, but we can believe that they have about them the eloquence and conviction of newly-met reality. If Milton composed them after he had won his struggle for serenity, he was torturing himself for art and risking a dangerous spiritual relapse. It would seem more likely that these impassioned utterances were part of the process by which he achieved control over his despair—the healing of confession, the capture of suffering in words. To write thus with blindness still a staggering blow would be relief; to write thus after the soul had found patience, after adjustment had been made, would surely be almost intolerable pain. The agony of Samson's words on blindness is the agony of Psalm 6, which Milton translated on August 13, 1653. Those words have the ring of raw experience—something very different from the controlled report on distress overcome, such as we may find in the sonnet to Skinner or in "When I consider how my light is spent."

The foregoing remarks, let candor add, are quite subjective and liable to critical blindness, for poetry can be fearfully and wonderfully made. Still, it is noteworthy that Milton did turn again to the writing of verse in 1652-1653, when his affliction was new; and in addition to eight psalms and two sonnets which we know he composed, he may have written further dialogue for an unfinished *Samson Agonistes.* No other literary design, not even *Paradise Lost,* could have had more relevance for him in this period of personal crisis. Samson's plight was more than ever his own plight. And Samson's story had an ending. If Milton, too, could achieve fortitude, could find renewed strength, could glimpse with sightless eyes God's ultimate use of him, all might yet be well. The working out of the drama was, in a sense, the working out of his own problem. And as the drama grew, as the years went by, we may be sure that Milton's varied experiences more and more determined the tone and emphases of the composition. The dark mysteries of God's providence, the incredible stupidity of "the common rout," the terrible responsibility of the chosen ones, the necessity for patience, the danger and dazzling power of intuition, the certainty of final triumph, whatever the cost—all these products of Milton's disillusion and stubborn faith combined to make a poem that is not a sermon, not a political allegory, not a disguised autobiography, but a profoundly moving drama touched with prophecy.

Having stressed the pertinence of the Samson story for Milton in the period 1647-1653, I must close with words of caution. A man writing a tragedy on a theme which has peculiar interest for him will inevitably express many of his own views; but if he is any sort of dramatist at all, he will also draw upon emotions which he has felt once and outgrown, ideas which he has held and since discarded, emotions and convictions which he has known vicariously in the writings of others or in the speech of friends—not to mention the attitudes which his creative ability enables him to imagine for appropriate characters and situations. In reading a poem like *Samson Agonistes,* therefore, we do both Milton and ourselves a grave injustice by labelling as autobiographical any passage for which there is not confirmation in Milton's undramatic work or in objective reality. An artist does considerably more than express his own feelings: he colors them, heightens them, modifies and distorts them, to achieve the effects he has in mind. His feelings are materials with which to work, and there is nothing sacred about their original shape or texture.

In *Samson Agonistes* Milton is a dramatist; although not challenging the position of Shakespeare in English letters, he is nevertheless a dramatist. As such, he identifies himself with Samson as any good playwright identifies himself with his characters; and when parallels of circumstance or of probable attitude make the identification natural, he is perhaps unusually eloquent. He also identifies himself with Manoa, Harapha, the Chorus, and Dalila. Manoa is an indulgent and aging parent, but he is not Milton's father. Harapha is a blustering bully, not a presbyterian minister, or Salmasius. Furthermore, Dalila is not Mary Powell or any other woman known to Milton; she is what the wife of Samson would have to be if violence is not to be done to the story: she is a despicable creature who betrays her husband. It is impossible to find a single definite, demonstrable parallel between Dalila and Mary Powell, and the fact needs to be stated twice for every ugly suspicion that crawls into print. On the other hand, as I have said, a playwright will draw upon emotions which he has felt once and since outgrown; and it is possible, even probable, that the shock and indignation and wounded pride which Milton experienced when Mary deserted him were recollected in tranquillity for dramatic purposes. If so, the passages which profited from feelings thus creatively recaptured are not truly autobiographical passages, and they will, moreover, forever elude us. Searching for them is not a legitimate business of criticism; futile speculation on their existence is not a legitimate business of biography.

Mood, theme, and dominant ideas are something else. If the conjectures here presented on the date of the drama can be accepted, *Samson Agonistes* becomes, for the first time, an expression of Milton's art and mind in the darkest, most troubled periods of his life. The mood of prophecy was still upon him, and a terrible anger. With his spirit straining to see the first signs of a regenerated England, to be achieved by lonely and enlightened champions, he had yet to win the serenity so luminous in his last sonnets—the serenity which, in my opinion, made *Paradise Lost* possible. The writing of *Samson Agonistes* must have been, however, a soul-cleansing experience. Although the drama is, above all else, a great and original work of art, who can doubt that its author, in creating it, achieved for himself something of the "calm of mind, all passion spent" ascribed finally to his chorus?

ERNEST SIRLUCK

SOME RECENT CHANGES IN THE CHRONOLOGY OF MILTON'S POEMS

This selection on the composition date of Samson Agonistes *is reprinted from* Journal of English and Germanic Philology, *LX (1961), 749-785. Three brief paragraphs which debate the position of Professor Allan H. Gilbert and the portions relevant to Milton's Sonnet VII and* Ad Patrem *have been omitted.*

There are two main arguments for dating the composition of S.A. in the period from the early 1640's to the early 1650's, both advanced in a special Milton number of *Philological Quarterly* (XXVIII, 1949). One, by William R. Parker, is entitled "The Date of *Samson Agonistes*"; the other, by Allan H. Gilbert, is called "Is *Samson Agonistes* Unfinished?" Mr. Parker subsequently published "The Date of *Samson Agonistes:* A Postscript," *Notes and Queries,* CCIII (1958), 201-202. Mr. Parker's argument, which is the more serious and has had considerable influence, may be considered first.

It begins with the contention (*a*) that there is no solid basis for the traditional late date for the poem. We have nothing from Milton about the date; neither Aubrey nor Wood mentioned the poem at all; "the Anonymous Biographer merely lumped it with seven other works 'finished after the Restoration'—an unhelpful comment. Toland . . . said nothing about the time of its composition. When Bishop Newton stated, in 1749, 'This I conceive to be the last of his poetical pieces,' he expressed an uncritical assumption. . . . *Samson Agonistes* was printed last; *ergo* it was written last. No one, of course, would dream of applying such dubious logic to Milton's *Grammar* or *History of Britain*" (*PQ*, p. 145). Next, Parker argues (*b*) that the traditional date is doubtful. For one thing, Edward Phillips, who said that *P.R.* was "begun and finished and printed after the other [*P.L.*] was published, and that in a wonderful short space considering the sublimeness of it," also said that "It cannot certainly be concluded when he wrote his excellent Tragedy entitled *Samson Agonistes*, but sure enough it is that it came forth after his publication of *Paradise Lost*, together with his other poem called *Paradise Regained*." Since it would be a much greater wonder if Milton had written both poems in so short a time, Parker concludes that the two statements together "make it quite clear that he, for one, does not believe the *Samson* to have been written after *Paradise Lost*" (*PQ*, pp. 146-47). Again, (*c*) "the years *immediately preceding or immediately following*" the publication of *P.L.* are highly unlikely ones for the composition of *S.A.* because 154 lines (about one-eleventh of the poem) contain rhyme, and when he wrote them Milton "could not have felt about riming as he did while composing the paragraph on 'The Verse' for *Paradise Lost*," with its attack on rhyme (pp. 147-49). Next, under the heading "The Autobiographical Fallacy," Parker (*d*) dismisses all critical and biographical inferences from the poem which point to the traditional date, arguing that the method is fallacious and the particulars unreliable. But, since "it is a game at which anyone can play blindfold, and . . . the scales of subjective criticism need balancing," Parker proposes his own biographical inferences from internal evidence. One dominant idea in the poem, Parker thinks, so heavily emphasized as to make it seem "a passion, a deep personal conviction of the author," is that God chooses a few individuals "for the fulfilment of His mysterious purposes." This, he says, points to the period 1648-54, when Milton's "belief in chosen ones amounted to an emotional necessity. . . . Cromwell was elected to power, not by the will of the majority, but 'by the special direction of God.' Milton wanted to believe that the great Protector was 'almost instructed by divine inspiration,' just as Samson acted 'from intimate impulse,' from 'divine impulsion.' The justification of success is, of course, a dangerous doctrine, and Milton found it increasingly difficult to hold as the Restoration grew imminent; and after the Restoration, he could not, in logic, believe it. . . . Neither *Paradise Lost* nor *Paradise Regained* contains such an emphasis . . ." (pp. 149-53). Again, (*e*) *S.A.* is, in Parker's view, not didactic in mood and tone (like the epics) but prophetic; and this would fit the Milton of the 1640's and early 1650's, but not the later Milton (pp. 153-55). Next, Parker gives other "Reasons for an Early Date." (*f*) Although most stylistic tests are "inconclusive," "the audacious metrical experiments" in *S.A.* link it with similar experiments in the ode to Rouse, and hence point to a period "as early as 1647" (pp. 155-56). Again, (*g*) "the *only evidence* of Milton's interest in dramatic composition dates from the period 1641-1645. Both . . . *The Reason of Church Government* . . . and . . . the Trinity Manuscript indicate clearly that Milton was contemplating writing a tragedy in 1641." When the pamphlets of 1643-45 were finished "and the poet enjoyed almost four years of freedom from pamphleteering (1645-1648), he almost certainly returned to his idea of writing a tragedy." If Aubrey and Edward Phillips can be taken at face value, Milton had in 1642-43 composed some ten lines for a drama on the subject of *P.L.*, having "evidently decided then that a drama could be brought to completion with less difficulty that a longer poem. Is there the slightest reason to suppose that he changed his mind in 1645?" (pp. 156-57). Further, (*h*) since Edward Phillips did not know when *S.A.* was written, Parker infers that it was "chiefly done" during some period when the nephew was not seeing much of the uncle. He believes that Phillips would have left Milton's care about 1646, "making it at least possible that *Samson Agonistes* was begun in the year 1647, when Phillips might have known nothing about it" (pp. 157-58). Now (*i*) Parker gives it as his "guess" that *S.A.* was "begun in 1646 or 1647, . . . discontinued in April of 1648, . . . taken up again for its possible *katharsis* in 1652 or 1653, . . . again discontinued in August of 1653. Whatever the exact facts, both the style and the characterization . . . persuade me that its composition was several times interrupted" (pp. 158-59). Parker anticipates (*j*) that "The reader may wonder at my inclination to link conjectured interruptions with experiments in translation. It seems to me that Milton's mood in April of 1648 was obviously unable to sustain original composition, and that it is clearly reflected in his translations of nine psalms into English riming verse. . . .The spirit of *Samson Agonistes* is everywhere in these psalms. . . .Milton's translations were exercises in morale as well as in linguistics; they compensated for unaccountable stoppages in direct personal expression." As for the psalm translations of 1653, they contain "a great variety of rime and metrical patterns, and strangely anarchic rhythms which may remind one somewhat of *Samson Agonistes*" (pp. 159-61). Finally, (*k*) "it is a simple matter to reconcile a conjectured early date with other facts of Milton's thought and art." Parker emphasizes that "Samson had 'quit himself like Samson' *before* he pulled down destruction upon the Philistines. The psychological development is the thing that makes the play. And this psychological development, the regeneration of the fallen leader, is Milton's invention; it is not even hinted at in the Old Testament story. It provides, therefore, a potential clue to Milton's choice of Samson as a subject for tragedy." The Trinity Manuscript and the published works show that Milton had been interested in the Samson story before 1646-48, but not very immediately; it was in these years, "when he realized that blindness threatened him, when the clergy were still damning his views on marriage and divorce, when he felt lonely and miserable and frustrated in his life's work, he may have wondered how Samson managed to rise above his troubles and fulfill, at last, his great purpose. The moment at which the poet first considered the mental process that led to Samson's regeneration was the moment at which the drama was conceived; for then, and only then, did the Old Testament story cease to be a possible plot, listed with a hundred others in a notebook, and become instead a compelling theme for tragedy." This is unlikely to have happened before Milton realized his own approaching blindness (i.e., about 1647). On the other side, "we can believe" that the passages on blindness "have about them the eloquence and conviction of newly-met reality," and it is unlikely that Milton would have risked writing them after he had achieved tranquility under the affliction (pp. 162-64).

Parker's arguments are best discussed seriatim. (*a*) He has not fully stated the external, objective basis for the traditional date, nor has he stated fairly that part which is reported. How is it that he passes from Toland (1698) to Newton (1749) without mentioning Richardson, whose *Life* of 1734 is so important an authority, who eagerly questioned so many persons who had been acquainted with Milton during his latter life (or who had known such acquaintances), and who was therefore able to give so many "fresh details that have the stamp of personal knowledge"? (Helen Darbishire, *The Early Lives of Milton* [London, 1932], pp. xxix-xxx). Richardson declares without any trace of uncertainty that *S.A.* was written after *P.L.* and *P.R.*: "His Time was Now Employ'd in Writing and Publishing, particularly *Paradise Lost,* and after That, *Paradise Regain'd,* and *Samson Agonistes*" (Darbishire, p. 275). As for Newton, why should he be presumed guilty of "an uncritical assumption"? He tells us that in order to present a reliable account he "not only read and compared" all written accounts of Milton's life and work but "also collected some other particulars . . . from credible tradition" (9th ed., 2 vols. [1790], I, sig. a3^{v}); among others to whom he talked was Milton's granddaughter Elizabeth. Nor is it clear that the element of opinion apparent in the phrase "I conceive" is concerned with uncertainty about whether *S.A.* was written after *P.L.* and *P.R.* Newton is discussing Milton's work in chronological order, and after having dealt with *P.R.* he says (I, lxiii-iv): "His Samson Agonistes is the only tragedy that he has finished, tho' he has sketched out the plans of several, . . . and we may suppose that he was determined to the choice of this particular subject by the similitude of his own circumstances to those of Samson blind among the Philistines. This I conceive to be the last of his poetical pieces. . . . There are also some other pieces of Milton, for he continued publishing to the last. . . . [In 1673] his poems, which had been printed in 1645, were reprinted with the addition of several others. . . . [In 1694] his excellent sonnets to Fairfax, Cromwell, Sir Henry Vane, and Cyriack Skinner, on his blindness, were first printed." Newton seems to me to be expressing no lack of confidence about when Milton wrote *S.A.*, but rather giving his opinion that although certain other poems were published for the first time at a later date, they had been written earlier. We may note in passing that in the articles of 1935 and 1952 which are discussed below, Parker takes as prime evidence of chronological order the sequence in which Milton arranged the poems of the 1645 and 1673 editions, but the present article (which comes between the other two) scorns the "dubious logic" which would assume that Milton placed *S.A.* after *P.R.* in the 1671 volume because it was composed later.

(*b*) If Edward Phillips thought *S.A.* written before *P.L.*, why did he not say so? What he says is that the date of composition is not known but that the date of publication is; if he thought that there was a great disparity between them—that is, that the latter gave a misleading impression about the former—would he not have said so? Incidentally, it is not very wonderful that he should be unsure of the date of *S.A.;* Miss Darbishire points out that dates are his weak suit: "he gets wrong both the year of Milton's birth . . . and the year of his death" (*Early Lives*, p. xiii).

(*c*) Some indication of the blatancy of the question-begging here may be obtained by observing that when Milton revised *P.L.* for the second edition and added four lines to introduce the newly separated eighth book, what he wrote was a quatrain with the first and third lines rhyming and the second and fourth assonantal. Actually, there is a considerable amount of rhyme in *P.L.*, as John S. Diekhoff has partly shown ("Rhyme in *Paradise Lost*," *PMLA,* XLIX [1934], 539-43). Parker knew of this article, but instead of being warned by it against his *petitio principii* he dismissed it in a footnote: "There are even rimes in *Paradise Lost,* but they are so inconspicuous and infrequent that a scholarly article was published to call attention to them" (p. 148). In fact, Diekhoff reported seventeen actual couplets, forty-five instances of rhymes separated by a single line, fifty-two instances of rhyming lines enclosing two not rhyming ("in several cases the enclosed lines themselves contribute to other rhymes"), twenty-seven instances of rhyming lines enclosing three not rhyming (some of the enclosed lines being themselves interlaced with rhymes), "many other rhymes . . . more widely separated," and a large number ("nearly two score . . . in the first two books alone") of rhymes at medial caesurae. To Diekhoff's count may be added two more couplets (II, 893-94; X, 544-45), seven more rhymes with a single intervening line (IV, 482-84; V, 349-51, 857-59; VIII, 171-73; IX, 228-30, 361-63; XI, 637-39), and ten more rhymes with two intervening lines (I, 553-56; IV, 729-32, 825-28; VI, 530-33, 601-604, 658-61; VII, 251-54; IX, 720-23, 1101-04; X, 712-15). Since Diekhoff does not list his twenty-seven rhymes with three intervening lines, nor the many which are more widely separated, nor any of the medial rhymes, it is not easy to know whether his count could be further enlarged. There are, however, well over four hundred line-end rhymes close enough together to be picked up by ear, and a very large number of caesural rhymes. It is not clear how we are to reconcile all this rhyme in *P.L.* with Milton's note explaining why he did not rhyme his poem (perhaps the answer is that as he used rhyme here it neither produced a "jingling sound" nor was it a "bondage"); but it is obvious that the presence of rhyme in *S.A.* cannot be used to prove that it belongs to an earlier period than *P.L.* We may add S. E. Sprott's remark

(*Milton's Art of Prosody* [Oxford, 1953], p. 37) that the rhyme in *S.A.* "occurs in lyrical choruses along with shortened lines, and the preface to *Paradise Lost* may not wholly apply."

(*d*) It may be thought a pity that Parker chose to "play blindfold" his "game" of autobiographical inference; without the blindfold he might have seen that "the deep personal conviction" which he found in *S.A.* was not as absent from the works written just before, during, and after the Restoration as he thought. In August 1659, Milton opened *Hirelings* with the declaration that the Rump, "after a short but scandalous night of interruption, is now again by a new dawning of Gods miraculous providence among us," restored (Columbia, VI, 43). The first edition of *Readie and Easie Way* (Feb. 1660) declares that while the majority of the nation who insist upon running "thir necks again into the yoke" may be worthy to be slaves, the minority must resist them by force, for they are "reservd, I trust, by Divine providence to a better end; since God hath yet his remnant" (ed. E. M. Clark [New Haven, 1915], pp. 18-19). "The justification of success" was never used more explicitly by Milton than in the second edition of *Readie and Easie Way* (see Columbia, VI, 140-41). The blindfold's harmful effects are most obvious in the reference to *P.L.* and *P.R.* All the heroes of Michael's preview of history in Books XI and XII of the former poem—Enoch, Noah, Abraham, Moses, Joshua, David, Jesus—were, like Samson, chosen by God, not elected by the will of the majority; and this is *a fortiori* so of the hero of *P.R.* The emphasis is heavy in *S.A.* (but not heavier than in *P.R.*) because the fallen hero's inner torment rises chiefly from the guilt of having betrayed God's trust.

(*e*) Not Moses and all the prophets could have understood this distinction, for were they not sent to "teach the good way" as well as to foretell the future? (Incidentally, does *P.L.* foretell the future less than *S.A.*?)

(*f*) What, precisely, can a comparison of the metrics of poems in different languages prove? But this general question aside, since Parker does not particularize his comparison, let us look at the conclusions of two prosodic studies which do. After examining all the relevant prosodic data, Sprott says (pp. 129-31): "Milton's most advanced prosodic theory is employed in *Samson Agonistes* . . . . [It] is metrically the pinnacle of its author's achievement . . . gathers up all his experience in previous works." Similarly, Ants Oras ("Milton's Blank Verse and the Chronology of His Major Poems," *SAMLA Studies in Milton,* ed. J. Max Patrick [Gainesville, Fla., 1953], pp. 128-97), says (p. 191): "The continuity of the statistical sequences is too striking, and the emerging patterns occur too persistently and seem too natural to be accidental. Certain features in particular, such as the treatment of feminine endings, of syllabized *-ed* endings, and of terminal pyrrhics, show a compelling logic in their development with which no order of composition very different from the traditionally accepted one seems at all compatible. . . . The second half of *PL* is linked in so many ways with *PR,* and *PR,* in its turn, with *SA,* that the chronological sequence *PL* VII-XII: *PR: SA* seems inescapable."

(g) What Milton contemplated writing at the time of *Reason of Church-Government* was a poem "so written to aftertimes, as they should not willingly let it die," but he was undecided "whether that Epick form whereof the two poems of *Homer,* and those other two of *Virgil* and *Tasso* are a diffuse, and the book of *Job* a brief model. . . . Or whether those Dramatick constitutions, wherein *Sophocles* and *Euripides* raigne shall be found more doctrinal and exemplary to a Nation" (Columbia, III, 236-37). As was long ago pointed out (see Hanford, *Milton Handbook,* pp. 181-82, and further reference there given), the fact that the only worked-up plans that happen to have been preserved in the Trinity Manuscript are for dramas does not mean that there were no plans for other kinds of poems. The subjects which were worked up in the Trinity Manuscript were not the Samson story but the stories of Adam and Eve, Noah, Abraham, Lot, Phineas, John the Baptist, and Jesus. If Milton did begin a drama in 1642, one can think of at least two reasons, neither particularly "slight," which might have made him turn to some other form if he attempted to return to poetic composition in 1645 or 1646: the closing of the theatres in 1642 and the increasing hostility of his own party toward plays. But these are all secondary matters; the main point here is that it is another *petitio principii* to say that Milton returned in any significant way to the writing of poetry at this time. There is no positive evidence for it; the negative evidence is against it, for there is nothing about it in the account of his writings in the *Second Defence.* (It must not be thought that this statement reported only published or completed works, for it includes the *History of Britain,* which was neither.)

(*h*) There is in fact nothing to show that Milton and his nephew were not seeing each other as much as usual during 1647, but there are quite other times when it is most unlikely that they did; for example, Edward Phillips was living away from London in 1664-65 (also in 1650-51, and he may well have been away at other times). And of course Milton was in hiding in 1660, and in Chalfont in 1665.

(*i*) Since the stylistic characteristics which persuade Parker of discontinuous composition are not given, it is impossible to examine them. We may however put against this impression of discontinuity of style Oras' numerical analysis of the style of *S.A.*, which concludes (p. 197): "Steady progression or regression is the most striking characteristic of the majority of these ratios. . . . This steadiness of direction suggests a subconscious unity of impulse and inspiration that could hardly have survived such prolonged interruptions of the process of composition as Professor W. R. Parker thinks probable." (See also the opinion of Sprott, quoted above.) There is no need to discuss the professed "guesses" about just when the work was taken up and laid down until it is established that there were such interruptions.

(*j*) With respect to the "anarchic" rhythms Parker thinks he sees in *S.A.*, we may add to the views of Oras and Sprott already quoted the opinion of F. T. Prince (*The Italian Element in Milton's Verse* [Oxford, 1954]), who says (p. 153) that because of the "severely logical . . . metrical construction" the affinities of S.A. are seen to be "only with the more disciplined of the Italian poetic dramas," and explains (pp. 164-65) that "the apparent freedom of the choruses" is a "legal, or even legalistic, freedom" whose governing law lies in the rules of Italian prosody. We have already dealt with the "conjectured interruptions" of composition. I agree that Milton's mood in April 1648—and, I would add, for several years before and some time after—was unable to sustain original composition, and that the psalm translations were exercises in morale as well as in linguistics.

(*k*) All the speculation and inference here is built upon a demonstrable error of fact. Milton did not invent the regeneration of the fallen Samson. Writing before the appearance of F. M. Krouse's *Milton's Samson and the Christian Tradition* (Princeton, 1949), Parker was unaware of the seventeenth-century view of Samson. Even so, he was somewhat categorical in ascribing the "invention" to Milton; it may be true that there is no hint of Samson's spiritual regeneration in the Old Testament, but there is in the New: the Epistle to the Hebrews, under the rubric "On faith: what it is; its powers; its heroes," includes Samson (11:32-34). Krouse gives many examples, from earliest Christian times down to the seventeenth century, of exegetes who declared that Samson repented of his sin after his captivity, was thereupon restored to grace, and as a regenerate saint brought down the temple under God's immediate impulsion; he also makes it quite clear that all this was a part of the popular seventeenth-century conception of Samson (see especially pp. 31, 37-38, 43, 45, 48-49, 77, and 78-79).

In his note of 1958 Parker returns to the Anonymous Biographer, whose comment he had in 1949 termed "unhelpful." He briefly recapitulates his 1949 statement about the absence of specific dating in the early biographers, and again says nothing of Richardson. Nor does he say anything of the effect upon his argument of the various studies published since and cited above. He only quotes the comment which he had previously "misread" and explains what he "now understands" it to mean: "It was now that hee began that laborious work of amassing . . . a *Latin Thesaurus* . . . ; Also the composing *Paradise Lost.* And the framing a *Body of Divinity* out of the Bible: All which, notwithstanding the several Calamities befalling him in his fortunes, hee finish'd after the Restoration: As also the *Brittish history* down to the Conquest, *Paradise regaind, Samson Agonistes,* a Tragedy, *Logica* & *Accedence commenc'd Grammar* & had begun a Greek Thesaurus. . . ." This, says Parker, distinguishes between two groups of works: the first three, begun after blindness and completed after the Restoration, and the remaining six, begun at some unspecified time and (except for the Greek Thesaurus) also completed after the Restoration. If there is such a distinction in the passage (so skillfully concealed that it has taken three centuries to become discernible) it would involve an early date for *P.R.*, but this does not deter Parker; instead, he cheerfully promises to make this consequence good in a subsequent article! He recognizes that the Anonymous Biographer contradicts Edward Phillips, who said that all three of the first group were begun before Milton's blindness; this he attributes to what he thinks the Anonymous Biographer's inferior knowledge of matters pertaining to 1640-43. He does not say why, if the Anonymous Biographer is wrong in respect of all three of the works about which he is explicit and confident, we should take his word (if one grants for the moment that Parker has correctly inferred what this word is) for the six works about which he is so vague and uncertain. It will be most interesting to see Parker's argument for redating *P.R.*, since so much of his argument (see [*b*] and [*h*] above) for redating *S.A.* derived from the contrast between Edward Phillips' uncertainty about when the latter was written and his confidence that the former was "begun and finisht and Printed after . . . [P.L.] was publisht."

As for the Anonymous Biographer's meaning, it seems to me that in this very summary, very incomplete, and, if Edward Phillips is right, very erroneous paragraph the author has taken as his basic framework the order of publication of the works he remembers. This he supplements by reporting three unpublished works, the two thesauri and the body of divinity, disposed among the published works in what he thinks to have been the order in which they were undertaken. The two great events to which this list of works is related are Milton's blindness and the Restoration. But the biographer got his original framework wrong in one respect: the *Grammar* should have come at the beginning of his list of works published after *P.L.*, instead of at the end. Otherwise the publication dates are in sequence: 1667, 1670, 1671, 1672. If the biographer at first omitted the *Grammar* (1669), and then bethought himself of it and tacked it on, it would not be very surprising: he omitted altogether the tracts of 1659-60 and 1673[1] and the letters and prolusions of 1674 (to speak only of published works).

[1] Article gives date 1773.

APPENDIX

SUGGESTED TOPICS FOR STUDY

Assignments of various range and depth pertaining to the materials of this text may be made to assess the student's judgment and acuity. For example:

Milton's Changes of (or Additions to) the Biblical Account of the Story of Samson

Milton's Development of Manoa (or Dalila; or Harapha)

The Samson Story in Selected English Poems

The Structure of Milton's Drama

Does *Samson Agonistes* Lack a "Middle"?

Is *Samson Agonistes* Autobiographical?

When Did Milton Write *Samson Agonistes*?

Samson Agonistes: Hebraic and Hellenic Features

Several assignments may begin in the text and progress to the use of other materials:

Samson in Art [Raphael, Rembrandt, Reubens, etc.]

Samson in Music [Handel, Saint-Saëns]

Samson in World Drama [Andreyev, Eulenberg, Wedekind]

Samson and Hercules

Samson and Job [See *The Voice out of the Whirlwind: The Book of Job,* ed. Ralph E. Hone, San Francisco, Chandler Publishing Company, 1960.]

Samson Agonistes and *Prometheus Bound* (or *Œdipus at Colonus*)

Samson in the Movies
Samson and Dagon (or the Philistines)

A SELECTED BIBLIOGRAPHY

ANNOTATED EDITIONS

Hughes, Merritt Y., ed. *John Milton: Complete Poems and Major Prose*, New York: Odyssey Press, 1957.

Percival, H. M., ed. *Samson Agonistes by John Milton*. London: Macmillan & Co., 1890.

Verity, A. W., ed. *Milton's Samson Agonistes*. Cambridge: University Press, 1892.

STUDIES

Bridges, Robert. *Milton's Prosody*. Oxford: University Press, 1921.

Carus, Paul. *The Story of Samson and Its Place in the Religious Development of Mankind*. Chicago: The Open Court Publishing Co., 1907.

Kirkconnell, Watson. *That Invincible Samson: The Theme of Samson Agonistes in World Literature with Translations*. Toronto: University of Toronto Press, 1964.

Krouse, F. Michael. *Milton's Samson and the Christian Tradition*. Princeton: Princeton University Press for University of Cincinnati, 1949.

Parker, William Riley. *Milton's Debt to Greek Tragedy in Samson Agonistes.* Baltimore: The Johns Hopkins Press, 1937.

Sister Miriam Clare. *Samson Agonistes: A Study in Contrast.* New York: Pageant Press, 1964.

Stein, Arnold. *Heroic Knowledge. An Interpretation of Paradise Regained and Samson Agonistes.* Minneapolis: University of Minnesota Press, 1957.

Tinker, Chauncey B. "*Samson Agonistes,*" in Cleanth Brooks, ed., *Tragic Themes in Western Literature.* New Haven: Yale University Press, 1955.

DOCUMENTING YOUR RESEARCH PAPER

FOOTNOTES AND BIBLIOGRAPHY*

THE READER of your research paper expects to find in it both your work and an accounting of the sources from which you have drawn your information. This accounting is your documentation. It is also your thanks, or at least your acknowledgment, to any people whose writings or other works have furnished you the information that you have organized into your paper.

Whether as thanks or as report of sources, your documentation must be explicit and specific. It must tell your reader where you found your information so that he can, if he wishes, appraise your sources, perhaps go to them himself and see whether you have conveyed their facts faithfully or reasoned soundly from them.

All of your sources are listed together in a bibliography at the end of your paper; this is *general* documentation. Any source you cite is named at the point where you cite it, usually in a footnote; this is *specific* documentation.

Most of your sources will be books or magazine articles, aside from the selections in this book.

DOCUMENTATION REFERRING TO A BOOK

A bibliography entry for a book will be organized thus:

May, Rollo. *Man's Search for Himself.* New York, 1953.

Period	Period	Comma Period
Name of the author, surname first for alphabetizing.	Title of book, in italic type or underscored to indicate that it is a publication.	City and year of publication. The name of the publisher may appear between the city and the date.

First line begins at margin; if there is a second line, indent it 5 spaces.

* Prepared by the general editor of Chandler Publishing Company.

The footnote for a citation from this book would be organized thus:

[1] Rollo May, *Man's Search for Himself* (New York, 1953), pp. 223–224.

Comma		Paren-thesis	Comma	Paren-thesis Comma
Index (number or asterisk).	Name of author, in normal order, as footnotes are not alphabetized.	Title of book, in italic type or underscored to indicate that it is a publication.	City and year of publication.	

Period

Numbers of pages that contain the information documented. Some people prefer to omit the abbreviation "pp."

First line of footnote indented as paragraph; second line at margin.

The order of the items in this information, the use of the index mark (raised number or asterisk), the punctuation, the parentheses, and the use of italic or underscores are customs that spare a writer the labor of writing many words and his reader some quantity of reading. The footnote would otherwise have to be something like:

This information comes from pages 223–224 of a book by Rollo May, entitled *Man's Search for Himself,* published in New York in 1953.

If you name the publisher of a book, the forms for bibliography and footnote are:

May, Rollo. *Man's Search for Himself.* New York: W. W. Norton & Company, 1953.

[1] Rollo May, *Man's Search for Himself* (New York: W. W. Norton & Company, 1953), pp. 223–224.

DOCUMENTATION REFERRING TO A PLAY

Any citation of a play almost necessarily refers to it as published in a book. Accordingly you cite a play as you would a book. To specify the location of a passage, the page number may be sufficient. But it may be more useful to give act, scene, and if possible line numbers. Hence:

Shakespeare, William. *The Tragedy of Coriolanus,* ed. William Allan Neilson. New York, 1906.

[1] William Shakespeare. *The Tragedy of Coriolanus,* ed. William Allan Neilson (New York, 1906), Act IV, Sc. vii, lines 2–3.

DOCUMENTATION REFERRING TO A MAGAZINE ARTICLE

If your source is a magazine article, your bibliography entry might read:

Kirstein, Lincoln. "The Future of American Opera," *Atlantic* 199:3 (March, 1957), pp. 50–55.

Comma Period		Comma	
Name of author, surname first.	Title of article, in quotation marks to indicate that it is not a separate publication.	Name of magazine, in italic type or underscored to indicate that it is a publication.	Volume and number.

Comma	Period
Issue, in parentheses.	Page numbers of the entire article.

First line begins at margin; second and subsequent lines indented 5 spaces.

Your footnote to this magazine article as your source might read:

[1] Lincoln Kirstein, "The Future of American Opera," *Atlantic* 199:3 (March, 1957), p. 54.

	Comma		Comma	
Index (number or asterisk).	Name of author, in normal order.	Title of article in quotation marks.	Name of magazine, italic or underscored.	Volume and number.

Comma	Period
Issue, in parentheses.	Page number to which the footnote refers.

First line of footnote indented as paragraph; second line at margin.

As is documentation from books, documentation from magazines is made briefer and less laborious by the customs of word order and punctuation.

DOCUMENTATION REFERRING TO A NEWSPAPER ARTICLE

Citations from newspapers cannot be so precise as citations from books or magazines, since many newspapers have several editions in a day and the same article may appear on different pages in different editions; even more troublesome, it may be rewritten, reheaded, or dropped in later editions, and it may not appear in the early editions of a given date.

A bibliography entry concerning a newspaper might therefore appear thus:

"State to Up Vet Home Loan Rate." *San Francisco Chronicle,* Sept. 17, 1959. Dated Sacramento, Sept. 16.

The corresponding footnote might be:

[1] "State to Up Vet Home Loan Rate," *San Francisco Chronicle,* Sept. 17, 1959; dated Sacramento, Sept. 16.

If the writer of this newspaper article were named, his name would precede the title of the article in both the bibliography entry and the footnote. If the story were sent to the *Chronicle* by a news service, such as United Press International or Associated Press, this fact should appear in parentheses at the end of both bibliography and footnote, in full or abbreviated:

... Sept. 16 (United Press International).
... Sept. 16 (UPI).

THE ESSENTIAL IN DOCUMENTATION

Information comes to the writer from so many sources that specimen bibliography entries and footnotes for all possible needs would overflow any book. So it is necessary to keep in mind the basic reason for documenting: namely, to give the source of a statement so it can be appraised, and located, by the reader. These are basic, though some other details may be put into the documentation.

If your bibliography entries and footnotes answer the following questions, they will be satisfactory:

1. *Who?* Who is the author who made the statement? What individual, collaborating group, or institution is the author? Or is the statement published in a work that does not identify the author?
2. *In what publication?* What book, magazine article, newspaper story, speech, broadcast program, or other? At exactly what point in this work? (Can a reader find your citation, from what the documentation tells him?)
3. *When and whence?* In what city and in what year was the book published? On what date was the periodical published?

The next sections contain numerous models for footnotes and bibliography entries, but all are guided by these three principles. Since almost every research project will require documentation referring to some source not covered by a model, you need to perceive the principles as they are demonstrated in the models.

EXAMPLES OF BIBLIOGRAPHY ENTRIES

The entries in a bibliography are ordinarily arranged in alphabetical order, as these examples are. To help in comparing them with corresponding footnotes, the footnote examples (pages 272-275 are numbered in series and the explanatory remark that follows each bibliography entry gives the number of the footnote.

Baker, Charles T. "Patients' Perceptions of Psychologists." Unpublished master's thesis, Ohio State University, 1953. [An unpublished doctor's dissertation or other research paper would be treated in this same way. See footnote 18.]

Boddy, Francis M., *et al. Applied Economic Analysis.* New York, 1948. [This book has six authors. If only one author card is carried in a library catalogue for it, the card will be in the name of the senior author, here given. See footnote 3 and pages 280-281 of this book.]

Bowman, Isaiah. *The New World.* 4th ed., Yonkers and Chicago, 1928. [An often revised book in political geography; marked differences between editions make it important to specify the edition used, as here. See footnote 6.]

Brahms, Johannes. *Concerto No. 2 in B Flat Major for Piano.* Alexander Uninsky, piano; Willem van Oterloo conducting The Hague Philharmonic Orchestra. Epic LC-3303, 1958. [For some purposes it might be unnecessary to identify the musicians presented on a phonograph record, but the information usually is significant. The record number and the "publisher" appear on the record label. See footnote 23.]

Doe, John. "Indexing of Dissertations." Paper read at methodology seminar, —— University, October 19, 1962. In —— University Library. [If this paper were not in a library and you were citing from your notes, you would write instead, "Notes of reading," or something of the sort. See footnote 19.]

Dumas, Alexandre, fils. Letter to Joseph Méry, Oct. 18, 1844. Unpublished. Collection of Simone André-Maurois. [Letters of famous men often are microfilmed for study, even if not published. If you use a microfilm letter, mention it; as, "Microfilm in —— Library." See footnote 20.]

"The Good ex-President," *Time* 74:14 (Oct. 5, 1959), p. 34. [A magazine article published without the author's name. It is therefore alphabetized according to its title, ignoring "The." See footnote 14.]

Gunther, John. "Inside Space." *John Gunther's High Road,* American Broadcasting Company (WABC-TV), Oct. 17, 1959. [A broadcast program in a series. The same form could be used for either radio or television. The station call letters and date might be enough in addition to the program name and the name of its "author." If no author, alphabetize on the program name. See footnote 26.]

Joyce, James. *Finnegan's Wake.* Folkways Records, FDF934, 1956. Tape. [It might be unnecessary to write "Tape," but may be useful. See footnote 25.]

Keats, John. *The Complete Poetical Works and Letters of John Keats,* [ed. Horace E. Scudder]. Cambridge, Mass., 1899. [Scudder's name does not appear in this book, but he is known to be the editor, hence the information is supplied but enclosed in brackets; if the fact appeared on the title page no brackets would be needed. Note that "Mass." is specified to avoid giving the impression that the book was published in Cambridge, England. See footnote 5.]

Kelly, Alfred H., and Winfred A. Harbison. *The American Constitution.* New York, 1948. [A book by two authors; observe that the second author's name is in normal order. Incidentally, this is the first edition of a book that was later published in a second edition; unless another edition is specified, the edition of a book is assumed to be the first. See footnote 2. See also the entry for Isaiah Bowman's book above.]

Kelly, George A. *The Psychology of Personal Constructs.* 2 vols. New York, 1955. [If your references were to only one of these volumes, you would write "2 vols., vol 1. New York, 1955." See footnote 7.]

Kirstein, Lincoln. "The Future of American Opera," *Atlantic* 199:3 (March, 1957), pp. 50–55. [Discussed earlier in detail. See footnote 13 and page 267 in this book.]

"Kite." *Encyclopedia Americana,* 1955 ed. [Encyclopedia article by an unnamed author. The names of editors and the like for a well-known reference book are not ordinarily needed. Neither is the page number in a book whose contents are alphabetically arranged. See footnote 12.]

Learned, Philip. Lecture given in English 346. Edwardian Criticism, —— University, May 17, 1962. Tape recording. [If there were no tape recording, an equivalent statement should appear: "Notes taken by John Doe, student," or the like. Observe that the course title is not italicized or enclosed in quotation marks. See footnote 21.]

Macaulay, Thomas Babington. "Bunyan, John." *Encyclopaedia Britannica,* 11th ed. [Macaulay signed this article simply "M"; the full name was gotten from the list at the end of the last volume. Observe the order of Bunyan's names; he is listed under Bunyan, not John. Observe that there are no page numbers or volume number, since neither is needed for locating an article in an alphabetically organized reference book. See also "Kite," above in this list. See footnote 11.]

May, Rollo. *Man's Search for Himself.* New York, 1953. [Discussed earlier in detail. See footnote 1 and pages 265-266 of this book.]

Ohneschatten, Dermann, Director, —— State Hospital. Interview, May 27, 1964. Tape recorded. [The subject of the interview could be mentioned, if important. See footnote 22.]

Poore, Charles. Review of Henry B. Kranz, ed., *Abraham Lincoln: A New Portrait. New York Times,* Oct. 17, 1959. [See footnote 16, footnote 17, and "Review . . ." below.]

Quintanilla, Luis. "Basic Tenets of Latin American International Policy." In Philip W. Buck and Martin B. Travis, Jr., eds., *Control of Foreign Relations in Modern Nations.* New York, 1957. [See footnote 8.]

Review, unsigned, of Henry B. Kranz, ed., *Abraham Lincoln: A New Portrait. Reviews of the Quarter,* vol. 21, no. 4 (Nov., 1959), p. 37. [To alphabetize the entry for this review at K for Kranz would suggest that Kranz wrote the review or that the entry was for the book rather than for the review. There is much variety of opinion about how to handle this kind of entry. If your reader-instructor has a strong opinion, follow his preference. See footnote 17.]

Shakespeare, William. *The Tragedy of Coriolanus,* ed. William Allan Neilson. New York, 1906. [See page 266 of this book, and see footnote 9.]

"State to Up Vet Home Loan Rate," *San Francisco Chronicle,* Sept. 17, 1959. Dated Sacramento, Sept. 18. [Discussed on pages 267-268 of this book. See footnote 15.]

Swedish Modern Jazz. Arne Domnerus and his group. RCA Camden, CAL-417, 1958. Record. ["Record" is unnecessary unless needed to distinguish the described item from a tape recording or other work of similar name. The record is a collection of works performed by one orchestra. If the name of one work or its composer were the important item, this information would be given first, followed by "In *Swedish Modern Jazz. . . .*" See footnote 24.]

Sypher, Wiley, ed. *Enlightened England.* New York, 1947. [An anthology. Any book identified by the name of its editor rather than an author would be presented similarly. See footnote 4.]

Two Thousand Years of Season's Greetings. New York: Photogravure and Color Company, 1951. [This is the kind of irregular publication sometimes called a "bulletin." Since it may be hard to locate, you help the reader by giving the name of the publisher. Since no author name is given, alphabetize it by the title. See footnote 10.]

We Discover the Dictionary. Coronet Films, 16V4906, 1949. Film. [The author's name, if one were given, would precede the title in this entry, and would govern the alphabetical position of the entry. "Film" may be unnecessary. See footnote 27.]

EXAMPLES OF FOOTNOTES

These specimen footnotes are numbered to help in referring to them for comparison with the corresponding specimen bibliography entries in the section preceding this.

[1] Rollo May, *Man's Search for Himself* (New York, 1953), pp. 223–224. [Book, single author. Discussed on pages 265-266 of this book.]

[2] Alfred H. Kelly and Winfred A. Harbison, *The American Constitution* (New York, 1948), p. 64. [Book, two authors.]

[3] Francis H. Boddy *et al., Applied Economic Analysis* (New York, 1948), p. 346. [Book with many authors, in this instance six. Unless courtesy or other special reason calls for them, the names of the junior authors are replaced by *et al.* See pages 280-281 of this book.]

[4] Wiley Sypher, ed., *Enlightened England* (New York, 1947), p. 451. [Book, single editor. This is an anthology, containing works of numerous writers, who need not be named in this kind of entry. To cite the work of one author included in such a collection, follow the model of footnote 8 below.]

[5] John Keats, *The Complete Poetical Works and Letters of John Keats* [ed. Horace E. Scudder] (Cambridge, Mass., 1899), p. 232. [Book by a single author in a version edited by another person. Observe the brackets enclosing the editor's name; these are present because Scudder is not named on the title page of the book but is known to be the editor; if the title page bore his name there would be no brackets; compare footnote 9, below. Note the "Mass." to prevent confusion with Cambridge, England, another publishing center.]

[6] Isaiah Bowman, *The New World,* 4th ed. (Yonkers and Chicago, 1928), p. 704. [Book, edition specified. Unless an edition is specified, it is assumed that the first edition is being cited.]

[7] George A. Kelly, *The Psychology of Personal Constructs* (New

York, 1955), vol. 1, p. 133. [Book, more than one volume. The citation here is to a page in one volume, and the number of volumes need not be stated; that information is in the bibliography entry. If your paper were to have no bibliography, this kind of footnote should read: ". . . 1955), 2 vols., vol. 1, p. 133."]

[8] Luis Quintanilla, "Basic Tenets of Latin American International Policy," in Philip W. Buck and Martin B. Travis, Jr., eds., *Control of Foreign Relations in Modern Nations* (New York, 1957), p. 188. [Work of one author in an edited collection of works by several authors.]

[9] William Shakespeare, *The Tragedy of Coriolanus;* ed. William Allan Neilson (New York, 1906), Act IV, Sc. vii, lines 2–3. [Play, in book form. If the printed version had no line numbers, a page number would be given. Discussed in the text of this book, page 266.]

[10] *Two Thousand Years of Season's Greetings* (New York: Photogravure and Color Company, 1951), p. 5. [Irregular publication, that is, one not published in the usual course of any publishing enterprise—the named publisher is an engraver-printer and this cited work is an advertising piece. The name of the publisher is therefore given even in a footnote plan which does not include names of publishers of standard books. If it had a named author, his name would be at the beginning, as usual.]

[11] Thomas Babington Macaulay in *Encyclopaedia Britannica,* 11th ed., *s.v.* "Bunyan, John." [Signed article in a reference book alphabetically organized. The abbreviation "*s.v.*" means "*sub verbo*" or "*sub voce,*" English "under the word" or "under the heading." The word "Bunyan" is as accurate a guide as a page number could be, and may be better since encyclopedias are sometimes repaged to make room for new entries inserted late in the life of a numbered edition. Macaulay's article on Bunyan fills two pages; if it were a very long article, and the citation to a single sentence or other brief passage, the reader might be helped by being given a volume and page number: ". . . 'Bunyan, John,' vol. 4, p. 805." Observe the spelling *Encyclopaedia.*]

[12] "Kite," *Encyclopedia Americana,* 1955 ed. [Unsigned article in a reference book alphabetically organized. See footnote 11 concerning the omission of page number. Observe the spelling *Encyclopedia* in the title of this work.]

[13] Lincoln Kirstein, "The Future of American Opera," *Atlantic* 199:3 (March, 1957), p. 54. [Magazine article. Discussed at length in this book, page 267.]

[14] "The Good ex-President," *Time* 74:14 (Oct. 5, 1959), p. 34. [Magazine article, unsigned.]

[15] "State to Up Vet Home Loan Rate," *San Francisco Chronicle,* Sept. 17, 1959; dated Sacramento, Sept. 16. [News article in a newspaper. Discussed in this book, pages 267-268.]

[16] Charles Poore, review of Henry B. Kranz, ed., *Abraham Lincoln: A New Portrait, New York Times,* Oct. 17, 1959. [Signed book review. Such reviews often have titles, either individual or departmental; it is usually unnecessary and confusing to give such titles.]

[17] Unsigned review of Henry B. Kranz, ed., *Abraham Lincoln: A New Portrait, Reviews of the Quarter* 21:4 (Nov. 1959), p. 37. [Unsigned review of a book, in a periodical—here an imaginary periodical. The bibliography entry corresponding to this footnote is alphabetized at Review.]

[18] Charles T. Baker, "Patients' Perceptions of Psychologists" (unpublished master's thesis, Ohio State University, 1953), p. 31. [Unpublished work, such as thesis or dissertation.]

[19] John Doe, "Indexing of Dissertations" (paper read at methodology seminar, —— University, October 16, 1962; in —— University Library). [Paper read but not published. See the specimen bibliography entry at Doe.]

[20] Alexandre Dumas fils, letter to Joseph Méry, Oct. 18, 1844, unpublished, in the collection of Simone André-Maurois. [Unpublished letter.]

[21] Philip Learned, lecture given in English 346, Edwardian Criticism, —— University, May 17, 1962, from a tape recording. [Unpublished lecture. If the lecture were cited from memory, or from the writer's notes, or from notes of another listener, that fact should be given instead of the reference to a tape recording.]

[22] Dermann Ohneschatten, Director, —— State Hospital, interview, May 27, 1964, from a tape recording. [Unpublished interview. No interviewer being named, the assumption is that the interview was with the writer. If the citation were not from a recording, that fact should be given instead.]

[23] Johannes Brahms, *Concerto No. 2 in B Flat Major for Piano,* Alexander Uninsky, piano; Willem Oterloo conducting The Hague Philharmonic Orchestra (Epic LC-3303, 1958), record. [Phonograph record. The word "record" may be unnecessary, or may distinguish between a disk and a tape recording of the same work and performance.]

[24] *Swedish Modern Jazz,* Arne Domnerus and his group (RCA Camden CAL-417, 1958), record. [Phonograph record, title without com-

poser's name. This record has several works by various composers and is thus comparable to a book of the type cited in footnote 8 above.]

[25] James Joyce, *Finnegan's Wake* (Folkways Records, FDF 934, 1956), tape recording. [Recorded book. To locate a cited passage more exactly, one might add "at 22 min." or the like. The tape does not contain the entire book. When a recorded work has several tapes, the one concerned may be specified, as "tape 3 at 17 min."]

[26] John Gunther, "Inside Space," *John Gunther's High Road,* American Broadcasting Company (WABC-TV, New York), October 17, 1959. [Television or radio broadcast; this footnote is for a television program. The network being named, the station call letters and city are extra information; but the latter would suffice if there were no network or the network were not known.]

[27] *We Discover the Dictionary* (Coronet Films, 16V4906, 1949), film. [Film. If the text at the citation does not make it clear that a film is meant, the word "film" is needed in the footnote, since many companies that distribute films also distribute sound tapes, disk records, and books having the same titles. Films usually are the work of writing-producing teams and are published without any "author" name; if an author is named, his name belongs first in the footnote.]

HOW TO FIND DOCUMENTATION DATA

Where do you get information for documentation?

Most books published in the United States and many published in other countries carry this information in the preliminary pages of the book itself. The title page normally has the name of the author (or authors), the title of the book, the name of the editor instead of or in addition to the name of the author, the name of the publisher, the volume number and number of volumes if the book has more than one, the edition number if later than the first, the city of publication, and sometimes the date. But the date may appear only in the copyright notice on the back of the title page, and there may be several copyright dates owing to renewals and revisions (if there are, use the latest). If the title-page date is other than the copyright date, give both dates (as "New York, 1938; title page dated 1949"). You and your reader, seeing this discrepancy, may reasonably wonder whether the title-page date is an effort to suggest that the book is more recent than it really is.

Often you have documentation information on a book even before you see the book itself, for library cards usually contain all of it, and

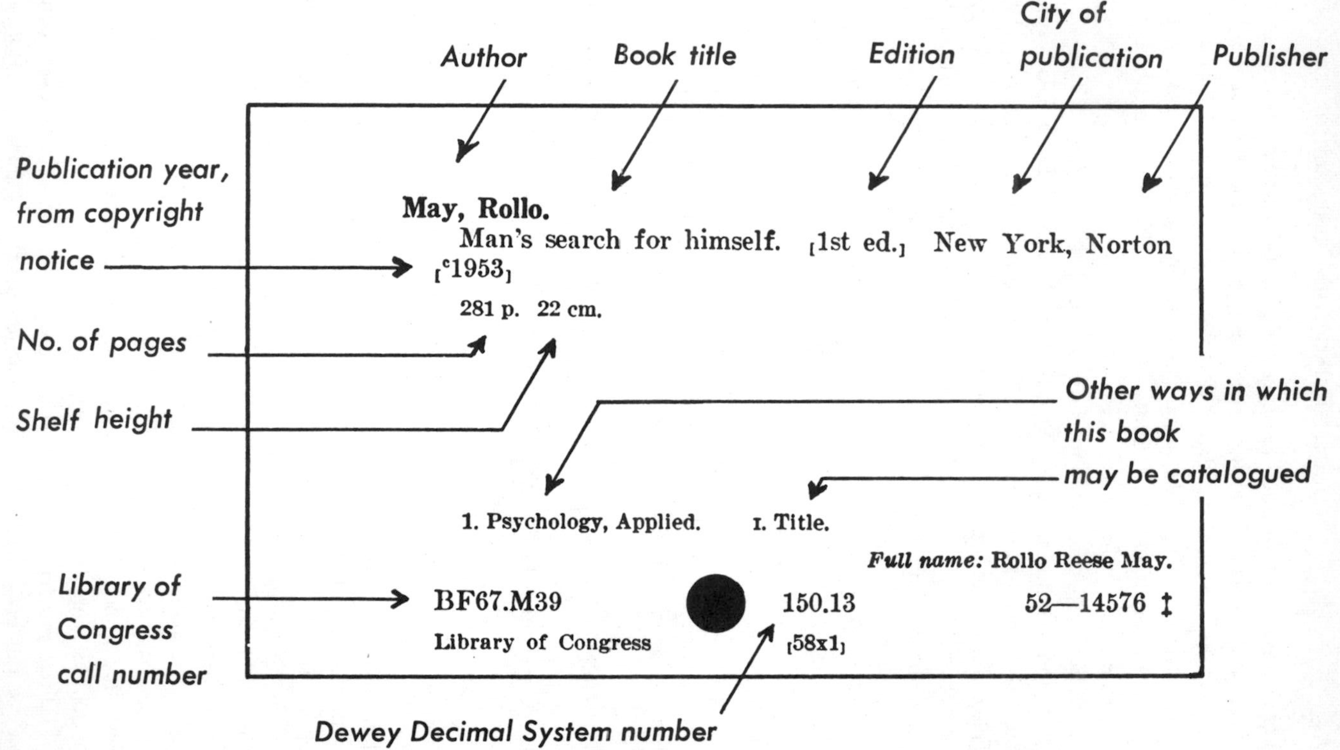
Author
Book title
Edition
City of publication
Publisher
Publication year, from copyright notice
May, Rollo.
Man's search for himself. [1st ed.] New York, Norton [c1953]
281 p. 22 cm.
No. of pages
Shelf height
Other ways in which this book may be catalogued
1. Psychology, Applied. I. Title.
Full name: Rollo Reese May.
Library of Congress call number
BF67.M39
150.13
52—14576 ‡
Library of Congress
[58x1]
Dewey Decimal System number

more, especially those cards prepared by the Library of Congress and distributed to libraries throughout the country. (See page 276.)

Magazines usually provide the bibliographical information in a note somewhere in the early pages, less often on the cover or on a page near the end of the issue. Finding it may take some hunting, since practice is not uniform. In most magazines it will be on the page with the table of contents. Also, as with books, a researcher often gets the information from a library card for the article before he has to search it out from the publication itself. He may also get it from the entry for the article in *The Readers' Guide to Periodical Literature.*

The title page of an unpublished dissertation or thesis will give you all the information you need for documentation, as will the file copy of a paper read at a scholarly meeting but not published. For letters, personal communications, lectures, interviews, and the like, you must formulate the documenting statement from information you get at first hand.

The label of a phonograph record gives you the name of the song, speech, collection, or other work recorded, the names of the composer and of the performing musician or his analogue, the name of the maker, distributor, or publisher of the record, his identifying number or code letters, the date of issue, and sometimes other information. You may have to get some facts from the album cover or record envelope, or from the distributor's list.

Documentation data for tape recordings and films will almost necessarily come from the label. Films usually carry it on the title frames at the beginning.

Radio and television programs contain almost too frequent mention of the program name, its principal personality, the call letters of the broadcasting station, and the name of the broadcasting system. You may thus get this information from the program itself. You may also be able to get it from the program listing in a newspaper or periodical. Sometimes you may get the script of a program from the sponsor or the broadcasting company; if so, the first page or two of the script will contain many of the documentation data.

RECORDING DOCUMENTATION DATA

You begin documenting your research paper before you begin writing it, even before you begin taking your research notes. If you were to collect material, write your paper, then try to work back to find where you got your material in order to document it, you would find the effort hopeless. When you decide to investigate a book or magazine article or other source, therefore, you should prepare a bibliography card immediately, recording all the documenting information you will need if you refer to the source—this before you take your first note! Then, when you write a note card, it should have a record of its source. The record need not be complete to identify it with your bibliography card—a short "slug" something like "May *Man's Search*" is enough. Thus your bibliography card would read:

May <u>Man's Search</u> M 150.13

May, Rollo. <u>Man's Search for Himself</u>. New York, 1953.

Then a note card might look like this:

May <u>Man's Search</u> 224

"... Courage is the capacity to meet the anxiety which arises as one achieves freedom. ..."

With the note card and the bibliography card, you are prepared to put accurate documentation into your finished research paper.

CITATIONS AFTER THE FIRST—BOOKS

When a writer must cite numerous statements from the same source at intervals throughout his paper, repeating long footnotes would become tedious for him and for his reader. When the first footnote has given full information, later footnotes may be shortened in many ways, providing the shortening does not make them confusing.

A second citation from the May book might come immediately after the first one, with no other footnote intervening. For such immediately succeeding footnotes, scholars have long used this style of shortening:

[2] *Ibid.,* p. 231.

This means "From page 231 of the same source given in the immediately preceding footnote." The abbreviation *Ibid.* for *ibidem* (literally, "in the same") is typical of the many abbreviations and Latin expressions that we have inherited and continued to use since early scholars established them. Because they are in some sense part of an omnilingual scholarly vocabulary, many instructors require their students to learn them and use them. But some people think of them as Latin and, if they or their readers do not know Latin, feel that the use of Latin expressions is pretentious or even dishonest. Such people would prefer to use some equivalent English-language form like

[2] May, p. 231.

—or even, if May's name is mentioned in the text, nothing more than

[2] P. 231.

The writer of a research paper does well to learn what preference his instructor has in matters of this sort, and to follow it.

If some citation from other source material were to intervene between the first and second citations from the May work, then the *ibid.* would be wrong, for "in the same" would point to the most recently cited work. The old scholarly usage would be

[3] May, *op. cit.,* p. 231.

This means, "From page 231 of the work by May which has already been cited." "*Opere citato*" is the unabbreviated Latin. Those who misgive Latin expressions might prefer to write any of four other forms:

[3] May, p. 231.

[3] May, *Man's Search*, p. 231.

[3] *Man's Search*, p. 231.

[3] P. 231.

The first-given form would serve if only one of May's books were being used as a source. If two or more were being used, it would be necessary to mention the title and to mention the author's name also, as in the second-given form, unless May's name were mentioned in the text. If the text mentioned May, but not the book title, the third-given form would be sufficient documentation. The last-given and briefest form would be correct and sufficient if the text language made clear what book and author were being considered.

When these English shortened forms are to be used, it is a frequent and helpful practice to tell the reader so in the first full footnote. Thus, after citing the source in full, you would add, perhaps: "This will here(in)-after be cited as May," or ". . . as May, *Man's Search*."

CITATIONS AFTER THE FIRST— MAGAZINE ARTICLES

The short expression *op. cit.* is not used when the source cited is a magazine article or other work not independent and complete in itself, such as an article in a symposium, an encyclopedia entry, or a newspaper story. For such sources, instead of *op. cit.* the footnote Latin is *loc. cit.* for *locus citatus,* Englished as "the place cited" or "the passage cited." Thus several alternative entries for the later footnote to a magazine article:

[3] Kirstein, *loc cit.*

[3] Kirstein, p. 55.

[3] Kirstein, "Future," p. 55.

[3] "Future," p. 55.

[3] P. 55.

These five forms of short documentation correspond in function to the similar five forms for books. But note that *loc. cit.* cannot be followed by a page number; such is the convention. The other forms may therefore be preferable as more specific.

CITING WORKS BY NUMEROUS AUTHORS

A Latin expression that often appears in documentation is the abbreviation combination *et al.* for *et alii,* which means "and others." Writers who are not alert in their Latin often punctuate this expression improperly; those who choose to use it need to remember that *et* is a word and that *al.* is an abbreviation.

The proper use of this expression is to save writing or repeating the names of two or more co-authors of a cited source. Thus a first and later footnote might be:

[1] Francis M. Boddy, Frank E. Childs, Wendell R. Smith, O. H. Brownlee, Alvin E. Coons, and Virgil Salera, *Applied Economic Analysis*, New York, 1948, p. 363.

[3] Boddy *et al., op. cit.*, p. 370.

Instead of *et al.*, those who object to Latin would use "and others":

[3] Boddy and others, p. 370.

If the names of the junior authors are not important for the citation, even the first footnote may have them packaged into *et al.* or "and others":

[1] Francis M. Boddy *et al., Applied Economic Analysis,* New York, 1948.

It is not courteous to use *et al.* in substitution for the name of a single author.

DOCUMENTATION WITHOUT FOOTNOTES

In some people's view the footnote is the most useful and explicit form of specific documentation, the least likely to be misconstrued, and the minimum civil acknowledgment that a writer can make to his source. With all these merits, footnotes are disliked by other people as obtrusive, overformal, distracting, and an extreme nuisance for the typist. Their preference is to put some or all of the specific documentation into the text itself.

In-text documentation for books, magazine articles, and other sources requires the same information that is given in footnotes. A writer citing a statement from a book might therefore write:

> . . . A definition of Rollo May (*Man's Search for Himself,* New York, 1953, p. 224) describes courage as ". . . the capacity to meet the anxiety which arises as one achieves freedom." Seen as such, courage is demanded . . .

The parenthetical documentation would be worded to accord with the text language. If it were to follow the quoted passage rather than precede it:

"The capacity to meet the anxiety which arises as one achieves freedom" (Rollo May, *Man's Search for Himself,* New York, 1953, p. 224) is a definition of courage as it is demanded from all of us. . . .

A writer uses footnote or in-text documentation as he and his readers prefer. If his readers are instructors who grade his research papers, their preference may well overrule the writer's. The general documentation is needed, in the usual bibliography form, to support either style of specific documentation.

Some writers attempt to have the best features of both kinds of documentation by using a footnote for the first mention of a source, then using brief parenthetical notes for later references. This practice might give:

> . . . May found that "the greatest block to a person's development of courage is his having to take on a way of life which is not rooted in his own powers" (*Man's Search,* p. 231). . . .

Or it might give:

> . . . May (p. 231) found that . . .

Either of these two parenthetical documentations might be replaced by the more traditional "*op. cit.,* p. 231" or if proper by "*Ibid.,* p. 231."

BRIEF DOCUMENTATION

It is often unnecessary to give a complete footnote for every citation from a source, yet necessary to document the citation. It seems redundant, when a text has mentioned an author's name or his book's title, or both, to repeat them in a footnote. The footnote then need contain only those facts not given in the text; but all the documenting facts must be given in one place or the other. For examples:

> . . . Rollo May, in his *Man's Search for Himself,*[1] defines courage . . .
>
> [1] New York, 1953, p. 224.
>
> . . . Rollo May[1] defines courage as . . .
>
> [1] *Man's Search for Himself* (New York, 1953), p. 224.

Specific documentation can be kept brief by using the general documentation, the bibliography, after notifying the reader that footnotes or in-text references identify the names of sources given in full in the bibliography. Thus a writer might refer to Rollo May's book thus, even on first mention:

> . . . Courage is "the capacity to meet the anxiety which arises as one achieves freedom" (May, p. 224). Seen as such, . . .

The reader is then expected to understand that he will find the source given in full in the bibliography, thus:

> May, Rollo. *Man's Search for Himself.* New York, 1953.

If several books by May were in the bibliography, the brief documentation would have to be explicit enough to prevent confusion. To this end, "May, *Man's Search*" would be used rather than "May" alone.

Sometimes the entries in the bibliography are numbered. If in such a bibliography the May book were to be numbered 221, then the citing note might read "221, p. 224."

DIVERSE PRACTICE IN DOCUMENTATION

Custom and agreement have not established uniform practice as to correct documentation. Readers' needs differ; scholars in different fields have different kinds of source material to identify and describe; and editors, teachers, and research directors have strong preferences which they can enforce on their contributors, students, and staff. The student writer who goes beyond this discussion in exploring documentation can find some additional and different recommendations in any of four books, especially:

ELINOR YAGGY, *How to Write Your Term Paper.* Chandler Publishing Company, 124 Spear Street, San Francisco, California 94105. Contains a thorough discussion of documentation forms, with numerous examples. Primarily for undergraduate writers.

BLANCHE ELLSWORTH, *English Simplified.* Chandler Publishing Company, 124 Spear Street, San Francisco, California 94105. An appendix on Writing the Research Paper contains directions for preparing a bibliography and for using footnotes, with a chart of model footnotes and corresponding bibliography entries in parallel columns. Primarily for undergraduate writers.

KATE L. TURABIAN, *A Manual for Writers of Term Papers, Theses, and Dissertations.* The University of Chicago Press, Chicago, Illinois 60637. Has chapters on footnotes and bibliography, with numerous examples. Primarily for graduates and advanced undergraduate writers.

WILLIAM RILEY PARKER, compiler, *The MLA Style Sheet.* The Modern Language Association of America, 6 Washington Square North, New York, New York 10003. Primarily for writers of material to be published in Modern Language Association periodicals. This has a supplement dealing with the preparation of masters' theses and doctors' dissertations. Widely accepted and authoritative, especially for papers on literary subjects.

THE DOCUMENTATION OF MATERIAL IN THIS COLLECTION

This collection, being a book of special character compiled for the convenience of students writing research papers, differs from general books and periodicals that might be found in a library. Footnotes and bibliographical entries describing sources in this collection must identify both the source and the collection.

There would be some question of propriety, or even of honesty, if a writer were to name an original source in a documentary citation without making it clear that he examined the material in a collection—whether this collection or another. A reader has the right to know whether a writer is working from original or secondary sources: whether for instance he has seen George Washington's actual diary or has seen only an edited version of the diary in print. For edited versions, even carefully and scrupulously edited versions, may depart from originals.

Notes – December 2

115-175 – (10-11)

278-289 (14-16) just are the ways...
293-325

[anti- (22) Many are the sayings...
652-709 (25-26) God of our Fathers

1010-1060 (35-36) – sex
1268-1299 (42-43) righteous/patience

[1380 —— p. 45]

1427– 1440 (46-47) – Go, Oh the Holy One

{1660-1709
{1745-1758 —— Denouement